Underground Harmonies

Susie J. Tanenbaum

Underground

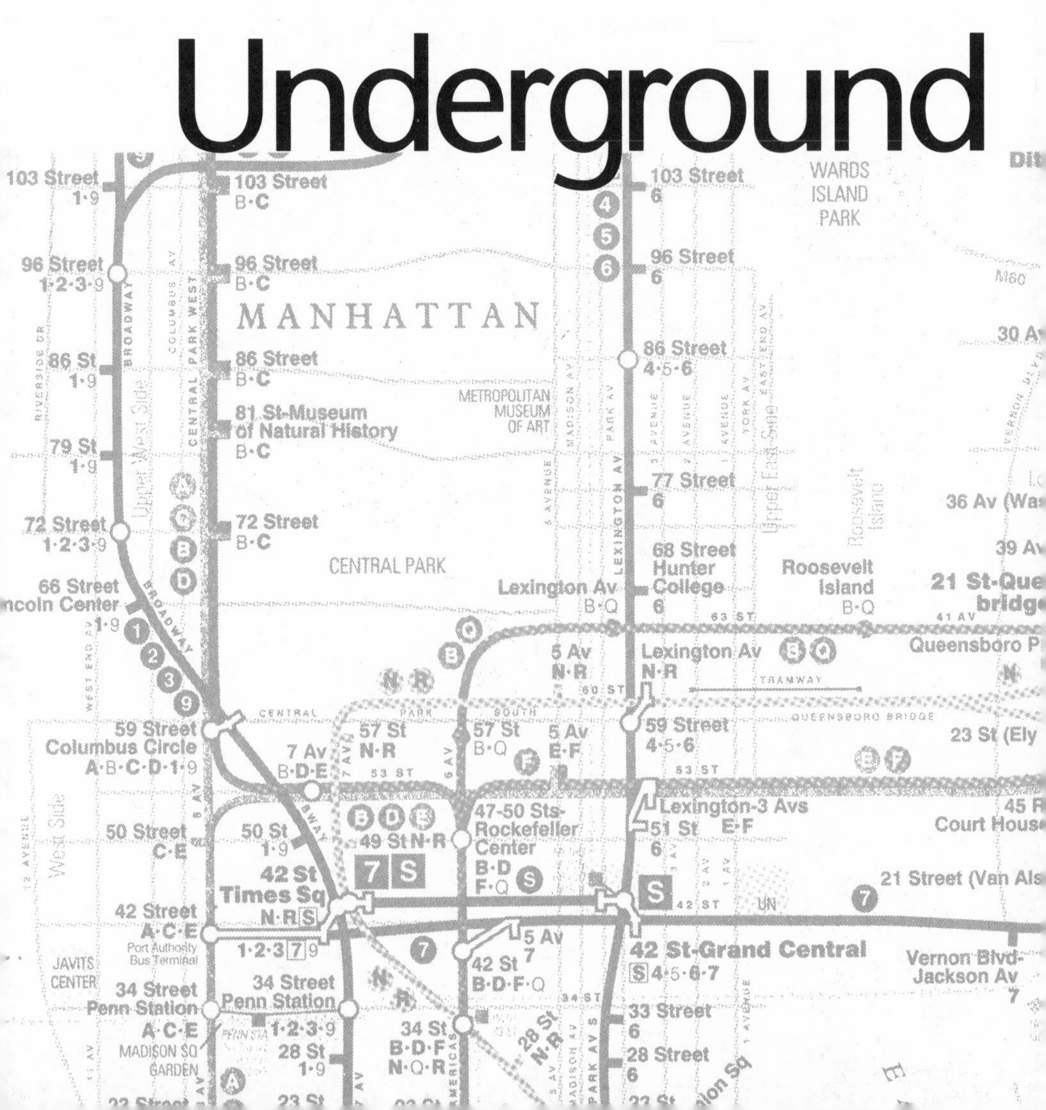

Harmonies

MUSIC AND POLITICS IN THE SUBWAYS OF NEW YORK

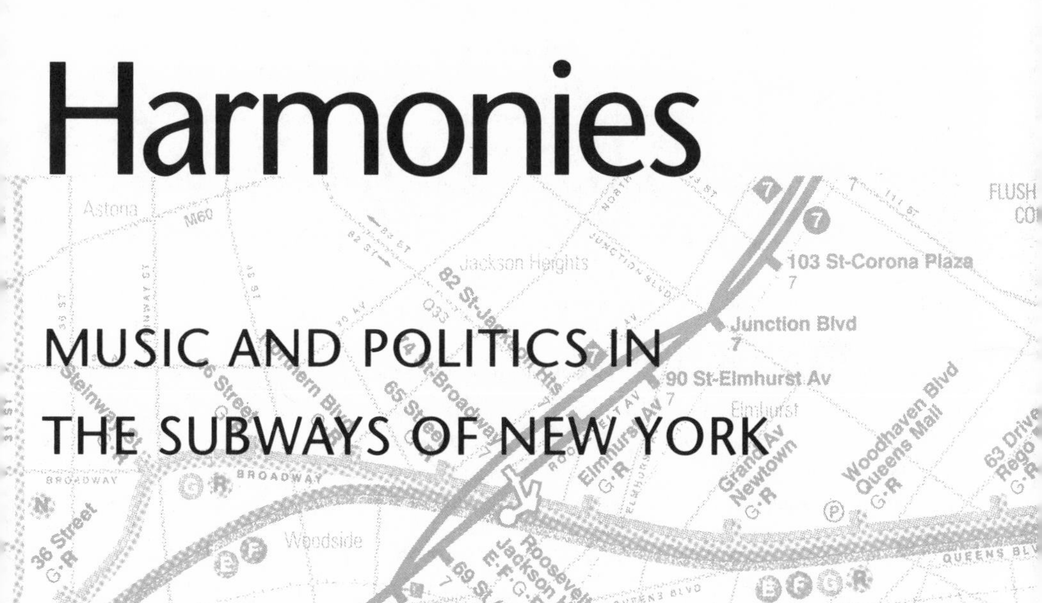

Cornell University Press   Ithaca and London

A volume in the series
Anthropology of Contemporary Issues edited by Roger Sanjek.

First published 1995 by Cornell University Press.

Library of Congress Cataloging-in-Publication Data

Tanenbaum, Susie J., 1965–
Underground harmonies : music and politics in the subways of New York / Susie J. Tanenbaum.
p. cm. — (Anthropology of contemporary issues)
Includes bibliographical references and index.
ISBN 0-8014-3051-8 (cloth). — ISBN 0-8014-8222-4 (pbk.)
1. Popular music—New York (N.Y.)—History and criticism. 2. Street music and musicians—New York (N.Y.) 3. Subways—New York (N.Y.) 4. Popular culture—New York (N.Y.) I. Title. II. Series.
ML3477.8.N48T36 1995
780′.9747′1—dc20 94-48428

Printed in the United States of America

♾ The paper in this book meets the minimum requirements of the American National Standard for Information Sciences—Permanence of Paper for Printed Library Materials, ANSI Z39.48-1984

To the memory of four friends and teachers
who imparted visions to the rest of us of
a more just, vital, and sustainable society.

Matthew David Edel (1941–1990)

Rebecca Levertov Shapiro (1949–1991)

Lisa Yudenfriend Aronin (1957–1993)

Rosalie Waldman (1942–1993)

In their terribly short time here, they did more
than their share to make that society a reality.

Para que comprendas
Estos sentimientos,
Canto las canciónes
Sobre nuestros tiempos . . .

Just so you understand
These feelings that I'm having,
I sing this song for you
About the times we're in.

—Ricardo Silva of Antara del Barrio,
"Lando de Respeto"
(translation by Julie Snyder)

Contents

Preface

One day in the fall of 1987, I was heading toward the exit of the Roosevelt Avenue–Jackson Heights station in the borough of Queens when I was drawn from my course by the sounds and sight of the group Antara. This, I soon learned, was folkloric music of the South American Andes. The melody emanating from Jalil Kifafi's *qena* (wooden flute) had me convinced that colorful birds were circling the yellow bulbs dangling from the girdered ceiling. Leyder Dorado strummed his *charango* (similar to a mandolin, often made out of an armadillo shell), and his quick hand motion imitated the rush of a waterfall. Kifafi, Dorado, and guitarist Francisco Rodríguez wore wide-brimmed sombreros and woolen ponchos, and in the dim light behind them I imagined I could make out the contours of Andean mountains. I had already gotten off the train, but it was then that I was, indeed, transported.

That was my first encounter with some of the musicians who sing and play in exchange for donations on platforms and mezzanines, in passageways and train cars in the city's subway system. There, in one of the dingiest urban spaces, was a paradigm of beauty. It was the ultimate New York paradox.

Antara adopted the Roosevelt Avenue mezzanine, and in subsequent weeks I stopped not only to listen to the music but to exchange nods and, between sets, to chat with Jalil Kifafi (who, fortunately for me, was fluent in English). We became familiar faces to each other. Antara's members gave me what urban ecologists would call "a sense of place"—an intuition that these were experiences worth preserving, even feelings of safety and belonging that I had not previously associated with a subway station.

As a rider I sensed that the musicians helped me to cope with my surroundings, but it took me a while to see subway music as a legitimate form of social and cultural activity, worthy of serious study. Perhaps I had assumed that important experiences could not possibly occur in a transportation terminal. Similarly, I overhear riders asking musicians whether they perform in clubs. Although intended as a compliment (and perhaps reflecting the riders' desire to watch the performances while seated), the question is consistent with Edward T. Hall's observation that our society tends to distrust "subjective feelings as a source of data."[1] We are accustomed to having our tastes sanctioned by cultural institutions, corporations, and government agencies. Moreover, the news media typically depict street performing and subway music as little more than tourist attractions, and major bookstores shelve the academic literature on street performing alongside travel guides.

Nevertheless, there are plenty of people who are thrilled by the largely unmediated experience of hearing live music in subway space and who express their interest and appreciation in many ways. For instance, as I conducted formal research I began to notice that in the presence of a musician the glazed stares on riders' faces were transformed into expressions of almost childlike wonder. I also observed many forms of social interaction and cross-cultural exchange among musicians, between musicians and audience members, and among audience members. In this book I document that contact, exploring what subway music means to its participants, and what it may mean more broadly as a "tolerance-building resource" in a city better known for its extreme individualism, its high rates of violent crime, and its racial tension.

In the following chapters I present the positions, sometimes conflicting, sometimes conflicted, of many actors in the subway music scene. There are the musicians, who want to earn money, express themselves, reach out to New Yorkers, or use the subways as a stepping stone to greater fame. There are the riders, who may welcome the pleasant sounds or resent the additional "noise." There is the Metropolitan Transportation Authority, which sponsors acts through the Music Under New York program, and its subsidiary, the New York City Transit Authority, which authorizes musical performances, both sponsored and spontaneous, underground. There is the court system, which prompted these quasi-governmental authorities to change their policies by affirming subway music as a form of free expression, but which also upheld their right to regulate it. There are transit police officers and station managers who, charged with maintaining order, silence musicians for breaking rules that may not even exist. And there are TA employees (other than transit police) and concession stand workers who have many opinions about the music that some of them have to listen to all day long.

My own point of view most closely resembles that of riders who think the musicians are extraordinary simply for having the courage to set up and who consider much of the music a pleasure and a relief from the heat, the stench, the waiting, and the deafening noise underground. To me, it is a theme song for our public life, a wake-up call from the mindless rush of the subway routine. Admittedly, my enthusiasm is heightened by personal associations, for instance with the complex cross-cultural exchanges that were routine when I was a student at the United Nations International School; with the obscure local radio and television shows that I have long found thrilling to "discover"; and with the folk jams and religious ceremonies I participate in where music is a vehicle of profound communication. Ultimately, though, this is an entirely different experience. Participating in subway music scenes has made me feel more alive as an individual and more hopeful about this city. Judging from my four years of fieldwork, I am not alone. Subway music, especially when performed spontaneously, improves urban life. While local government attempts to upgrade the "quality of life" in New York through policies that encourage strangers to trust one another even less, subway music scenes demonstrate, to the contrary, that a meaningful sense of social order is achieved when strangers have opportunities to encounter each other face-to-face and feel strengthened by their shared experiences. I believe Evelyn Blakey, a jazz vocalist, expresses a similar idea when, after welcoming her audience to "Cafe Subway," she declares: "For the music washes away the dust of everyday life."

The help of many people made this book possible. I am most deeply indebted to Roger Sanjek, professor of anthropology at Queens College and editor of the "Anthropology of Contemporary Issues" series at Cornell University Press, for inspiring and shepherding my study from its inception through to publication. Candace Kim Edel, professor of urban studies at Queens College, frequently welcomed me into her home, edited my interview questions, and helped me interpret my data. At Cornell University Press Peter Agree, Carol Betsch, Kay Scheuer, Susan Kuc, Nancy Curvin, Linda Wentworth, Mary Lash, and copy editor Judith Bailey gave my work an exceptional amount of attention and respect. Photographer Dennis Connors devoted days to tracking down musicians, and he captured their magic with his own.

Many people were consistently cordial and helpful in answering my questions and obtaining documentation for me. Some of them have since gone on to other work. At the Metropolitan Transportation Authority, Susan Weiner, Wendy Feuer, Gabrielle Schubert, Rob Wilson, Erica Behrens, Peter Harris, Jeanette Redmond, Douglas Sussman, Tito Davila, Drora Kemp, and the Real Estate Division were most helpful. At the New York City Transit Authority, I thank Veronique Hakim, Carol Harris, Kenneth Lewis, and the Station Design Department. Lieutenant Eugene J. Roach and Inspector Ronald R. Rowland in the Office of the Chief and Lieutenant Jeffrey McGunnigle in the Special Services Bureau of the Transit Police Department were delightful and their help was indispensable. My thanks to David Treasure at Metro-North Commuter Railroad, Lucy Shorter at the Massachusetts Bay Transportation Authority, and George Sanborn at the State Transportation Library in Boston. I am also grateful to Devra Zetlan, Stephanie Makler, Joan Nichols, and Joanne Scutero at the Municipal Reference and Research Center, and to Kenneth Cobb at the Municipal Archives, New York City Department of Records and Information Services; to David Osborn, Susan Deninger, and Roberto Ferreiras at the LaGuardia–Wagner Archives; to Kathleen Collins at the Transit Authority Archives; to Tom Harrington at the New York Transit Museum; and to the staffs of the New York Public Library (Central, Annex, and Performing Arts branches), the New-York Historical Society, and Hunter College Library.

Three "special informants" shared knowledge and views that are woven into the text. Stephen Baird, who began as a street singer in the early 1970s, is founder of the Street Artists' Guild, a street performer–run organization based in Boston and Cambridge, Massachusetts. Information from Baird comes from an interview at his home on August 19, 1991, from his visit to New York City in August 1992, and from mailings and telephone conversations between 1991 and 1994. Gina Higginbotham coordinated the Music Under New York program for the Metropolitan Transportation Authority, first as an employee of the

MTA consultant MPL Productions, and since 1993 as head of her own company, Performing in Public Spaces. She provided information in a formal interview in November 1990, in subsequent conversations at MUNY special events and auditions, and over the telephone. She also furnished me with MUNY mailings and other promotional materials. Steve Witt is a subway folk guitarist as well as leader (and father) of his group, the Family Colors, which is on the roster of the MUNY program. I interviewed him in January 1992. Witt also writes a column, "The Street Singer's Beat," for the newspapers *Downtown* and *Street News*, and he supplied me with plenty of back issues.

For vital information, insights, and assistance, I thank David Sanjek, director of the Broadcast Music, Incorporated, Archives; Paul Chevigny, professor of law at New York University; Arthur Eisenberg, legal director of the New York Civil Liberties Union; Robert T. Perry, an attorney, law professor, and street performance advocate; attorneys David Goldstein and George Sommers; Marshall Berman, professor of political science at the Graduate Center of the City University of New York; Pete Seeger, folk musician and activist; Andrew Jackson, executive director of the Langston Hughes Community Library and Cultural Center; Steven Zeitlin, Eric John, Benjamin Salazar, and Roberta Singer of City Lore; Gene Russianoff, staff attorney, and Joseph Rappaport, Straphangers' Campaign coordinator, New York Public Interest Research Group; Joel Patraker and Islam Muhammad of the Council on the Environment Green Market program; Elizabeth Brown, associate director of metropolitan studies at New York University; Stephen Steinberg, professor of urban studies at Queens College; my friends, mentors, and preliminary editors Elizabeth Hovey, Marla Bretschneider, and Daniel C. Lynch; my research assistants, Gwynn Kessler, Malcolm Howard, Andi Jamison, Barry Joseph, Jami Rosen, and Bridget Wolf; and Arne Abramowitz, Rabbi Mordekai Shapiro, Vice Chancellor Julius C. C. Edelstein of CUNY, Alex Lopez, Tom Tyburski, Jesse Moskowitz, Gladys Beyruti, Bill Weinberg, Jean McClelland, and the Jackson Heights Community Development Corporation.

I express my appreciation and affection to my mother, Helga Weiss, my sister, Adena Tanenbaum, my brother, Michael Tanenbaum, and to extended family and friends for their ongoing support.

I acknowledge the transit police officers, TA employees, concession stand workers, and subway riders who spoke with me, including those whose names I never learned or cannot disclose. In particular, riders

Teresa Vélez de Carpio, Clotilde Vargas, and Méry Quintero gave generous answers that my questions hardly merited.

Above all, I offer my gratitude to the subway musicians and street performers I have been privileged to meet, who explained to me how they break down the "Fourth Wall" of anonymity in our urban public spaces and who, in the process, helped me to break down my own. They are: James Aaron, Mustafa Abdul-Aleem, Dave Achong, Los Africanos, Wilfredo Alvarez, Ancestral Messengers, Los Andinos, Antara del Barrio, Anthology, Caleb Arruda, Asheba, Peter Barkman, Jason Black, Evelyn Blakey, Steven Blue, the Brewery Puppet Troupe, Sam Brown, Jorge Cabrera, the Roy Campbell Sextet, Lloyd Carew-Reid, Carmen, Michael Christopher, Bobby Davis, Bruce Edwards, the Family Colors, Kimber Fuller, Michael Gabriel, Antonio Gomez, Carlos Gomez, Fidél Gonzalez, Luis Gramal, Jim Graseck, Bob Grawi and Pip Klein, Sean Grissom, Jessel Harris, James Humphrey, Hinantillan, JC, JR, Curt Jardine, Sayyd Abdul al-Khabyyr, Kenneth Lewis and Alexander Earl Griffin, Roger Manning, Eduardo Martinez Guayanes, Zane Massey, Dave "The Wolf" Merk, Michael Minto, Carlos Munhos, Nicole, Charles Nix, Robert Ogarro, Olmedini the Magician, Albert Owens, Luis Pauta, Reniel, Alice Tan Ridley, Roger Ridley, Wendy Saivetz, Spirit Ensemble, Elijah "Carolina Slim" Staley and Jeremiah, Sur Manta, Annette Taylor, Dr. Thunder, Robert Turley, Tutone, and Tony "Pots and Pans" Walls.

Special thanks are due the musicians and riders who taught me how to speak Spanish. It would be a cliché, and inaccurate, to say that they opened doors for me. The doors in their communities were already open: they showed me how to enter.

SUSIE J. TANENBAUM

New York

Underground
Harmonies

Introduction

Venturing Down

The New York City subway system has become a locus of activities that seem to have nothing to do with transit. Unlicensed vendors set up their wares on easily collapsible cardboard display cases, visible representatives of an "underground economy" that grew apace with the economic crisis of the 1980s.[1] Panhandlers are living reminders of political leaders' failure to address that crisis adequately. Members of the Nation of Islam preside over tables of books and incense, and Jews for Jesus and Straphangers' Campaign volunteers distribute leaflets. And then there are the musicians.

In the subways, as in the streets (really sidewalks) above, performance includes magic, comedy, mime, and breakdancing, but music is the predominant entertainment form. Like the vendors, panhandlers, religious devotees, and political activists, musicians are drawn to the subways by the prospect of making contact with riders. They set open instrument cases, shoulder bags, upturned hats, plastic buckets, or tin cans in front of them to collect donations. As they perform, some riders rush past to catch a train; others pause momentarily; but often people gather to listen and also to smile, talk, laugh, sing, cry, even dance, and applaud.

This book is about New York City subway musicians. It explores who these individuals are and what motivates them to perform in an urban space that was not designed with their activity in mind. This book is, moreover, about New York City subway music, an urban ritual that challenges the way we think about public space by promoting spontaneous, democratic, intimate encounters in one of the city's most routinized and alienating environments.

Early in 1990 I began to investigate this phenomenon; four years later I was still researching it. I collected much of my data through anthropological fieldwork, conducted primarily in the following stations:

Times Square (42nd Street and Broadway)

Port Authority (42nd Street and Eighth Avenue)

Grand Central (42nd Street and Lexington Avenue)

Citicorp (53rd Street and Lexington Avenue)

Bloomingdale's (59th Street and Lexington Avenue)

Herald Square (34th Street and Sixth Avenue)

Roosevelt Avenue–Jackson Heights in Queens[2]

These are multicomplex stations, where riders from various parts of the city either transfer to other trains or converge on their way to and from shopping and work. In these stations and in Grand Central Terminal, the commuter railroad above Grand Central Station where I also gathered data, the heavy pedestrian traffic flow attracts an exceptional number of musicians.

The first of my research strategies was simply to find musicians and chat with them when they took breaks. I met Michael Gabriel and Robert Ogarro in this way; the duo was playing steel drum and bongos against the back of a staircase on the 59th Street and Lexington Avenue BMT platform. A few days later I encountered Antonio Gomez, a blind violinist, at one end of that long, narrow platform and, inaudible to him, an Andean trio at the other end. One weekend I watched two Andean groups take turns playing in a corner of the wide mezzanine at Roosevelt Avenue. Over the months I continued to encounter musicians, and this approach proved to be the most productive and personally satisfying of all, revealing much about their backgrounds, practices, and commitments. To avoid inhibiting the flow of conversation, I often waited until afterward to make notes and reconstruct statements. As musicians began to see me as someone genuinely interested in understanding what they were doing (which variably pleased or amused them), I felt increasingly at ease returning to ask additional questions or simply to observe and enjoy the scenes they initiated. In many cases the musicians and I developed ongoing dialogues that crystallized into public (and sometimes private) friendships.

I feel it is important for me to acknowledge that, as a young woman, I have been attracted to a phenomenon whose principal actors tend to be young men. Similarly, I doubt it is entirely coincidental that the authors of the two principal books on street performing are women, one of whom uses adjectives such as "good-looking" to describe her subjects.[3] Gender issues certainly figured into my contact with musicians, at various points facilitating or obstructing communication. For instance, a male researcher might have found it more difficult than I did to slip into the role, for better or worse, of "groupie" and to spend hours asking musicians about their lives. A few musicians used sexist language or behavior toward me; as we came to know each other, I began to sense which comments were playful, which were demeaning, and which I should confront. Conversely, I developed admiration and affection for musicians, and at times I wondered whether in doing so I had overstepped my bounds as a participant observer. Ultimately, I hope that any gender-bound ideation on my part simply motivated me to explore why so many riders lower their protective walls and display emotion when they encounter subway musicians. Indeed, regardless of gender or sexual orientation, there is something romantic about crossing paths with people who make their art, and themselves, so accessible.

In 1990 I also began to approach subway riders. I spoke to those who donated money to musicians on platforms, and I had more prolonged talks in audience "circles" on station mezzanines and in Grand Central Terminal.[4] Some of these conversations were so informative that I marveled at my ability to be in the right place at the right time, but of course my experiences simply demonstrate that New York is populated by individuals with unique and useful insights into their lives and their city.

Usually when I initiated contact with riders I introduced myself as a researcher and explained my work, but in spontaneous conversations I often postponed my disclosure until the end. The second approach helped me to gauge whether riders' responses were designed to "please" me. In fact my impression is that they were not. The countless times I exchanged—or observed other audience members exchanging—glances, raised eyebrows, and smiles further confirmed my impression. Indeed, though many riders gave subway music little conscious thought, they considered it a positive experience and, when asked, said that it mattered to them.

The first musicians I met were from the South American Andes, and as my research proceeded, I became better acquainted with them and with some of their colleagues from the same region. I attended a *peña*, an evening of music and poetry with political overtones, at a Manhattan church; the members of the group Antara had invited me to see them play there. Later, I met the Andean group Los Andinos, and three Latina riders, friends of the group, invited me into their homes. As our friendships developed (and my Spanish vocabulary increased), we began to discuss subway music in light of larger cultural, economic, and political issues that are familiar to many Latin American immigrants in New York. These discussions help account for the relative emphasis in this book on what subway music means to riders with origins in the Andes. My informal research among subway musicians and riders was supplemented by conversations, outside the immediate fieldwork setting, with homeless advocates, relatives, and other friends.

I had come to think of subway music as an example of what Lawrence Levine calls a "shared public culture," where people of vastly different backgrounds participate in a single cultural event. At the same time, I realized, if subway music occurs inside the city's rapid transit facilities, it must raise unique legal and political questions about the places in which a shared public culture can exist.[5] That is when I began to arrange formal interviews.

I met with the MTA general counsel, the director of the MTA Arts for Transit Office, officials and patrol officers in the Transit Police Department, station managers, lower-level TA employees, subway concession stand workers, and civil liberties attorneys who have counseled the musicians. These interviews helped me to identify the diverse, sometimes conflicting interests that the MTA and TA have tried to balance through regulation since the 1980s. They also helped me to assess the extent to which the authorities[6] enable diverse interests to coexist in an environment that by its very nature seems to militate against all interests.

I used formal techniques as well to interview Stephen Baird, founder of the Street Artists' Guild of Boston and Cambridge, Massachusetts; Gina Higginbotham, coordinator of the MUNY program; and Steve Witt, a folk guitarist and leader of the Family Colors. And I formally interviewed candidates at the annual MUNY auditions, which I attended regularly beginning in 1990.

In time I saw a need to supplement the informal and formal interviews with surveys. In December 1992 I designed and administered a one-page questionnaire to twenty musicians in the MUNY program. The following winter I designed three surveys: one for riders, one for musicians, and one for TA employees. My aim was to verify and update information I had collected in previous years as well as to gather a broader range of opinions on the personal and political effects of subway music than informal interviews had allowed. This sample data provided purely descriptive information that revealed noteworthy patterns across responses.

Four volunteer research assistants helped me to conduct the subway rider survey: Gwynn Kessler, a doctoral student at the Jewish Theological Seminary; Malcolm Howard, a freelance journalist, radio producer, and musician who sometimes plays in the subways; Andi Jamison, then a senior at Stuyvesant High School in Manhattan; and Barry Joseph, at the time a graduate student in the American studies program at New York University. Kessler and Howard also assisted me on the subway musician survey. I approached TA employees alone. Ultimately, conducting these surveys acquainted me with the subway music scene, and with the subways, to a greater extent than I had previously managed.

My research assistants and I distributed a seven-page survey to forty-five riders, most of whom completed it while we waited. In an effort to maximize the diversity of responses, we approached riders at various points, including inside subway cars, on platforms where they were waiting for trains, and on mezzanines in subway music circles. We administered the survey to those who did not feel confident about their English literacy, and I translated it into Spanish for three respondents. Questions probed riders' personal views, their interactions with musicians and other audience members, and their opinions about the regulation of subway music. We distributed two versions of this survey: the first consisted mainly of open-ended questions while the second provided a greater number of multiple-choice answers. Riders were more inclined to respond to the close-ended questions, although responses gathered with the open-ended version were extraordinary.

We distributed an eleven-page survey to subway musicians, both MUNY members and freelancers. They answered open-ended questions about their backgrounds, their patterns of activity underground, their contact with transit police, station managers, and MUNY, and their goals and commitments. Because I wanted to document as broad a range of experiences as possible, my assistants and I generally approached only one member of each musical group. Most musicians preferred to complete the survey at home. We either arranged to retrieve it, or I asked the musicians to mail it back to me. In six cases we administered the survey as an interview. Malcolm Howard taped three of these for possible use in a public radio broadcast. In the end I used twenty completed copies.

Finally, I distributed a six-page survey to TA employees. It resembled the rider survey in structure and content, although I gave employees the option of answering "whatever the TA says" to certain close-ended questions. They usually asked me to retrieve it on a subsequent day. I administered it to five respondents and had illuminating conversations in the process. In the end I collected thirty completed copies.

My experience in distributing this last survey illustrates the somewhat ambiguous power structure at the TA and the political nature of the environment in which subway music occurs. Three station managers were extremely helpful, but in very different ways. The first one, who had known about my project for three years, told me to approach his employees directly. The second introduced me to his station supervisors and instructed them to complete the survey. The third initially advised me to clear my project with the TA Customer Relations Department, then, on second thought, decided that my survey was "harmless." He proceeded to make extra copies and distributed them himself. As for the TA employees who completed the survey, two all but thanked me for seeking out their opinions on policy matters. At such moments I felt that, whatever its outcome, conducting this study had been worthwhile.

In analyzing the data, the work of scholars in many disciplines proved useful. I developed a conceptual framework by combining ideas from urban anthropology, sociology, social history, cultural studies, constitutional law, political theory, urban planning, urban ecology, and folklore. I cannot think of a more suitable approach to a topic that defies categorization. Similarly, I was drawn to different writing styles; in the following chapters I combine traditional exposition with informal storytelling. It seems to me that juxtaposing techniques is appropriate in a book that is, at base, about transcending barriers and making spontaneous connections.

This book begins by situating New York City subway music in the context of social, cultural, and political developments of recent decades; identifying its main characteristics; and reviewing the relevant literature. Chapter 2 outlines the music's history to show that there are two types: official subway music, which celebrates and promotes the subway system, and freelance subway music, a descendant of street performing. Chapter 3 profiles musicians, exploring their personal characteristics, their reasons for performing underground, their impact on subway space, and the cultural transformations in which they are involved. This chapter also presents riders' reactions, focusing on the music's ability to evoke personal memories and promote distinct forms of group solidarity.

Chapter 4 describes the dynamics of the audience circles and explores how subway music challenges dominant paradigms about legitimacy as it relates to community, culture, and public space use. These considerations set the stage for the second part of the book, which directly addresses the politics of the subway music scene. Chapter 5 discusses the Music Under New York program, which lends support to selected performers. Meanwhile, TA regulations govern unsponsored, freelance music in particular. Chapter 6 traces the legal, political, and cultural debate over the authorization of subway music in the 1980s, which peaked in 1989 when musicians challenged the constitutionality of the TA regulations in federal district court.

Chapter 7 examines the role of the transit police in enforcing the regulations and reveals that officers' practices are often shaped by a lack of information. Chapter 8 presents the views of two populations that encounter subway musicians daily—TA employees and concession stand workers—to assess the effects of the music on the broad, informal social network underground. The Conclusion presents the street performers' community in Boston and Cambridge, Massachusetts, as a possible model, describes current legal and political organizing activity among street performers and subway musicians in New York, and offers policy recommendations fitted to the particular cultural and political setting of the city's subways.

Ultimately, my hope is that the issues presented in this book will interest participants in the subway music scene as well as social scientists who are debating the politics of public space use and attempting to define "quality of life" more inclusively for this city.

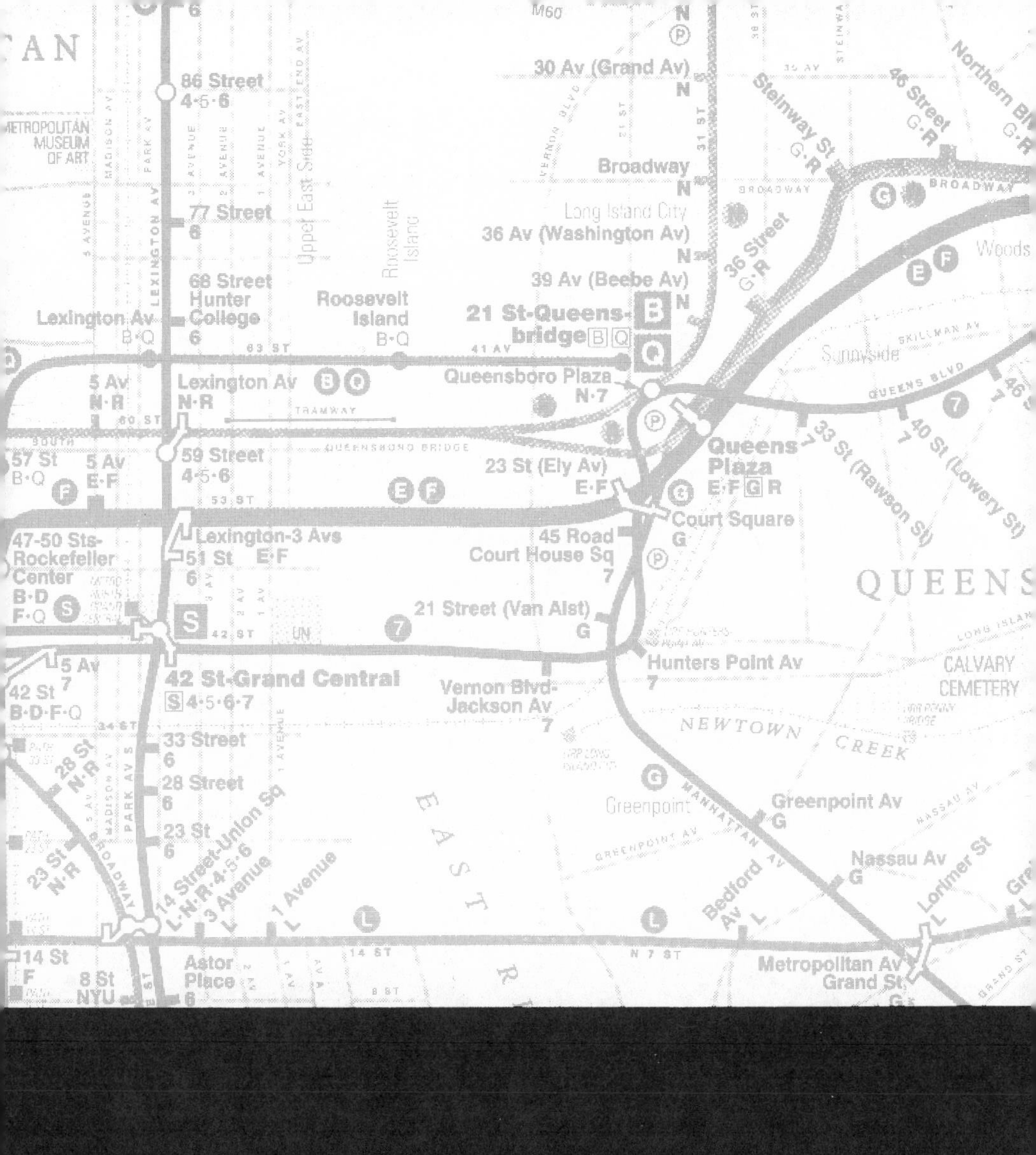

PART I

MAKING MUSIC UNDERGROUND

1

Setting Up

January 14, 1992, 5:30 P.M., 59th Street and Lexington Avenue BMT Platform

It was rush hour and the trains were delayed. A virtual sea of people waited on the platform, but an oasis had formed around Trinidadian steel drummer Michael Gabriel and his partner Roland. With riders peering over both of his shoulders, Michael nimbly tapped the surfaces inside his fifty-gallon silver pan. Roland, who wore a large Rastafarian cap, sat on a milk crate and with a single drumstick he thumped the bottom of a white plastic construction bucket that jutted out between his legs.

I stood next to a white-haired woman in a crisp pink raincoat. "When I was expectin' my daughter," she commented to me in a melodic accent, "the musicians in my town were practicing through the night for Carnival. They were playing calypso like this and, when my daughter came out, she had the music in her blood!"

I asked her what she thought of subway music.

"It makes the waiting easier," she said. "Sometimes I don't realize I'm waiting an hour for the train!

"We need it. What do they say? Music soothes the savage breast? It's soothing. It's relaxing. I think of sandpaper on wood. Smoothes the rough edges. We need music. It's like water. Like waves on a sea. Music is a blessing.

"I don't have to dress up and go to Carnegie Hall. I get it right here."

Subway music grew out of the ancient art of street performing, whose practitioners declare themselves in plazas, in parks, and on sidewalks in towns and cities throughout the world. Despite their long history, however, official government attitudes toward them have rarely been favorable. "Street performance," Sally Harrison-Pepper notes, "is viewed as an event that is marginal, inconsequential, unworthy of documentation, even a threat to the image of the city, established structures of commercial theater, or other businesses."[1] New York is not much of an exception in this respect. At the turn of the century, street music saw its heyday in this city, but by the 1930s an order from the mayor's office ended the issuance of licenses to musicians. The ban was not lifted for over three decades. True to the street performing tradition, the latest revival promotes gatherings; yet, ironically, it results from the severe political, cultural, and social dislocations since World War II and particularly during the last three decades.

In the late 1950s and 1960s, as the United States emerged from the political and cultural repression of the McCarthy era, African American people and young white college students began to call attention to the racial discrimination endemic to their nation's domestic and foreign policies. The civil rights movement drew on the African American communal tradition of singing to promote solidarity, and the antiwar movement turned to what sociologist Simon Frith calls the "radical tradition of American folk music."[2] The streets of major American cities became political forums, where activists expressed their views through protest songs and guerrilla theater. Participants discovered that the street setting facilitated highly democratic forms of expression and exchange; even after the original civil rights and antiwar activities subsided, some decided to continue with versions of their own.[3] The Bread and Puppet Theater, which incorporates broad political themes into its annual summer festival in rural Vermont, is one of many entertainment troupes that began by performing guerrilla theater on the streets of major cities like New York.

Gentrification produced the second form of dislocation. In the 1970s, corporations and suburban residents began to reverse the postwar exodus from center cities.[4] In New York, their return stimulated the real estate market, and skyrocketing rents forced avant-garde jazz clubs and other small musical venues to shut down—or at the very least to save money by paying their musical entertainment less or nothing at all. Musicians' problems were compounded in subsequent years by the administration of Mayor Edward I. Koch, which refused to repeal the city's antiquated cabaret laws that restricted live music in restaurants and clubs by setting strict limits on the number of musicians and the types of instruments allowed.[5] In addition, technological changes steadily reduced opportunities to perform. According to Paul Chevigny, a civil liberties attorney, the rising popularity of discotheques "signalled the ultimate divorce of dancing and live music."[6] Sam Brown, a seasoned alto saxophone player who in ten-gallon hat and cowboy boots doubles as a shoeshiner on the 42nd Street side of the New York Public Library, recalls that jazz musicians like himself turned to the streets and subways during this period to find an audience.

Immigration is a significant factor in the proliferation of street performing in New York, just as it was at the turn of the century. The United States has changed its immigration policy with respect to non-European nations, and increasingly Latin American people, displaced by severe political and economic crises at home, have settled in this city.[7] By the end of the 1980s, Latino musicians, particularly from the Andes region, had joined their North American counterparts in New York's streets and subways, contributing an indigenous tradition or, in the words of subway musician Ricardo Silva, "a new spirit" to the scene. In the 1990s immigrants from the former Soviet Union as well as from other Eastern European and Asian nations have also joined them. In short, African American and immigrant musicians are largely responsible for the city's distinctive street performing and subway music traditions.

In the 1980s New York also became aware of hip hop—what David Toop describes as a subculture or an "attitude" first developed in the early 1970s by African American and Latino youth in the South Bronx and Harlem who, through personal and collective cultural expression, resisted the gang warfare that plagued their neighborhoods. In Toop's words, "Since nobody in New York City, America or the rest of the world wanted to know about the black so-called ghettos—the unmentionable areas of extreme urban deprivation—the style was allowed to flourish as a genuine street movement."[8]

During the 1970s hip hop incorporated many forms of expression and identity, including rapping ("rhythmic talking over a funk beat"), breakdancing, graffiti, and a particular fashion style. Young men called DJs built sound systems, which they brought to house parties, high school dances, and parks to produce musical collages out of an eclectic mix of existing recordings. The DJs' music encouraged fierce verbal and dance competitions which, Toop says, contained elements that can be traced back through centuries of black culture.[9]

In 1979 an independent black label released the Sugarhill Gang's "Rapper's Delight," which quickly climbed the record charts and secured a place for rap (or, as Toop says, a marketable form of rap) in the popular music industry. Meanwhile, young breakdancers and moonwalkers took their craft downtown to the Times Square theater district and into the subways, engaging in what Toop calls "the bottom line of street survival."[10]

Strangely enough, breakdancing is sometimes dismissed as a fad that disappeared after 1984. A Chicago judge even held that the end of breakdancing (which can easily be interpreted to mean the return to invisibility of disadvantaged African American youth) meant his city could safely consider authorizing street performing.[11] Yet breakdancing and hip hop drumming remain familiar and popular sights and sounds in New York's streets and subways. Plastic bucket drummer Larry Wright, who was "discovered" and cast in a television commercial and a feature-length film, is perhaps the best known representative of this style underground. Hip hoppers' particular forms of expression, and the ways in which some people—particularly people in positions of authority—have responded to them, raise important questions about the roles of race and class in the New York subway music scene. The point to be stressed at present is that hip hop is a significant part of this scene.

Initially, many street musicians saw the subways as a winter refuge; they resurfaced above ground in the spring. Many still adhere to this seasonal pattern, especially during the summer months when the heat in the stations makes performing, let alone waiting for trains, close to unbearable. But some musicians choose to perform underground all year round, which suggests that the subway system constitutes a performance space with an appeal of its own.

Apart from scheduled events in semi-public arcades and shopping malls, subway music is the one true example of indoor street performing. Indeed, the subways are formidable, both in terms of size and function. "With 722 miles of tracks," says Clifton Hood, "New York City's subway is the longest rapid transit system in the world, larger than the London underground, the Paris metro, the Tokyo subway, and the Seoul subway." It operates 6,400 cars through 469 stations, and serves an average of 2.7 million riders a day.[12] In this specialized setting, live music may seem out of place, if not dangerous, compared to street performing, which often blends in with the recreational atmosphere of today's parks and plazas.

But like the streets, the subways shape and are shaped by live performances.[13] The acoustics underground, for example, accommodate both intimate and scattered audience circles. And the labyrinthine structure of such stations as Times Square leads to surprise encounters with musicians; according to William H. Whyte, "It is the unexpected that seems to delight [urban people] most."[14] Moreover, despite the fact that it tends to look and smell like a sewer, the subway system inspires musicians. Classical violinist Jim Graseck talks about listening for, and playing in, the silences between the trains. And in Grand Central Terminal, the "Carnegie Hall of the subways," alto saxophonist Sayyd Abdul al-Khabyyr pauses during a piece to allow his sound to resonate. "I try to utilize this entire space," he says. "I even know what key it's in."

Sally Harrison-Pepper appropriately calls the New York subways a "moving performance space."[15] Yet it is also a space that demands a considerable amount of standing and waiting. Perhaps it is in this respect that subway music most differs from street performing. It makes the waiting easier for many riders. It relieves their anxieties and even gives them a feeling of safety in their dismal surroundings. Moreover, New York's subway system never closes; late at night, when the platforms might otherwise be deserted, musicians with unconventional schedules perform and offer these various benefits to riders. Thus, subway music is worth studying in its own right.

Subway music has hardly been documented, and even the street performing tradition has largely been excluded from the official historical record. As Sally Harrison-Pepper aptly observes, "Much of the history of street performance . . . is found in laws that prohibit it."[16] Indeed, references surface in books that discuss particular musical genres. In *The Rap Attack*, David Toop describes the public space culture and street performing traditions of African American communities, from the rent parties of the 1920s to doo-wop in the 1950s to rap in the 1970s. Toop also identifies films, such as *Flashdance*, which have incorporated breakdancing into their story lines.[17]

Simon Frith mentions street performing in *Sound Effects: Youth, Leisure, and the Politics of Rock 'n' Roll* when he explains the debate

Jim Graseck, a classical violinist, entertains riders by imitating the closing-door signal on a platform in the Herald Square station. Photo by Dennis Connors

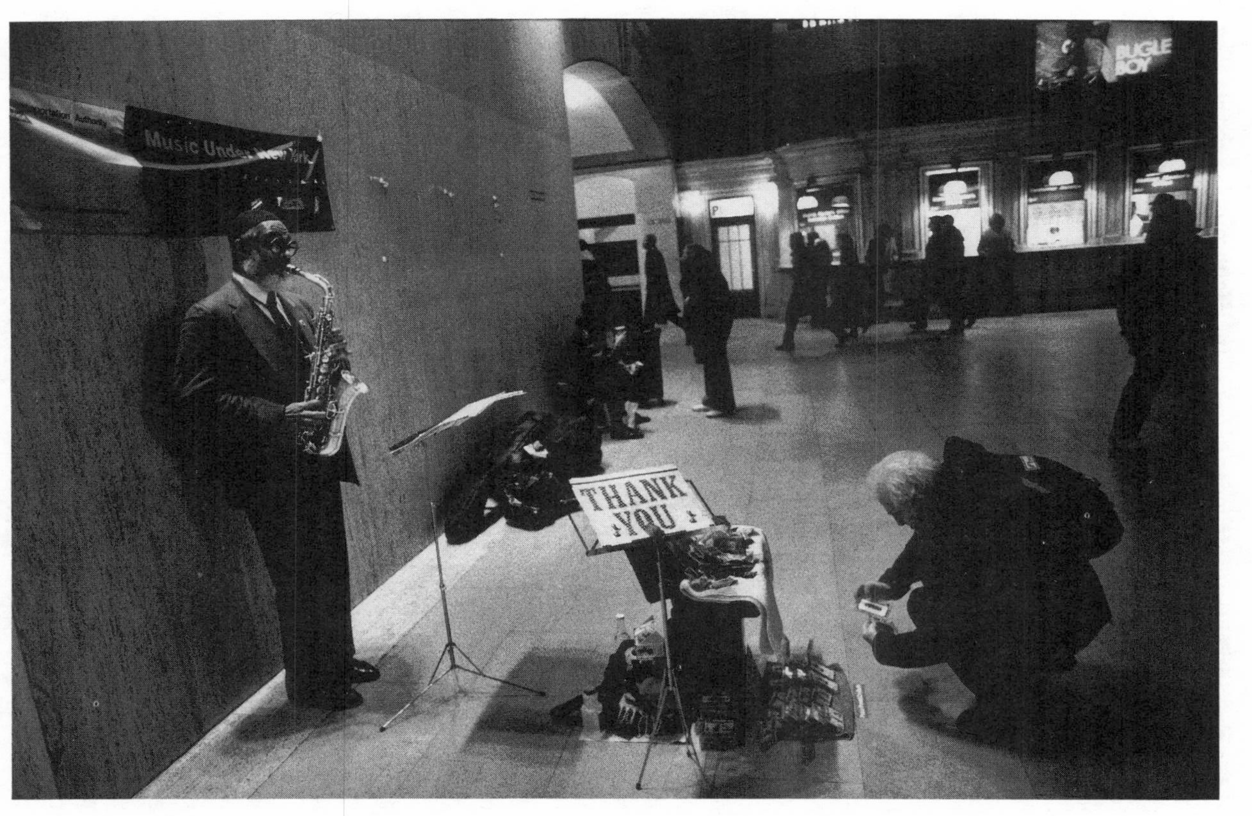

Sayyd Abdul al-Khabyyr, saxophonist, performing on the main concourse at Grand Central Terminal. Notice the Bugle Boy ad in the top right-hand corner of the photograph. Photo by Dennis Connors

about the authenticity of mass culture. In *Highbrow Lowbrow: The Emergence of Cultural Hierarchy in America*, Lawrence Levine traces the disappearance of a shared public culture, which he says existed in the United States until the turn of the century. At that time, he reports, immigrant musicians, in particular Italian organ grinders on the streets of New York, were singled out by the social elite as the cause of the nation's cultural decline.[18] Stephen Baird, founder of the Street Artists' Guild in Boston and Cambridge, finds information about the history of his calling in record liner notes and in musicians' biographies.

Fortunately, inspired by the street performing revival, two authors have published highly informative books that explore the social and cultural significance of the phenomenon. *Passing the Hat: Street Performers in America* (1980) is a broad ethnography in which Patricia Campbell draws on her travels with the "pioneers" of the 1970s. In street performers she sees a hope for increased democracy and freedom in a society imprisoned by its own consumerism and greed.

Sally Harrison-Pepper's book, *Drawing a Circle in the Square: Street Performing in New York's Washington Square Park* (1990), is a detailed analysis of nonmusical performances in a well-known public space in Greenwich Village. Harrison-Pepper describes the ways in which successful street performers "transform city 'space' into theater 'place.'" But she contends that street music is not truly street performing. Musicians, she says, tend to be students or temporarily unemployed indoor artists and are consequently less committed to the streets. Musical pieces, moreover, set the parameters of these performances; according to Harrison-Pepper, "street music only happens to occur on an urban stage; the larger message is that the environment is mostly to be ignored."[19]

Indeed, many street and subway musicians have access to other venues or make contacts that lead to private engagements. Yet, performance elsewhere does not necessarily indicate less commitment to the streets and subways. In fact, a number of subway musicians, experienced in both worlds, reflect on the different impact of artistic expression in the cultural establishment and in public space, and on the complex relationship between them. Harrison-Pepper herself singles out the Folk Singers' "Riot" of 1961, in which musicians protested the city parks commissioner's attempt to ban spontaneous cultural gatherings in Washington Square, as a catalyst of the street performing revival.[20] Ultimately, urban public space itself politicizes musical performances by rendering them immediate and democratic. The following chapters document the various ways in which subway musicians, like other street performers, integrate cues from their environment, handle unexpected interruptions, and involve themselves in public life. This book also explores how music—a form of communication that transcends barriers at the same time as it conveys particular cultural messages—promotes complex and specifically urban forms of engagement in the subways.

Campbell and Harrison-Pepper identify the essential characteristics of street performing, and these apply to subway music as well. Most, although not all, of these performers are men, which is why Harrison-Pepper uses the male pronoun to describe them, and why I follow her practice.

The prototypical street performer has a moral and political philosophy about his work. He performs in public space to challenge established ideas about what legitimate culture is and where it can be found. He presents new ideas before anyone is willing to invest in them. He encounters his audience directly, obviating the need for advertisements, agents, auditions, or opening night reviews. He democratizes his art by making it accessible to everyone, regardless of income, race, gender, or age.

In street performance, the audience is a part of the event. In contrast to most other forms of live entertainment, the presence of the audience creates a stage. Moreover, by giving or withholding applause, comments, and money, the audience advises the performer on how to perfect his art and improve his street skills. Together, performer and audience articulate conflicts and hopes that exist in their city at that particular stage of its history.

Both Campbell and Harrison-Pepper found that, despite the tremendous diversity among street performers and their audiences, they tended to resemble this model. My task was to test the model underground.

Surprisingly little has been published about the history of the New York City subway system, and even less has been written about its social history. Two of the best-known efforts, Brian Cudahy's *Under the Sidewalks of New York* and Stan Fischler's *Uptown, Downtown*, alternate between the broad political implications and the minute details of subway construction; they consider riders primarily in aggregate terms or in the context of subway trivia. To be fair, Cudahy prefaces the latest edition of his book with a reference to musicians: "The subway today is not without occasional musical interludes. From time to time, roving musicians entertain passengers with impromptu recitals on instruments conventional and otherwise."[21] Clifton Hood documents the roles of the public in the political battle to build the subways. In his chapter "The People's Subway," he describes the popularity of the system in the 1920s and 1930s among a cross section of New Yorkers as well as among artists who depicted riders as representing "the 'Truth' about humanity."[22]

A few social histories and ethnographies explore what people have done in the subways aside from riding the trains, and what the subways have meant to them. In the 1950s Edmund Love wrote *Subways Are for Sleeping*, a profile of bohemians who spent a large portion of their days and, evidently, nights underground. More recently, in *Getting Up*, Craig Castleman provided a vivid account of graffiti artists and their encounters with the transit police. City Lore's booklet, *I've Been Working on the Subway*, is a compilation of oral histories of TA employees.

Perhaps the most elaborate and entertaining work of this kind to date is *Subway Lives: 24 Hours in the Life of the New York City Subway*, in which Jim Dwyer describes the myriad official and unofficial interactions that overlap underground. He asserts that "the subways have become the great public commons of the city." Only there, he says, "can the full spectrum of city life—with all the bewildering diversity of its pathologies and its glories—be glimpsed, felt, and at times even understood."[23]

Dwyer refers to musical performances in the subways with varying degrees of approbation. He talks about Tom Thomasevich, the conductor who sings Elvis tunes in his train car; the saxophone player from Mars, who performs in the cars and vows to hurt riders' ears unless they give him money; and an Ecuadorian group in the Times Square station, which can be seen as a symbol of immigrants' contributions, past and present, to New York.[24]

The news media are another source of information about contemporary street performing and subway music. Sally Harrison-Pepper notes that in the late 1970s "New York newspapers and journals responded to the street performance craze with a wealth of articles and photographs."[25] They singled out such "urban folk heroes"[26] as European-born Philippe Petit, renowned (and notorious) for performing his tightrope act one morning between the Twin Towers of the World Trade Center, and Jim Graseck, whose street and subway fans more recently filled Alice Tully Hall in Lincoln Center and Carnegie Hall for his debuts. Michael Lydon, a subway musician and rock author, explained some of the primary motivations for playing underground in his article "New York City Subway Orpheus" (*Atlantic Monthly*, 1990), and Steve Witt, a modern-day Woody Guthrie, combines interviews and personal insights in his column "The Street Singer's Beat," in the Manhattan newspapers *Downtown* and *Street News*.

Nationally broadcast news programs including *The MacNeil-Lehrer News Hour, ABC World News Tonight*, and National Public Radio's *Morning Edition* and *All Things Considered* covered the public policy debate in the late 1980s, which peaked in 1989 when musicians challenged the MTA and TA in court. Unfortunately, the media all but lost interest once the legal battle ended. Recent features have not always been so insightful. On December 30, 1992, syndicated talk show host Phil Donahue featured street performers and subway musicians on his program, offering, he announced, "a real stage." Some of the most promising work may be coming from students in journalism, film, and sociology who are producing documentaries and dissertations on the effects of street performing and subway music on urban life.

It is certainly tempting to try to evaluate the quality of subway performances, in particular to note that the musicians are often at least as talented and creative as their counterparts in more established venues. One subway rider I interviewed, a visitor from Baltimore, remarked that he had paid a fifteen-dollar cover charge at a jazz club back home where the music was not nearly as good as what he had just heard performed in Grand Central Terminal. In this book, however, I discuss quality and taste only as they figure into the views of the musicians, riders, and authorities. I am more interested in sociological effects—in how people respond to subway music and what it means to them.

My choice was greatly influenced by the work of anthropologist Ruth Finnegan. In *The Hidden Musicians: Local Music in a Small English Town*, Finnegan studies music through its *practices*, created and transmitted between local performers and their audiences, rather than through musical scores or the lives of "professionals," as is generally the custom in both classical and popular music scholarship.[27] Through this approach, she discovers that performing in and attending local cultural events are ways people, especially urban people, interpret and make sense of their society. Similarly, I relied on audiences as a major source of information and interpretation.

Finnegan concludes her analysis by considering the nature of music itself: "It is tempting to write in facile mystical terms, but there does seem to be a sense in which the process of joining together in music, with all its problems and conflicts, really does unite people 'in harmony'—to follow the significantly common musical metaphor—in some unique and profound way which, except perhaps in religious enactment, is seldom found in other contexts."[28] I, too, found this type of harmony in the circles around subway musicians. Normally, New York subway riders approach each other to ask for directions or to commiserate about service, but those listening to the music exchange gestures and words signifying approval, appreciation, "a respect," as one rider put it.[29] Considering that varieties of Andean, reggae, and soul music (all of which are performed underground) originated as part of sacred ritual, it is not so surprising that subway music often promotes reactions and interactions that could indeed be described as "religious."

Historically, government has distrusted live music in intimate settings, considering its intensity a threat to the prevailing social order. In *Gigs: Jazz and the Cabaret Laws in New York City*, Paul Chevigny analyzes the social and cultural underpinnings of the laws that restricted live music in jazz clubs from 1926 to 1990. In the 1980s Chevigny represented jazz musicians in court, and in his book he explains the strategy they used to have the laws overturned. Many of the issues he raises are central to the politics of subway music as well.

The cabaret laws were a combination of licensing requirements and zoning restrictions, limiting the establishments and neighborhoods in which live music was performed as well as the people who were allowed to play there. Interestingly, Chevigny says, by the time the board of aldermen passed the ordinance in 1926, cabarets no longer existed in New York. These restaurant-theaters for the social elite had been replaced by speakeasies, and white New Yorkers were traveling uptown to Harlem to hear black musicians play jazz. Indeed, the aldermen admitted that they aimed to curb the "'wild' people" who frequented jazz clubs. According to Chevigny, the cabaret laws encoded stereotypes of black culture in an effort to prevent mixing between the races. "Such an enforcement of status is characteristic of lawmaking about the arts," he says. "Those who legislate voice their sense that one style is socially acceptable and that another is not, and by their acts make the discrimination come true."[30]

Over the years the city introduced various enforcement tools that further degraded jazz and censored the musicians. Local 802 of the American Federation of Musicians harbored its own prejudices against the music, which it considered "lower class": when in 1955 the union persuaded the mayor and the City Planning Commission to amend the zoning resolution to allow "incidental music" performed by ensembles of up to three members in non-cabaret districts, it requested the provision for flutes and keyboards only, not for horns and drums, the traditional instrumentation in jazz. In fact, the union assured the city that the change would not encourage "congregating by undesirable elements," thus recasting old racist attitudes in vaguer forms that were consistent with the city's contempt for "degenerates" and corruptible elements (p. 70).

During the mayoralty of John Lindsay and the fiscal crisis of the 1970s, enforcement was relaxed, but in the 1980s Mayor Ed Koch empowered the Department of Consumer Affairs to close down unlicensed clubs. In 1983, under new sympathetic management, Local 802 decided to take action to increase the number of venues for all its members. When lobbying for legislative change proved slow and largely ineffective, the union resolved to attack both the licensing and zoning provisions through litigation in state court. Counseled by Chevigny, the plaintiffs argued that musical performance is a form of expression entitled to protection under the First Amendment to the Constitution. While the city has the right to regulate the time, place, or manner of such expression to advance a "substantial government interest," it cannot discriminate against content; the cabaret laws, explained the plaintiffs, were discriminatory since the restrictions on instruments and ensemble size changed the "emotional impact" of the music. An acoustical engineer testified on the musicians' behalf that noise concerns could not be used by the defense to validate the cabaret laws. In an era when flutes and keyboards may be amplified with electronic devices, he contended, a distinction cannot be made between horns and drums, on the one hand, and incidental music, on the other. In point of fact, while lobbying the city council the union had helped to pass an ordinance setting a decibel limit on club music, which was being enforced effectively.

For its part, the city argued that the three-musician limit in non-cabaret zones prevented traffic congestion and thus maintained the "quality of life" in those neighborhoods. Justice David Saxe accepted the argument. He granted the musicians a preliminary injunction, lifting the ban on horns and drums but not the restriction on ensemble size. Convinced that no arguments remained, the city moved for a summary judgment to dismiss the case before trial. Meanwhile, the plaintiffs collected more affidavits, including one from an engineer formerly with the city Department of Environmental Protection stating that no studies existed to prove any correlation between small clubs and traffic problems. In 1988, Judge Saxe surprised everyone by declaring the incidental music exception unconstitutional (pp. 118–27).

As Chevigny aptly points out, however, the sequel illustrates the disparity between litigation and politics. The court victory meant nothing until the city implemented the changes, and the Koch administration attempted many bargains to postpone or even reverse the outcome of the case. Finally in 1990 Mayor David Dinkins, a jazz aficionado, approved an amendment to the city zoning resolution and swiftly nullified the cabaret laws (pp. 148–53).

Chevigny speculates on why it took the city so long to abandon the discriminatory laws. A legal change in this case presupposed a cultural change, namely, an increased acceptance in society of vernacular music—artistic expression that is more popularly based and that tends to originate in non-Anglo communities. In addition, Chevigny explains, the Koch administration presumed that clubs so small could not be major cultural resources; if they were, the government reasoned, surely they could afford to pay the price of licensing and regulation (pp. 11, 177–78).

This analysis clarifies why street and subway musicians have fared so poorly, even worse than musicians in the jazz clubs. Street music was banned in New York in the 1930s, at the same time that the cabaret laws were put into effect; like jazz, it was discriminated against in official campaigns against vernacular culture and "undesirables." In that period, too, street musicians were explicitly equated—and outlawed—with beggars.

The transit system has its own set of rules, and until 1985 spontaneous performances were banned entirely underground (although they took place there nevertheless). Over the next five years, musicians succeeded in having their activity constitutionally protected by the courts as a form of free expression. These rulings and the popularity of vernacular music pressured the TA to revise its regulations. In 1989, the TA authorized subway music, subject only to time-place-manner restrictions. Yet in contrast to the cabaret laws, and demonstrating how inconsistent government policy can be, the TA allowed horns and drums while it banned amplification devices on subway platforms.

Musicians challenged the amp ban in court, arguing that it discriminated against particular musical styles. A federal judge ruled in their favor, enjoining the MTA and TA from imposing the ban. On appeal, however, the authorities argued that the amp ban helped to ensure public safety, a substantial government interest. The court of appeals reinstated the ban.

Whereas the musicians in the cabaret case won the right to perform in locations designed for their activity, subway musicians raised a public policy question that is fairly recent and controversial: Can a transportation terminal double as a performance space? It would seem that the MUNY program and the TA regulations affirm that possibility, but the authorities' actual positions remain ambiguous. Transit police officers, relying on official policy or inventing their own rules, invoke arguments about safety and sanitation to move or "sweep" musicians out of the stations. Thus the old denigration of vernacular culture and "undesirables" has been encoded underground. Despite the risks, however, hundreds of musicians, MUNY and freelance, proceed to set up underground. One can only imagine how much more music would resonate through the stations were it not for the unpredictability of the authorities.

Chevigny explains that the negative attitudes toward vernacular culture emerge from a principle called "controlled community." Often embedded in urban planning, controlled community maintains that cities are safer and better when they are quiet and empty, and when strangers are kept away. Its counterpoint is the urban diversity ideal, which holds that cities are more exciting and, even, safer when public spaces are filled with people engaged in diverse activities (pp. 94–95). Controlled community was refuted in the cabaret case, and it certainly does not belong in the subways, where we learn to negotiate and share the city. In this book, I consider how it would be in the authorities' own interest to nurture urban diversity, particularly the involvement that is characteristic of subway music scenes, and to see subway musicians as major cultural resources.

Among the millions of riders who enter the subways each day, there are of course those who ignore or actively dislike subway music. Even as they raved about the musicians, certain people I interviewed felt compelled to add: "And then there are some who are *awful*!" In this book I mean to acknowledge the many different opinions people hold about creating social order, or harmony, underground. Similarly, I am interested in the politics between musicians and the authorities but also, more broadly, in the web of activities and negotiations that make subway space work.

The spectrum of opinion on subway music is complex, at times surprising, even contradictory. Folk singer Pete Seeger, for example, believes that subway music programs and regulations are acceptable, if not necessary, while some transit police officers all but ignore the rules. In 1990 the MTA defended the regulation of subway music as an effort to "balance several, sometimes competing interests," but a 1988 customer survey from the MTA offices had revealed that 70 percent of the riders polled liked subway music.[31] This matrix of views and practices, embedded in the larger matrix of life underground, is good reason to problematize subway music—to understand what it is, what it does, and what it means for the subways and the city.

2

The Beat Goes On: History

In New York City, subway music predates the subway ride. Alfred Ely Beach is responsible for this turn of events. He built the precursor to the city's subway system, and his story has assumed almost legendary proportions. Beach, who founded and edited *Scientific American*, was also an exceptional inventor. In 1868 he received permission from the state legislature to construct a set of underground pneumatic tubes through which mail could be moved. His permit was subterfuge, the perfect disguise for his true intentions. He wanted to build a pneumatic subway that, much like the proposed mail dispatch, would use compressed air to shoot carloads of passengers through the tunnel. But under the corrupt governance of the Tammany Hall political machine, especially boss William Marcy Tweed, Beach would never have been granted a permit for his own project. In spite of the need for improved transportation in New York, Tammany did not welcome competition with the existing surface transit lines, since the administration was receiving kickbacks from them.[1]

Permit in hand, Beach rented the basement of Devlin's clothing store (on the corner of Broadway and Murray Streets, facing city hall), formed his own crew, and dug the subway tunnel in secret. To allay possible fears among the general public about the safety of venturing below ground, before operations began he initiated a "public relations blaze" by building the "Saloon," an elegant waiting room adjacent to, and twice as large as, the tunnel.[2] The *New York World* described it as "120 feet long by 14 in width, the floor covered with oil-cloth of a pretty pattern, the walls hung with pictures, an expensive clock in the centre, elaborate chandeliers along the walls, comfortable settees at each side, and at the further end a space railed off for the occupancy of the ladies, with one of Chickerling's grand pianos for their amusement while waiting for the train."[3]

Of course, the Victorian-style Saloon bears little resemblance to today's subway stations. But the Beach legend demonstrates that in New York City, music making in the subways has a long, if not an extensive, history. It challenges the impression, which might otherwise prevail, that subway music began in the 1980s either through spontaneous generation or in the public relations offices of the MTA.

Indeed, two types of subway music have existed over time. The first, which I call "official subway music," occurs at ceremonial events involving politicians and transit executives and aims to promote the subway system. The second, "freelance [independent] subway music," closely resembles street performing in terms of form, content, and effect. In this chapter, drawing on surviving records and verbal accounts, I trace both traditions.

Official Subway Music

Starting with the groundbreaking for the city's first subway tunnel in 1900, New York politicians and transit executives marked significant stages in construction with dedication ceremonies. "Tunnel Day," as the groundbreaking was called, took place outside city hall where a huge crowd listened to a band play "The Star-Spangled Banner," heard speeches delivered by the "high priests" of transit, and watched Mayor Robert Van Wyck deposit the first shovelful of dirt from the excavation site into his silk top hat, to save as a souvenir.[4]

In that era, the subway system was envisioned as a major public monument. Patrician politicians saw station and line openings as occasions to call attention to the subways' (and, by implication, their own) role in stimulating development that would transform New York City into a major metropolis.[5] These ceremonies were meant to promote civic pride. The dedication site was draped in red, white, and blue bunting, and bands were contracted to play patriotic anthems. Otherwise, government found music to be an intrusion at such solemn events.

The opening of the first subway line in 1904 is a case in point. A "simple ceremony" was held in the aldermanic chambers at city hall where politicians, representatives of the Rapid Transit Commission, and officials from the privately financed Interborough Rapid Transit Company (IRT) spoke before fifteen thousand invited guests.[6] Meanwhile, the general public stood in City Hall Park, waiting to catch a glimpse of the dignitaries as they emerged and descended into the new station for the inaugural ride. (The crowd had to wait an additional five hours before "ordinary" people were allowed to enter the subways.) Many spectators had brought whistles and horns with them to celebrate the event, but the *New York Times*, which tended to represent the views of the social elite, reported that "everybody who had a whistle to blow had in mind the Mayor's request." They had been asked to remain silent while the speeches were delivered inside.[7] Ironically, Mayor George B. McClellan was attributing "the greatest honor and the greatest glory . . . to the spirit of the people themselves, without which this work would never have been undertaken, and without which it could never have been brought to a successful conclusion."[8]

Of course it can be argued that the sheer size of the crowd warranted a degree of government control and a police presence. But the rigidly hierarchical nature of the inauguration suggests that at least in the context of public ceremonials, the politicians considered the masses and their spirited music making to be sources of disorder. (By contrast, the relatively populist *Evening Post* reported, "as the public knew quite well that it could not go below ground before 2:30 o'clock, the most the policemen had to do was to answer foolish questions.")[9]

Later that evening was "carnival night in New York," according to the *Times* (acknowledging New Yorkers' excitement but using a term that in subsequent articles about subway line openings would be directly linked to rowdyism and vandalism). "Every noise-making instrument known to election night was in operation" at a celebration in Times Square.[10] And according to Clifton Hood's account of inauguration night, "high-spirited boys and girls took over part of a car and began singing songs, flirting, and fooling around."[11] Already on the first day of operation, some New Yorkers considered music making to be consistent with traveling underground, whereas politicians and transit officials could not envision holding even a dedication ceremony inside the subway system.

In subsequent years, dedications assumed a more festive air, partly, it seems, because the events were arranged by the local civic and merchant associations that had pressed for subway construction in the first place. In Brooklyn civic groups organized parades and turned the subways' arrival into a neighborhood event. Bay Ridge celebrated both the groundbreaking and the opening of the Fourth Avenue line in this way. At the groundbreaking in 1912, the Brooklyn Rapid Transit Company (BRT) lent its band to a procession featuring the area's children who marched in military formation dressed as Uncle Sam, Martha Washington, and Little Miss Brooklyn.[12] Through these events Brooklynites expressed their excitement about the new rapid transit system and reinforced their neighborhood and civic pride. Ultimately, however, as the folklorist Susan Davis explains, "those concerned with law and order" see a need "to pacify and regularize the people's use of the streets for demonstrations and marches."[13] The parades conformed to that type of control, which is why the BRT band could participate; it was heard only at ceremonies presented at clearly demarcated times and places.

The subway line dedications of the 1920s and 1930s rarely incorporated music. In fact, the celebratory mood of these events was often dampened by political tensions between elected officials and the private financiers of the IRT and the Brooklyn-Manhattan Transit Corporation (BMT), the successor of the BRT. In 1924, for instance, Mayor John F. Hylan used the opening of the 14th Street subway as a bully pulpit to rail against the IRT and to advocate a unified subway system that would be not only owned but operated by the city.[14] In 1932, when the first line of the municipally run Independent (IND) subway system opened along Eighth Avenue, no official ceremonies were held at all, perhaps because the local administration's corruption had recently been exposed and Mayor James Walker had resigned. The West Side Association of Commerce lost no time in criticizing city government for failing to celebrate this momentous event.[15]

Whether or not government participated, affluent merchant associations and major hotels continued to organize their own celebrations. These events began to feature forms of entertainment that promoted the participants' businesses and provided opportunities for leisure. In 1926 when the Fifth Avenue station of the Queensboro subway extension opened, the Hippodrome ran movies about the development of the area, narrated by members of the Forty-second Street Property

Owners and Merchants' Association.[16] On December 14, 1940, Mayor Fiorello LaGuardia, who thoroughly enjoyed public events, presided over the dedication of the Sixth Avenue subway, the last IND line to be opened.[17] It included a ribbon-cutting ceremony at the turnstiles and an inaugural ride that terminated at Radio City Music Hall, where management provided a free "entertainment program to celebrate the opening of the new line."[18]

Although LaGuardia succeeded in unifying the city's subway lines into a single municipally owned and operated system, he, like his predecessors, failed to make rapid transit financially self-sustaining. After World War II the stations and the service greatly deteriorated. Moreover, the increasingly complex forms of crime and racial conflict surfacing on the streets of New York were beginning to erupt underground. These conditions, together with the competition of the automobile, contributed to a steady decline in subway ridership.[19] In 1953, the New York City Transit Authority was established as a public benefit corporation to operate the city's mass transit system,[20] and TA executives looked for ways to improve public perception of the subways. Repeatedly they used vernacular culture, and specifically music, as a promotional tool.

In December 1956 five TA workers "serenaded" riders with Christmas carols inside subway cars. "Reaction," said the *Times*, "varied from 'excellent' to 'baloney,'" but generally, riders expressed "surprise" and "pleasure." A photo caption even stated that "passengers joined in song."[21] This appears to have been the first official attempt to emulate freelance subway music, which already existed underground. Yet evidently, in spite of its success, the TA never attempted to repeat this particular type of direct contact and interaction between employees and riders.

During the same period, the TA discovered a new form of official subway music, intended to foster the impression that riding the subways was a pleasant experience. It began to broadcast recorded Christmas carols and popular tunes over the public address system at Grand Central Station. "If the public likes the idea," the *Times* reported, "the Transit Authority will continue the practice and expand it to other subway stations."[22]

After 1956 the TA piped music over the loudspeakers at the Jay Street station in Brooklyn (where the TA headquarters are located). In December 1964, at least two riders wrote to complain and request that the practice be terminated. One customer, Miss E. Laurel, who signed her letter "A Weary Traveler," was incisive:

> Early in the morning, between 7:30 and 8:00 A.M., with the trains and station jammed beyond belief, a person is not in the mood for that asinine, superficial blasting of recorded "music"—we get enough of it from neighbors' radios and TV's, over the whole weekend, and every night and morning, as it is. . . . Isn't there enough noise in the City of New York, Brooklyn, Queens, etc.—with people jam-packed in tiny rooms—with not enough privacy—without having to endure the noise of canned music in the public streets? And in the subways?[23]

That month, the TA instructed personnel at the Jay Street station to stop broadcasting the music.[24]

Almost thirty years later, the TA revived the idea, this time to make the subways seem not only more inviting but safer. The proposal was unveiled in 1991, soon after one of the worst train accidents in the subways' history had occurred. The TA openly admitted that it thought recorded music would soothe riders' nerves. But many riders accused the TA of trying to sanitize its own image by directing public attention away from persistent problems with service.[25] In fact, some riders feared the piped-in music would drown out the spontaneous performances they had become so accustomed to encountering underground. One woman, a source told me, phoned the TA and asked, "And what will happen to the musicians down there?"

Freelance Subway Music

From the start, freelance subway music was unscheduled, diverse, variously motivated, and until the 1980s, unauthorized. To the extent that it is an outgrowth of street performing, its history begins in the earliest cities. According to Patricia Campbell, the history of street performing *is* the history of urban civilization, because as long as cities have created public meeting places and thoroughfares, performers have staked a presence in them. "But," Campbell notes, "because such entertainers were beneath polite notice, their existence was seldom documented in serious literature, and we have to infer the teeming theatrical life of the streets from oblique mentions, occasional pictures, and the mark their passing has left on language ('charlatan,' which originally meant 'one who draws a crowd,' or 'mountebank'—'he who climbs up on a bench')."[26] Nevertheless, Campbell cites historical records of street performing in ancient Egypt and Greece, which even document the performers' practice of collecting donations by "passing the hat."[27]

Many street performers and subway musicians in the United States trace the origins of their craft back to medieval Europe. England was known for its buskers, Germany for its minnesingers, and France for its troubadours. At least three of the subway musicians I interviewed used the French term while discussing their artistic heritage.

Troubadours were itinerant poets who composed songs of courtly love for the aristocrats (or for the wives of the aristocrats) who supported them financially. Many of their songs also commented on their society. Troubadours led a precarious existence. "The common folk loved them and welcomed the glimpse of magic they brought to their grim lives," Campbell says, "but the nobles feared such free spirits and regularly persecuted, jailed, and burned them—although they first chose the best for their own households."[28] Steve Witt has heard that as they traveled between competing towns, they were killed for divulging political information.

Troubadours also broke down cultural barriers. As itinerant musicians they sang ballads describing their homes and their journeys. According to Robert Briffault, the troubadours of southern France exchanged literary techniques with the Moorish poets of Spain.[29] If Briffault's account is accepted (his contemporaries challenged it), then the troubadours' practice can been seen as a precursor to the fusion of cultural traditions which subway musicians engage in today, and which will be explored in the next chapter.

There is a difference of opinion among contemporary street performers who trace their artistic roots to Europe on whether the troubadours are their true ancestors. Stephen Baird rejects the claim because troubadours almost exclusively came from and played for the aristocracy. Instead, he believes his predecessors were the medieval minstrels and jongleurs—musicians, jugglers, mimes, and acrobats—who represented and performed for all classes and who organized and trained themselves in craft guilds. Moreover, in previous eras different ethnic groups supported their own itinerant musicians. Eastern European Jews, for instance, had Klezmer groups, which traveled among the shtetls to play at weddings, bar mitzvahs, and other communal events.[30] Spiritual descendants maintain the street performing tradition in Europe, with varying degrees of government sanction, to this day. One New York subway musician who has performed abroad reports that "Europe is especially busker-friendly."

Evidence of street performing can be found on every continent. David Toop traces rap singers' verbal wizardry to the griots, experienced musicians, poets, storytellers, and historians on the savannahs of west Africa. For generations they have delivered the news and enforced social codes among villagers through a combination of traditional recitation, extemporizing, and wit.[31] In Amy Tan's novel *The Kitchen God's Wife*, the narrator describes a market scene in pre-Communist China in which two young boys toss coins to an organ grinder's monkey: "The monkey picked them up, bit them to see if they were true, tipped his hat to the boys, then handed the money to his owner, who gave him two dried lizards that he crunched on right away. We all clapped."[32] If street music is broadly defined to include the chants and rhymes that merchants traditionally sang to call attention to their wares, then street performers can also trace their origins to marketplaces the world over.[33]

In New York City, many contemporary street and subway musicians have emigrated from the Andes region, which includes Colombia, Ecuador, Peru, Bolivia, and parts of Chile and Argentina. Their music making derives from the pre-Columbian, communally based traditions of indigenous Andean culture, but it also reflects very recent changes in Andean attitudes toward indigenous culture and the meanings attached to it.

In the rural highlands of southern Peru, explains Thomas Turino, an ethnomusicologist, monthly fiestas are "at the center of communal social life." Men form wind ensembles and provide music for these celebrations, which often mark religious holidays or life-cycle transitions. The fiestas are generally prepared by the older community members, and the fate of their local musical traditions is becoming increasingly uncertain as young people migrate to the cities.[34]

Throughout much of Peru's history, ruling elites have asserted the superiority of Spanish-criollo culture and promoted negative attitudes toward "Indian" highland tradition as a way of marginalizing and oppressing the indigenous population. Only in this century has Andean music emerged in Peruvian cities, largely because of reforms instituted during the administration of President Juan Velasco (1968–1975). These reforms extended the promise of social mobility to young rural Andeans who migrated to Lima, and new policies heightened acceptance of highland culture in the cities.[35]

During the Velasco period, radical student groups in Lima formed traditional *sikuri* (Quechua term for *sampoña*, or panpipe) ensembles as a way to express solidarity with the long-oppressed indigenous population and to reject foreign cultural imperialism. In the vanguard of these groups was the Asociación Juvenil Puno (AJP), the first to perform spontaneously in the streets of Lima (beginning, notably, with a protest against the Velasco government). AJP challenged the notion that "folklore" had to be contained in government-sponsored spaces where it remained nonthreatening to those who continued to harbor cultural prejudices.[36]

Meanwhile, worsening economic conditions spurred further migration to Lima. As the number of migrants increased, so did their political presence; by the mid-1970s they felt comfortable enough to display their highland identity publicly, and *sikuri* ensembles proliferated. During the 1980s, university students and migrants gathered together for regular Sunday afternoon panpipe performances held in city schools and vacant lots.[37] Some of the Latino and Latina subway riders I spoke to told me that similar kinds of street performing have developed in Ecuador and Bolivia in connection with their particular patterns of urban migration.[38]

The Andean musicians who perform in New York City streets and subways have drawn musical inspiration from these and a broad range of other experiences. Ricardo Silva, who plays *qena* (wooden flute) underground as a member of the group Antara del Barrio, often attended the Sunday afternoon panpipe performances while he was growing up in Lima.[39] Silva says, however, that he was influenced at least as much by Nueva Canción (New Song), a musical movement of social protest which originated in the 1960s in Argentina and Chile and which Velasco welcomed into Peru. Nueva Canción musicians did not always use traditional Andean instruments, but through their lyrics they rejected both foreign imperialism and local dictatorships by encouraging pride in indigenous culture. Inspired in part by this movement, Silva formed Del Pueblo del Barrio, one of the first groups in Lima to fuse Afro-Peruvian, Andean, and rock music. Since then he has contributed these ideas to Antara del Barrio, and the group has

Ricardo Silva, originally from Lima, Peru, is the virtuoso *qena* player with Antara del Barrio. Here, the group is performing under the auspices of Music Under New York. Photo by Dennis Connors

helped to develop what is now recognized in New York streets and subways as an "Afro-Andean" sound.[40] Thus custom and innovation have produced a contemporary street performing phenomenon in Andean cities, as well as an Andean street performing tradition in cities around the world.

In the United States, street performing began in colonial times. Among other functions, it served as a way to deliver the news. Stephen Baird reports that at the age of twelve Benjamin Franklin sang political broadsides, and tested out ballads he had composed, on the streets of Philadelphia.

Even earlier, African American slaves were planting the seeds of a street performing tradition in New York. A Works Progress Administration document states that "'country slaves' (Long Island and New Jersey) and . . . 'city slaves' (Manhattan) . . . introduced Negro dancing and singing in this city at the Catharine Market." They accepted donations for their performances.

> Sometimes bystanders hired them to do a "jig of breakdown," paying them in collections taken up and from amused tradespeople who had stopped to watch. The dancers brought along boards, called shingles, upon which they performed. . . . Music was usually provided by one of their party, who beat a rhythm with his hands on the sides of his legs. Tom-toms were also used in their music making. . . . The talent displayed by these dancers made one awed observer exclaim that the blacks danced as though they "scarcely knew they were in bondage."[41]

Within a racist performance frame, African American slaves were some of New York City's first street performers. While dancing and playing music, they negotiated their oppression by developing their own social unity.[42] They made use of one of the few avenues of creative expression available to them, and the tradition they helped to develop ultimately formed the backbone of American music.[43]

After the Civil War, African American people migrated from the rural South to such major cities as New Orleans, Chicago, and New York. Stephen Baird notes that emancipated slaves were barred from most professions and musical venues, and consequently street performing was one of their few means of economic survival. At the same time, by singing the blues, playing jazz, and tap-dancing in public spaces, they further developed the art forms that had originated in their families and communities.

At the turn of the century, Louis Armstrong was born in New Orleans in the red-light district of Storyville. During that period, African American people were politically disenfranchised and lived under jim crow segregation that restricted them socially and economically. Young men like Armstrong apprenticed themselves to peddlers and hustled to contribute to their families' incomes. Despite poverty and racism, however, the community's cultural traditions were rich. Growing up, Armstrong watched the performances that were integral to his district's street life. Ragtime bands held contests on street corners. Peddlers and their apprentices—including Armstrong—attracted customers by improvising melodies about their wares. "Old timers" sang among themselves in their public meeting places.

At age ten, Armstrong joined a quartet, vocalizing for pennies a few times a week on the streets of Storyville. They passed the hat, and Armstrong delivered his earnings to his mother. "The group seems to have existed for at least two years," says James Lincoln Collier, "and if we allow that it either practiced or performed in public two or three times a week, the experience might have amounted to several hundred hours of improvised part-singing. That would have constituted a substantial course in ear training—far more than most conservatory instrumentalists get today. . . . Certainly the singing experience was important to developing whatever talent was already there." It constituted the first musical training of one of America's most admired jazz entertainers.[44]

Bessie Smith was born in the 1890s in Chattanooga, Tennessee, to an impoverished family. Orphaned at the age of nine and left without any means of support, Smith sang in the streets for small change, accompanied on guitar by her brother Andrew. Another brother, Clarence, was a dancer and comedian on the black minstrel circuit, and he arranged for Smith to audition. Thus began her career as "the Queen" of jazz and blues.[45]

African American migration to northern cities increased in the 1920s and again in the 1940s as people looked for jobs created in each period by an expanding wartime economy. According to Stephen Baird, a number of African American people continued to perform on the streets in those decades, and when they were accepted into clubs or were featured in MGM films, their street audiences followed them indoors. Their success can be seen as an ironic twist of fate or, more precisely, as an ironic twist in a discriminatory socioeconomic order. Yet perhaps most ironic of all is that racial discrimination drove these artists (and many others who did not become as widely known) into the streets to perform, where they earned money, developed their talent, and contributed to American cultural life.

Like the African American migrants, European immigrants who settled in New York saw street performing as a way to survive economically. Decades before New Deal legislation established a social welfare system to address the needs of many of America's poor and disabled, street performing enabled immigrants to earn a living despite language barriers—an explanation that is still offered by some of today's subway musicians.

Composer Irving Berlin's life provides a window into that period. Israel ("Izzy") Baline and his family had escaped the Cossack pogroms against the Jews of Russia by immigrating to the United States. The Balines settled on the Lower East Side, but within a few years Izzy's sister and father died. He dropped out of school (where, one teacher had reported, "he just dreams and sings to himself")[46] and sold newspapers on the streets to contribute to the family's earnings. Ashamed over his inability to provide much financial support, he left home and immersed himself in the street life of the Lower East Side. "Through this painful and dangerous rite of passage," writes Laurence Bergreen, "he would gradually discover his sense of self and worth in a difficult and demanding world" (pp. 14–15). With limited education and experience, Baline paid for a space in a homeless boys' lodging house by engaging in a secular version of the career that his father, a cantor, had pursued.

Baline became a busker, singing popular ballads in exchange for pennies on the streets and in front of sailors, prostitutes, and laborers in the saloons on the Bowery. One of his street contacts brought him to the attention of a well-known busker named Blind Sol, who paid Baline to accompany him into the saloons and attract attention—as well as donations—from the rather indifferent clientele. "A good night's work netted Izzy no more than fifty cents," says Bergreen. "The only advantage of this arrangement was that Izzy became acquainted with the pianists, whom he coaxed to show him a musical trick or two" (p. 21).

In that era, entertainers moved fairly easily between local performance venues. Thus, Baline landed a job as part of the chorus in the musical *The Show Girl*, and a contact on the Bowery referred him to Harry Von Tilzer, a songwriter who hired him as a Vaudeville hall "boomer," a "hired hand," Bergreen explains, "who sat in the audience, disguised as a paying customer, and who applauded furiously when the cast sang the choruses of songs. A dedicated boomer even tried to encourage the audience to stop the action onstage by repeating the choruses or singing along with the none-too-surprised actors" (p. 18). Pete Seeger adds that Irving Berlin and such other budding performers as George Burns joined quartets singing on the Staten Island Ferry.

Around the turn of the century, New York was hospitable to street performers. It served as the headquarters of Italian organ grinders, also known as hurdy-gurdies. Vocalists, accompanying themselves on guitar, mandolin, or violin, sang in tenement courtyards where housewives, listening from above, showered them with wrapped coins.[47] Even before greater New York City was consolidated, local ordinances authorized organ grinders and street musicians to perform and accept voluntary donations if they paid an annual license fee and met a residency requirement.[48] One ordinance set the limit on hurdy-gurdy licenses at eight hundred, indicating that organ grinders were not merely tolerated but, in fact, numerous and popular.[49]

The hospitality, however, did not extend underground. Already in 1904, IRT regulations explicitly barred freelance musical performances from subway cars and stations. Rule 416 stated: "Playing upon musical instruments and collecting or receiving compensation therefor, in this Company's trains, will not be allowed," and rule 439 continued: "Soliciting alms, playing upon musical instruments, and collecting or receiving compensation therefor, at stations, are prohibited."[50] Through these and similar regulations, IRT officials made clear that the subway system's primary function—transporting people safely and efficiently—was its only function.

Interestingly, the IRT rules were published even before the subway system opened. How could transit officials have predicted that freelance subway music would come into being? Consistent with Sally Harrison-Pepper's observation that the history of street performing can be found in the laws that prohibited it, the IRT rules appear to signify that freelance musical performances were already taking place in transit facilities. Indeed, in 1890 the Manhattan Railway Company rule book explicitly banned music making on its elevated lines.[51] Additionally, performances may very well have taken place in the city's surface transit system. In *Highbrow Lowbrow*, Lawrence Levine says that Walt Whitman recited Shakespeare on Broadway omnibuses.[52] Even before 1890, local transit regulations prohibited soliciting and begging,[53] terms which by the 1930s were explicitly defined to cover freelance subway music. Thus, the original transit officials may have promulgated rules less out of a sense of certainty about the single function of the subway system than out of concern that patrons would find multiple uses for it.

Transit regulations prohibited freelance subway music, but they did not entirely suppress it. In the early years, a derivative form of street performing emerged underground. The musicians did not collect donations, but their performances were highly spontaneous and democratic. They considered self-expression and direct encounters with riders to be ends in themselves.

Apart from the youths who sang and flirted on the night the subways first opened, perhaps the oldest surviving account of this form of music dates back to the period that Clifton Hood has dubbed "the people's subway," inasmuch as New Yorkers of various racial and socioeconomic backgrounds rode together rather peacefully around the clock. In *A History of the New York City Subway System*, Joseph Cunningham reports: "Since all express service ended at 1:30 A.M., many wondered what happened in the wee hours. A series of surveys in 1929 revealed that bored riders became friendly. Political arguments and discussions went on, also poetry recitations, singing and dancing. Orchestra members often played. Amusement park visitors on their way home considered this a pleasant diversion for only 5¢."[54]

If the freelancers described so far were prototypes of today's subway musicians in terms of spirit, freelancers of the Depression era, who played in exchange for donations, were prototypes in terms of form. During the Great Depression, itinerant activities of all kinds proliferated underground. The WPA commissioned a group of unemployed authors to write a *Guide to New York*, which included the following rather desperate description of the subways: "Greater drama resides in the endless flow of activity that crowds the cars and platforms. Beggars, singers, banjo-players, and candy-butchers vie for a few pennies, howl bargains, or stumble silently past the apathetic passengers. Occasionally, a particularly bright singing troupe or an unusually pathetic cripple will meet with warm response."[55]

Destitute and disabled New Yorkers recognized that the subways were a major public thoroughfare with a constant traffic flow they could tap for potential customers and contributors. Subway musicians share this economic motive today, and some government officials as well as riders continue to draw parallels between musicians and homeless people in the subways—a comparison that elicits a range of responses from both parties (see Appendix 1).

Early on, New York City government called attention to the similarities between street performing and begging. As indicated by the residency requirement in the ordinances and by a prohibition against actively soliciting donations, local administrators did not want to issue licenses to "vagrants" who were too "lazy" to hold a job and were therefore "unworthy" of assistance. In February 1935 Mayor LaGuardia reinforced the equation by instructing the commissioner of licenses not to authorize any more organ grinders (fourteen had already received permission to play that year). Hurdy-gurdies were given the option of applying for permits at no cost—if they met the requirements set by the Department of Welfare.[56] Meanwhile, the Department of Licenses discontinued the licensing of street musicians generally.[57]

LaGuardia's ban, as it is called, provoked a public outcry. Newspapers as distant from the scene as the *Boston Globe* carried editorials.[58] Interestingly, the upper-crust *New York Times* served as a major forum for the opposition. In response to the mayor's argument that hurdy-gurdies did not fit the image of the "progressive" or modern city, the editors stated: "In this highly institutionalized age, the organ grinder is an exception, a protest and an escape." As for LaGuardia's contentions that in the age of the automobile street music created safety hazards and in the age of radio it had become obsolete, the *Times* retorted: "Abolish the last street organ on the day when New York's last dumb-bell tenement is torn down."[59]

Letters from readers elaborated on the positive effects of hurdy-gurdy music. It evoked pleasant memories, promoted cross-cultural exchange, delighted the children, and lifted adults' spirits.[60] (Over fifty years later, subway riders would repeat each of these responses.)

On January 1, 1936, all itinerant street music licenses expired in New York. The *Times* reported that a German marching band was issued a summons for playing on a Harlem street corner on New Year's. Later that month, hurdy-gurdies pleaded their case on *NBC Radio*. Metropolitan Opera soprano Mary Lewis, declaring that hurdy-gurdies had inspired her to pursue a career in music, advocated on their behalf. Yet, LaGuardia was unmoved. At his first press conference of 1936, he is reported to have reiterated: "I'm not going to license begging." By 1938 the rule book of the city Board of Transportation prohibited musical entertainment under the heading "Peddling and Begging."[61] Pete Seeger confirms that "the overall attitude [equating street music with begging] had extended underground." The street music ban officially remained in effect for over thirty years.

Although LaGuardia stands out as the mayor who championed the rights of immigrants, minorities, and the poor, he did not always rise above the bigotry of his fellow public officials to denounce their narrow-minded notions of social order or to defend immigrant culture and vernacular music. In an era when nationalism and cultural distinctiveness caused alarm in this country, LaGuardia himself downplayed and even denied his Italian and Jewish heritage. Near the end of his life, the mayor is said to have confessed that his aversion to street musicians began in childhood, in Prescott, Arizona, when other children, spotting an organ grinder, yelled: "Hey, Fiorello, you're a dago too. Where's your monkey?"[62]

In the late 1940s, folk musicians began to hold gatherings in Washington Square Park, using traditional music to address new social and political realities. In the 1930s American folk music had figured prominently in the Old Left's efforts to build the populist and labor movements. In the 1950s it served as a form of protest against the cultural censorship of the McCarthy era, at least until blacklisting censored many of the musicians. And by the 1960s the New Left had revived folk music as a vehicle for expressing solidarity with the civil rights and antiwar movements.[63] The gatherings in Washington Square continued through the 1960s after hundreds of musicians and other New Yorkers had staged what Sally Harrison-Pepper refers to as the "Folk Singers' Riot." Their rallies, protests, and vigils succeeded in blocking the parks commissioner's attempts to restrict their public forum.[64] Some contemporary street performers single out the folk music and antiwar movements as the catalysts of the street performing revival in America.

The first signs of the folk revival may in fact have emerged in the New York subways. In early 1941 the Almanacs, which Joe Klein calls "the first urban folk group," were playing spontaneous music underground. The members at that time were Pete Seeger, Woody Guthrie, Lee Hays, and Millard Lampel. Klein describes them in his biography of Guthrie:

> They certainly must have seemed an odd-looking group as they traveled from place to place in the city by subway, their guitars and banjos slung jauntily over their shoulders. In 1941, guitars weren't nearly so common in New York as they'd later become. In fact, a half dozen people carrying, sometimes even *playing*, guitars in the subway was about as likely a sight as a tuba sextet. The Almanacs created waves of curiosity wherever they went, and usually were more than happy to oblige their fellow passengers with a song or two about the world situation. Some of their best performances were in subway stations; the acoustics were wonderfully resonant. Pete Seeger would get so excited when the group was out and together and playing around like that, he'd dash up the down escalators in the subways . . . like a kid.[65]

In a more recent conversation, Pete Seeger qualified this account. He told me the Almanacs never deliberately went underground to play; the trains were so loud that it was difficult to hear much of anything. In fact, only in the 1980s did the TA replace entire fleets with quieter trains. The renovation, although not necessarily intended to do so, has made it easier to talk and to listen to music underground. The Almanacs did play on platforms "for our own amazement," Seeger said, while waiting for trains on their way to "left-wing fund-raisers." They would select "any old country song," a Leadbelly tune, or make up their own melody, then take turns improvising lyrics about the subways. Seeger concedes that when they played riders smiled and talked to them, but he maintains that the contact was limited and unsolicited. Nor did the Almanacs solicit donations at these times.

Both the written and the oral records on the Almanacs shed light on what spontaneous music has historically contributed to the subways and to urban life. Within the context of the industrialized city, time spent in the subways is essentially wasted and empty. It derives value in relation to riders' destinations, where they will usually engage in production or consumption. By contrast, the Almanacs' practice and riders' reactions suggest that passing moments throughout the day also matter. They can add pleasure and meaning to people's lives. And in the course of "playing around," the Almanacs engaged a cross section of New Yorkers—not just members of the political Left—in cultural, if not also social and political, transformations-in-progress.

During the postwar era, major record companies all but stopped producing "race" music—the term used to denote music composed and performed by African American people—and focused on catering to the white pop market. Within a matter of years it became clear that a significant number of white teenagers were tuning in to local black-run radio stations to listen to rhythm and blues. Consequently, the major companies began producing "cover versions," imitation rhythm and blues songs performed by white entertainers. To a great extent, this history of appropriation is the history of rock and roll.[66]

By the end of the 1950s the first wave of rock and roll had subsided, and the musical "lull" that followed was filled by vocal harmony groups.[67] Independent labels signed some of the young African American men who were singing on the street corners of New York.[68] Meanwhile, some singers gave themselves exposure by performing in the subways.

Rabbi Mordekai Shapiro, an Orthodox Jewish spiritual leader and teacher, remembers encountering "fantastic" a capella groups in 1960 when he was a teenager riding the A train from Utica Avenue in Brooklyn to religious school. The groups sang doo-wop inside the subway cars on Sunday mornings, when they were less crowded. The singers were mainly African American, but Rabbi Shapiro recalls that one group included two young white men whose partners teased them about being off key (in line with David Toop's descriptions of the black oral traditions of "signifying" and "the dozens").[69] These groups did not solicit donations—they sang "for the fun of it"—but the rabbi distinctly remembers riders, mainly white adults, offering them money, as if to say, thanks for brightening my day. "That was a time," Rabbi Shapiro soberly remarks, "when people still knew how to treat each other like human beings." In this way African American subway musicians promoted positive social interaction between black and white New Yorkers, introduced the general public to emergent forms of popular music, and by extension did their part to prod the segregated music industry to evolve. Ultimately, says Bobby Robinson, an African American music producer, doo-woppers, and later rappers and breakdancers, "were trying to express themselves and they made up in fantasy what they missed in reality."[70]

John Vliet Lindsay incorporated street music into his mayoral campaign in 1965.[71] He soon learned that what he had done was illegal. Once elected mayor, Lindsay signed an ordinance eliminating the requirement that street musicians be licensed.[72] At base this change in public policy reflected a growing acceptance in society of vernacular music in general and street entertainment in particular.

During that period, courts began to uphold the First Amendment rights of people distributing political leaflets in transportation terminals. Meanwhile, however, the TA promulgated a new rule book that reinforced the ban on freelance subway music and other types of spontaneous performance by attaching fines and even jail terms to them. In a tongue-in-cheek article, the *New York Times* indicated that, despite the ban, performers could be spotted underground: "For tap dancers, tenors and choral groups performing impromptu matinees on the downtown IND, the message is simple: 'Entertaining passengers by singing, dancing or playing a musical instrument' is banned."[73]

Apparently, the new penalties did not make the ban more effective than it ever was. There are rumors that during the 1960s a few musicians were "discovered" in the subways. By the late 1970s, some of the musicians I interviewed were already performing underground, dodging or negotiating with the transit police to avoid paying fines for breaking the rules. Yet not until the mid-1980s did society accept vernacular music and public space activity enough for subway musicians to be able to have their performances seen and protected as free expression. At that point the TA eliminated the total ban and the MTA created the MUNY program. Many of today's musicians perform underground out of economic need and a desire to be "discovered," yet a number of them also express a commitment to public space comparable to those who entertained in the stations decades ago.

In every era, Stephen Baird has discovered, the demise of street performing is predicted. First "it was the printing press. Then it was the lightbulb! Then radio, records, TV, and videos." Baird concedes that each of these technological innovations increased choice and competition among forms of entertainment. "But," he says, "that doesn't stop the need for self-expression, and that sure doesn't stop the need for group participation in a live event. . . . That's what a street performer does. He puts people into contact with each other."

The historical record reveals that street performing and freelance subway music emerged and reemerged over time, and that even when unauthorized they elicited positive public response. Moreover, the performers advanced new art forms, prodded political structures to change, and added meaning to single moments in individuals' lives. Stephen Baird says that street performing, and by extension subway music, demonstrates political, social, and cultural significance by "challenging authority," "questioning society," and helping members of the public "articulate who they are."

Given that subway music is bound up with the street performing tradition, does it in fact have a history of its own? This chapter has shown that at the very least it does politically, as two distinct types, official and freelance, enjoyed different degrees of government sanction. Even today, of the city's three major public spaces—streets, parks, and subways—it is only in the subways that two types of musical performance regularly occur, namely, freelance and MUNY. Does MUNY signal that government has accepted the existence of freelance subway music—or adapted it to serve other, official, interests?

Before examining the politics of subway music directly, it will help to develop a clearer picture of today's subway music scene—who the musicians are, why they perform underground, and what role they fill in their own eyes, as well as in the eyes and ears of the public.

3

The Partners: Subway Musicians and Their Audiences

One of the most salient features of local music making scenes is the integral role of the nodding, clapping, singing, dancing, even instrument-playing audience. Subway music is no exception. It is a participatory phenomenon, an exchange between musicians and riders—"partners" in subway music scenes.

In this chapter I profile the main participants. I investigate how musicians use and negotiate subway space with one another and with riders, what motivates them to stake out a presence in such a hostile environment, and how they feel about being unconventional community artists. I also examine the varied reactions of riders to the music, focusing on what it means to a number of them to be exposed to and engaged in such an unconventional community art.

Musicians

"Other than the love of freedom," writes Patricia Campbell,

> there are no common characteristics of personality, background, or life-style that describe the average street performer. . . . Some have grown up in the life as waifs surviving by their talents. Others have chosen to drop into it from flourishing careers in law or medicine or teaching. Still others are actors and musicians waiting for the big

> break. A surprising number are college graduates, but some have almost no formal education. Some work only when the spirit or the landlord moves them. Others follow a rigid schedule. Not all love the street—a few spoke bitterly of their life as outcasts. Not all are committed to it for life or make their whole living from it. But in every city I visited I found a hard core of people who had dedicated their lives to the street, who saw themselves as bearers of a tradition, and who were articulate and thoughtful about their place in the world.[1]

To better understand who New York's subway musicians are, in the winter of 1993 I designed and distributed (and in some cases administered) a survey, which twenty of them completed—eleven soloists, three members of duets, and six members of larger groups. Six respondents were strictly freelance musicians, four performed only under the auspices of the MUNY program, and ten performed for MUNY and also "doubled" as freelancers. Most had started performing underground between 1987 and 1991, although one had begun as early as 1979.

The respondents' musical training provides one index of their diversity. Of the sixteen who answered this question, five had learned to sing or play from family members, usually parents; five had studied in school, in music conservatories, or with "master teachers"; two had sung in church; one had developed her talent in "school and the streets"; and three were self-taught. This learning primarily took place in the United States, Peru, Ecuador, Brazil, Argentina, and Trinidad. Clearly, the paths that brought each respondent to New York's subways reflected unique combinations of political, social, economic, and personal issues.

And yet, despite these differences, it is possible to identify common characteristics related to who the musicians are (gender and age), what they play (instruments and styles), when and where they play (times and places), and why they play (motivations and goals). Using these descriptive categories, it becomes apparent that what might otherwise seem to be a random occurrence in fact displays a recognizable pattern.

Most subway musicians, like most street performers, are men in their late twenties and early thirties. In *Sound Effects*, Simon Frith explains that itinerant musicians have traditionally been bohemian and free—of domestic responsibilities, that is. Women generally did not have the option of assuming this role; they were expected to stay by the hearth and raise the family.[2] The gender imbalance is characteristic in other parts of the music world as well. In their analysis of rock and roll, Steve Chapple and Reebee Garofalo advance the more critical argument that society has long denied women easy access to instrumentation and to the structures of power in the music business. Considering that rock began as a countercultural force (albeit one that articulated male fantasies), they contend, the limited number of women performers and executives in the rock universe is especially ironic and should call attention to the continued need to address gender discrimination in the popular music industry.[3]

Five of the twenty subway musicians I surveyed were women. Fifteen of the respondents, including these five, agreed that fewer women than men perform underground. When asked why this might be the case, almost three-quarters (nine) gave reasons similar to Frith's, attributing their absence to almost "natural" differences in gender roles. One subway musician, a woman, responded: "Because it takes a very special person to play in the subway. Some women are afraid." Another woman implied that female musicians have the power to change the situation: "Women have not made the connection that to perform in the subway is not a dirty thing to do." Fewer than one-quarter (four) of all the respondents provided answers along the lines of Chapple and Garofalo's analysis, explicitly stating the belief that gender discrimination and the threat of sexual harassment might be keeping women from performing in the subways. Of these four, three were men, two of them white. One of them concluded: "We all lose as a result of women musicians not feeling as comfortable playing in the streets and subways." The MUNY program consultant, Gina Higginbotham, observes that the acoustics of the subways can be good for women with soft voices. On the other hand, MUNY member Wendy Saivetz plays in Grand Central Terminal and avoids underground stations in part, she says, because "I get lost in the noise." Ultimately, as more musicians have come to perform underground, the number of women among them has increased.

Older men are also an exception to the young male rule. A few are Argentinean and they play tango on accordion and keyboard. Some violinists performed with prestigious orchestras in China until their musical careers were constrained or halted by Mao Zedong's Cultural

Alice Tan Ridley sings rhythm and blues in Grand Central Terminal at the Hot and Crusty spot, named for the bakery across the way. "Tan" has been known to move people to tears; once she lent her own handkerchief to a man in her audience. Photo by Dennis Connors

Some Argentinean musicians perform tangos in the subways. Photo by Dennis Connors

William Hong, originally from China, plays violin on the Times Square IRT platform. Photo by Dennis Connors

Revolution.[4] Most older performers, however, are African American jazz and blues players, many of whom are veterans of the local venues that are now, to a great extent, a part of New York's past.

The range of instruments and styles of music is exceptional, but certain ones predominate, and others are absent altogether. In Boston and Cambridge street performance primarily reflects North American folk traditions, which explains why hammer dulcimers and acoustic guitars are relatively common around Harvard Square; by contrast, saxophones and *sampoñas* (panpipes) are very familiar sights and sounds in New York streets and subways, evidence of the particular cultural history of this city.

Survey respondents reported playing many styles of music: jazz, Andean, Caribbean (reggae and calypso), gospel, blues, rhythm and blues, funk, folk, country, bluegrass, and classical. Moreover, some of them indicated that they use the same instruments to perform distinct genres. Combinations included "classical and jazz" on tenor saxophone, "US standards and European operettas" on accordion, and "country, bluegrass, blues, reggae, rock & roll, folk and jazz" on acoustic guitar.

When instruments cross over into a different culture, many of the musical conventions from the original culture travel with them. Cultural crossover is not new: it occurs when historical developments bring two distinct populations together. This pattern has occurred repeatedly in the United States, most notably when white audiences have taken interest in African American music and the white music industry has appropriated it in a practice colloquially known as "blaxploitation."

Contemporary scholars are finally documenting the racist history of the American popular music industry, but some of them are finding it important to address blaxploitation as one thread in the complex tapestry of cross-cultural musical exchange which has long characterized our multicultural society. Thus Robert Cantwell calls bluegrass "an Afro-American ensemble form in the body of traditional Appalachian music."[5] Chapple and Garofalo (and other rock historians) explain that Carl Perkins and Elvis Presley created rockabilly, the precursor to rock and roll, by fusing the country music and the rhythm and blues they had learned from white and black musicians in the Deep South.[6] Currently, New York City subway musicians from many different cultural backgrounds meet in the stations and "jam" together. The result is what I call "fusion" music, characterized by the interfacing, blending, and transforming of traditions.[7]

Fusion is a combination of apprenticeship and improvisation. Paul Chevigny describes these dynamics in the context of jazz clubs as musicians "play[ing] for one another" and "inventing the music together" in a "democratic, unpretentious" atmosphere.[8] But as the economic viability of clubs that accommodate this vital activity remains uncertain, the subways appear to be supplementing, if not replacing, them as apprentice spaces. Virtually all (eighteen) of my survey respondents said they had watched or played with other subway musicians, and over one-third (five) of the fourteen who performed in duets or larger groups also reported that they had met some of their partners underground. The fusion that occurs in the subways is exceptionally complex, since it draws from such a broad range of cultures. Nevertheless, it is important to note that subway music scenes include the people but not all the musical forms of the city's many racial and ethnic groups.

Some of the musicians routinely change partners; others stay together to develop and sustain a new sound. Robert Ogarro plays bongos and conga drum with different musicians who perform various types of roots music, identified as part of African or African American culture. "Don't you know I can't be out here for very long before someone comes up and asks to play with me?" Ogarro once remarked. His partners include Trinidadian steel drummer Michael Gabriel, jazz clarinetist JC, and the members of the Afro-Caribbean group Los Africanos. In 1994 he even played with the Andean group Anthology. Ogarro also solos on bongos and the *kalimba* (an African thumb piano). Not every subway musician is able to adapt to different styles, he believes, and he attributes his versatility to the fact that he was raised in this city. "New York is one of those rare places [where] you can experience so many different traditions and cultures in one place. . . . It's one of the best musical learning places in the world."[9]

Recent immigrants also participate in fusion. Jessel Harris, a young steel drummer from Trinidad, has taught Larry Wright, an African American teenager who drums hip hop rhythms on plastic buckets, to play calypso. I have heard Wright integrate these rhythms into his subway performances.

Some instances of fusion involve musicians from more divergent

Robert Ogarro, roots percussionist, meets and engages in fusion with a wide variety of subway musicians. In 1994, for instance, he began jamming with the Andean group Anthology. Here Ogarro performs on the Times Square IRT platform. Photo by Dennis Connors

backgrounds. Jason Black, a white American guitarist, plays duets with Dave Achong, a Caribbean violinist he met underground, who dazzles audience members with his improvisations. Their repertoire is eclectic, ranging from classical to popular, and their pieces often sound like bossa nova, a style with which Black is familiar because his wife is from Brazil.

Antara del Barrio, which roughly translates as "the flute of the neighborhood," formed in 1989 when the traditional Andean group Antara and the Afro-Peruvian group Del Pueblo del Barrio met in the subways. Antara del Barrio combines ancient and contemporary instrumentation and styles. In 1991 it was not unusual to see Ricardo Silva playing the *sampoñas* and Rubén Isola next to him on electric bass. As guitarist Francisco Rodríguez explains, the group's repertoire reflects the members' separate experiences in their countries of origin—Chile, Colombia, Peru, and Argentina—as well as their joint experiences in the United States. The musical result, says Rodríguez, is something "más universal" (more universal), so universal that Silva has woven a familiar snatch of George Gershwin's "Summertime" into one of the group's compositions. Antara del Barrio's universality clearly reflects the cultural interface occurring in the United States, especially in New York.

Government-sponsored and freelance musicians exert different degrees of control over the presentation of their performances. Members of the MUNY program can usually assure themselves of performance spaces. They request times and locations—called "spots"—two weeks in advance. MUNY assigns spots on station mezzanines and in commuter railroad terminals for three-hour intervals.

Freelancers structure their schedules in relation to more immediate, personal considerations, and they base their decisions on insights gained through experience. Most of my respondents said they perform three to five consecutive days a week. Those who freelance perform anywhere from one to eight hours at a time, although most limit themselves to three hours, the same time allotted to MUNY members. Over one-third (seven) of the freelancers perform at various times of day and night, least often in the morning. Some of the people I interviewed, however, did prefer mornings—Jim Graseck begins at 7:30 A.M., Anthology at 6:30 A.M. Their performance times reflect their preferences and also unspoken negotiations with riders, as these explanations indicate:

Antara del Barrio plays a fusion of ancient and contemporary styles, here, on the main concourse at Grand Central Terminal. *Left to right*: Francisco "Pancho" Rodríguez, from Chile, on guitar; José Maria Santalla, of Bolivia, on tambourine and percussion; Leyder Dorado, from Colombia, on *charango*; César Ferreyra, from Peru, on conga and *cajon*; Maurizio Najt, from

> "'Cause it fits my schedule."
>
> "There's money to be made each day."
>
> "I have found that people are paid from Wednesday to Friday and by Sunday they have spent all their excess cash."
>
> "I generally do better in evenings on platforms when people are going out to have a good time."
>
> "The city never sleep."

Ten respondents like to perform on subway platforms. Seven of them are soloists and their preference stands to reason. Soloists often have a difficult time attracting riders' attention on mezzanines (although the novelty of their instruments or their music can make a difference), whereas platforms, with their stationary crowds and traffic in and out of trains, guarantee musicians an audience and thus increase the chances of receiving donations. In the words of one respondent, "You get more of a flow and more money." A soloist in my sample praised the platforms for providing a "captive audience," but the term raises questions about the rights of riders who would rather not hear the music. (I address this issue in Chapter 6.)

The same number of respondents (ten) prefer to perform on station mezzanines. Six of them are members of duets or groups. Three of them also perform on platforms, but their responses suggest that mezzanines satisfy particular spatial and aesthetic needs of both musicians and audiences. The same respondent who praised platforms offered a positive assessment of mezzanines: "It's like a stage and people aren't just running."

None of the respondents preferred to perform in subway cars. One soloist described the logistical problems: "Too close a space, and very difficult to stand and perform." Yet, a vocalist in the sample said: "I never did, but for me it sounds like fun."

The TA prohibits all public space activities in subway cars,[10] but anyone who rides New York's subways knows that they go on nonetheless. Panhandlers and vendors may be the most familiar figures, but homeless advocates, magicians, and musicians also make presentations there, and pass the hat as well.

Those who sing or play in the cars tend to perform between express stops in order to present an entire piece and avoid the traffic flow in and out of the doors. There are saxophone players, violinists—one of whom taps the rhythm on a tambourine under his foot—and a variety of vocalists. A young hip hop trio performs a show in the 42nd Street shuttle train which produces a great deal of applause. The saxophone player from Mars, mentioned earlier, exploits the captivity of his audience and is paid for keeping quiet, but other musicians receive donations from appreciative riders. One of them, Teresa Vélez de Carpio, described a performance by the violinist with the tambourine. The riders in the car gave him so many donations that he played another piece for them without passing the hat again.

Only four of my respondents perform in passageways, which, one said, are "good for the 'quick' donation. You perform for them truly 'in transit.'" But money is not necessarily the deciding factor. Indeed, it is not unusual to find a few musicians playing in passageways that are virtually deserted. While conducting fieldwork I met three solo saxophone players who said they perform in these spots because of the acoustics. They like the sound their music makes as it bounces off the opposite wall and fills the space. A subway guitarist who plays in the 42nd Street (Bryant Park station) passageway connecting the IND and IRT lines added, "This is where I started out." Some freelancers carve out niches in the system that, in time, feel safe and familiar to them.

Many musicians have definite opinions about places to perform. A number of the most highly prized spots, such as the one on the main concourse at Grand Central Terminal, are reserved for members of the MUNY program. My survey respondents preferred midtown mezzanines and platforms, although 125th Street in Harlem and Christopher Street in Greenwich Village were also mentioned. Their positive and negative opinions of particular spots attested to their intimate knowledge of the physical and social environments of the subways and commuter railroad terminals. Some places, they said, have the "noisiest trains," others "non-receptive crowds." Yet others are "quiet and warm in winter." And "Grand Central is the Carnegie Hall of the system, Penn [Station] is like a theater and Astor Place is like a downtown club." Visitors also have their preferences. During his periodic stays in New York, Mustafa Abdul-Aleem, a roots musician and educator from Tennessee, sets up on the BMT platform in the Times Square station, which, he says, is the best performance space in the entire system.

Problems can occur when musicians become territorial, when they act as if they own a spot. Territoriality can be a disadvantage if riders lose interest in musicians they encounter every day. Yet it is also true

A guitarist known as "Chuck the Wolf" plays in the passageway connecting the IND and IRT lines in the 42nd Street (Bryant Park) station. Photo by Dennis Connors

Mustafa Abdul-Aleem, a roots musician and community artist visiting from Nashville, Tennessee, considers this spot on the Times Square BMT platform to be the best in the system. Photo by Dennis Connors

that some riders become regular patrons of familiar musicians, supporting them as they develop their art, or at the very least as they struggle to survive. One rider I interviewed described the thrill of coming across "her" group on her daily commute.

Territoriality can cause problems between musicians. During fieldwork, some of the musicians spoke of colleagues who "set up" on them, that is, found spots nearby and tried to drown them out with excess volume. They said that a few groups had threatened physical violence. (One of my sources admitted to having responded in kind.) At least one subway musician actually knocked a colleague out in a territorial dispute. Most of the conflicts I learned about occurred between musicians of similar backgrounds, although in a few cases they involved racial or ethnic difference, perhaps reflecting tensions that exist in the city at large. On the other hand, some musicians make the best of these situations. Carlos Gomez, originally from Brazil, is a blind accordionist who plays regularly on the Citicorp platform. Some Andean groups (among others) have been known to set up on him. But by listening to them play, Gomez has learned South American melodies and has added them to his own repertoire.

Survey results reveal that musicians handle territorial disputes within a two-tiered system. Members of the MUNY program have permits to perform in designated locations; when they find freelancers performing in a spot at their scheduled time, they tell the others to leave. Some MUNY members rely completely on their priority status; one woman commented: "Hasn't ever happened where it was a problem. I had the permit and that was that." Others use it in combination with a set of personal ethics; another woman said: "I give them one more tune then I set up my band and give the other group a donation if possible."

For the most part, freelance musicians negotiate spots according to what subway guitarist Michael Christopher called "the unspoken law." Asked what they do when they encounter others singing or playing where they intended to perform, freelancers among my survey respondents provided examples of their etiquette. "Move on to another spot," one said; "you have to respect the other musicians." Another said, "If they can't hear, we sing on the same platform—[it depends on the] acoustics of the station." A third explained, "At times I ask how long shall they be playing for. Sometimes I join in and jam along." Even subway musicians who are not well acquainted tend to show each other a mutual respect that is unexpected in subway space.

Why do musicians play in the subways? They generally share three broad motivations and goals: to earn money, to make artistic discoveries, and to reach out to other people.[11]

Certainly, the prospect of earning money draws musicians to the subways. As one told me, "I can rehearse and get paid!" Yet, fewer than half (nine) of my respondents listed money as a prime motivation for performing underground.

Subway musicians may conjure up the sympathetic (and sometimes accurate) image of the starving artist. They also variably resemble entrepreneurs, praised for their resourcefulness, or panhandlers, condemned for being idle. Ultimately, they fall into a category outside the established work structure. By the 1980s many courts had affirmed that street and subway music are protected forms of expression under the First Amendment to the Constitution and that the musicians may collect donations while expressing themselves in order to survive.[12]

Both MUNY members and freelancers depend on their audiences for donations. Most musicians perform a small repertoire many times over (because they want to rehearse selected pieces or they have limited musical experience), but since each successive wave of riders hears it as new, the potential for donations is not limited by the repetition.

Money, moreover, is a powerful form of feedback from the public, a tool riders may use to help regulate subway music. Steve Witt believes that an "untalented" or inconsiderate musician eventually leaves the subways because riders withhold their donations. From another perspective, donations are a vehicle through which audience members exercise *their* freedom of expression, encouraging the performers they appreciate. In addition to money (frequently dollar bills nowadays), spectators find other ways to communicate their approval. James Humphrey, who plays Christian folk music, says that riders have placed letters and flowers in his guitar case. Anthology was playing on the Citicorp mezzanine one day when a Puerto Rican woman approached them and asked one of the members to leave the station with her. The two soon returned with a complete chicken and rice dinner that the woman had bought for the group.

An air of mystery surrounds subway musicians, and it has a great deal to do with their financial status. Many riders wonder how much the musicians earn and whether they can make a living from subway music alone. It is difficult to gauge how much the average subway musician earns, since it is hard to define an average subway musician. Moreover, earnings are erratic, especially during economic downturns.

Like most wage earners, many musicians were reluctant to disclose to me how much they earned, and not necessarily for fear that the Internal Revenue Service would find out (some of them do file tax returns). One, however, said openly that he earns "good money," and another believes he earns more than many of his contributors. Although exact figures are elusive, some patterns emerged.

When asked if they had other kinds of paid work, almost three-quarters (fourteen) of my survey respondents said that they did not. At least eleven, though, make contacts with riders that lead to paid indoor gigs. Most of the soloists reported earning up to $20 an hour or between $35 and $50 a day. Two, however, earn well over $50 a day, and two usually make over $30 an hour. This drastic differential in earnings might reflect varying degrees of talent and street skills, but it probably has more to do with the fact that these last four soloists are MUNY members and thus have access to the prime spots.

Among the duet and group members, one reported earning $10 to $20 an hour, another up to $20 a day, and four well over $50 a day. The top earners also sell ten to twenty-five cassettes or compact discs during performances. By the late 1980s it had become relatively common for subway musicians to display cassette tape or compact disc recordings of their repertoires while performing. These recordings are produced independently at the musicians' expense. Musicians currently sell cassettes for eight to twelve dollars and CDs for ten to fifteen dollars apiece. TA rules prohibit them selling, but many do anyway. One of the Andean groups told me that in effect it has no choice. These sales form the basis of the members' livelihood; they cannot support their families on donations alone.

One group in the MUNY program reports that, on the main concourse at Grand Central Terminal, it can sell eighty tapes at eight dollars apiece over the course of its performance. This means that, in addition to donations, the group earns $640 in three hours. It is unlikely, however, that even this astounding rate of success translates into wealth. First, many obstacles, from physical exhaustion to police harassment, make it difficult for most musicians to perform in the subways more than a few hours a day. Thus, estimates of hourly pay do not translate into a forty-hour work week. Second, the main concourse of Grand Central Terminal, also known as the "Carnegie Hall of the subways" because of its relatively refined atmosphere and exceptional acoustics, is well traveled by New Yorkers and by suburbanites waiting for commuter trains. Only MUNY members are al-

Carlos Gomez, who is blind, plays his accordion eight hours a day, six days a week, in his regular spot on the Citicorp platform. Photo by Dennis Connors

lowed to perform on the main concourse, and at present, even they are scheduled there little more than once a month. Finally, groups must divide this money among their members, each of whom must help to cover such expenses as studio time and tape reproductions. Whatever is left over constitutes their earnings, which some use to support spouses, children, and extended family. Thus even the most successful musicians earn only a modest living through this activity.

Certain subway musicians are less vulnerable to downturns in donations: those who have dedicated their lives to playing music. Of these, one subgroup feels morally and politically committed to performing in subway space, and the other would prefer regular access to a more established venue. (There is overlap between the two.) Generally, these musicians have sufficient social and financial support (for instance, from other gigs) to survive periods in which their unstable incomes are more severely limited.

Three other subgroups play music in the subways primarily because they need the income. The first consists of disabled individuals such as Carlos Gomez, who is blind. Gomez has become a permanent fixture on the Citicorp platform; he plays his accordion there eight hours a day, six days a week to support his disabled wife and his family. "I'm collecting endless disappointments," Gomez says, bitter about the limited number of riders who assist him and about riders who equate subway musicians with panhandlers, only to reject them both.

The second subgroup comprises homeless or otherwise destitute people who sing or, in fewer cases, play instruments. Panhandling is illegal in the subways, whereas subway music is constitutionally protected (see Appendix 1). Thus in legal terms it is "safer" for panhandlers to sing their requests for aid. In cultural terms music making legitimates the act of soliciting donations in the eyes of some subway riders and, often, in the panhandlers' own eyes. One very thin white man who sang folk-rock songs in subway cars during the summer of 1993 acknowledged this need for legitimacy when he announced: "People, I don't want to beg."

Some subway musicians identify a third subgroup in their midst, the "merchants." This scornful term is used to denote musicians with limited talent, who seem to have no other aspiration than to earn as much as they can, who sell poor-quality cassette tapes or cassettes that they did not record. But the critics fail to observe that the merchants often draw crowds as large as their own and that the decision to sell poor-quality or nonorginal cassettes may have more to do with limited ac-

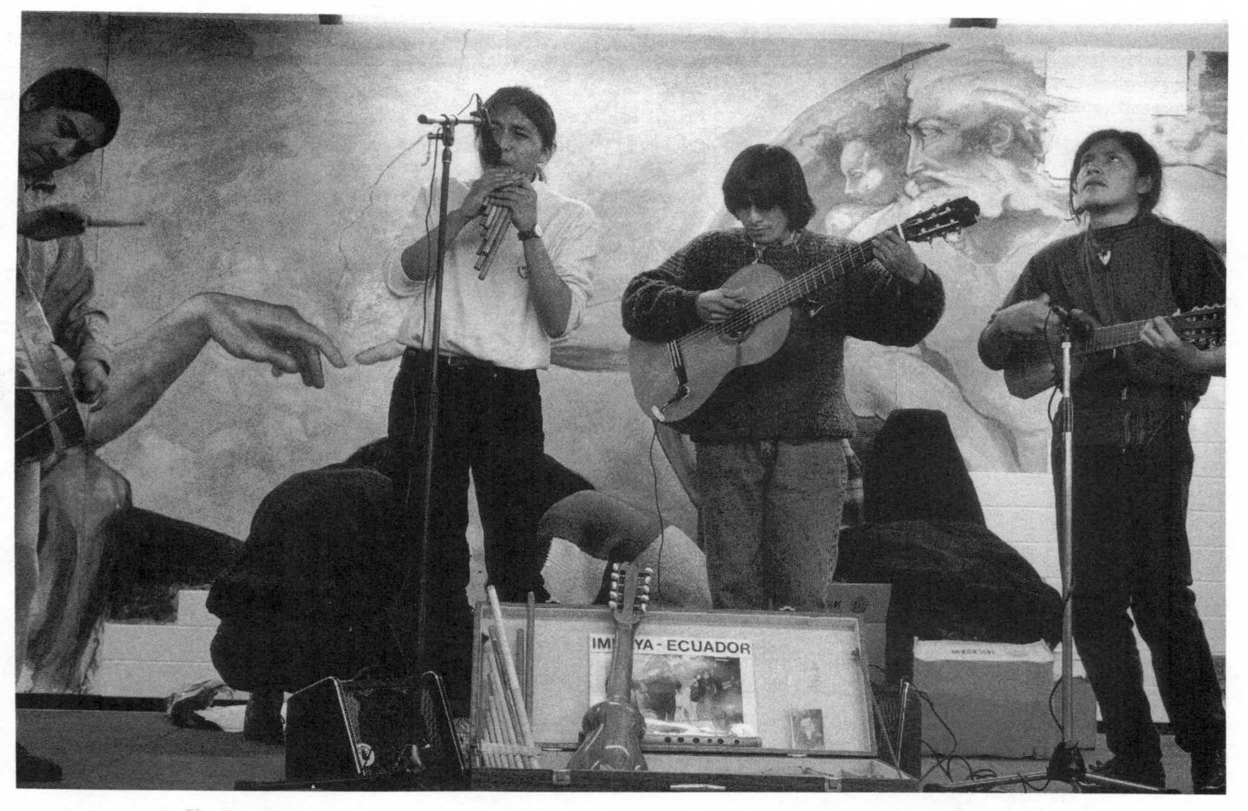

Grupo Imbaya, from the traditional community of Otavalo, Ecuador, performs on the 34th Street and Sixth Avenue (Herald Square) mezzanine. They are standing in front of a mural, a replica of Michelangelo's work in the Sistine Chapel, which has since been removed as part of station renovations. Photo by Dennis Connors

cess to recording technology than with talent. The most appropriate application of this label is to musicians from the Ecuadorian community of Otavalo—men and women distinguishable by their long black braids who take up temporary residence in New York to earn money by selling sweaters, crafts, and instruments as well as by playing traditional Andean music in public spaces. Some hear about New York's subway music circuit even before arriving in the United States. Yet one Otavaleño, Luis Gramal, says that his group plays in the subways not only to make money but to disseminate their art and thus to preserve their culture.

Over two-thirds (sixteen) of my respondents said they enjoy performing in subway space because it facilitates artistic discoveries. The subways are a kind of workshop, a cross between a concert hall and an open rehearsal. Musicians are guaranteed an unusually broad audience whose members provide direct feedback by donating, commenting, or walking past. Some report that this interchange enhances both their artistic and personal development. As Jessel Harris remarked, "You don't know who's in your audience. It makes you a stronger player, a stronger person." After learning to face the unpredictability and diversity of the subways, says Anthology member Marcial Olascuaga, formal gigs become relatively easy.

The notion that local music making *is* musical training is integral to aural traditions in African American, Latin American, and North American folk cultures—all of which are well represented in New York's subway music scene. Part of that traditional view is the incorporation of sounds from other players. Through fusion, many subway musicians discover new directions for their personal styles and cultural conventions.[13] In some cases, audience members participate directly in this fusion. For instance, in 1993 a trumpet player saluted jazz vocalist Evelyn Blakey as she welcomed her audience to "Cafe Subway" on the 42nd Street and Eighth Avenue (Port Authority) mezzanine. Although they had never met before, Blakey invited him to jam with her band. The trumpet player hesitated. "I can't play with you now." "Sure you can!" Blakey exclaimed. "This is my public rehearsal." With that, he sat in on her session.

Musicians are not the only ones to make artistic discoveries in the subways. Sometimes they themselves are "discovered." That is, a representative from a recording company, a television or film outfit, or a nightclub emerges from the crowd to offer forms of work that may provide more pay and wider recognition. Larry Wright was "discovered" in this way and cast in a Levi's jeans commercial as well as in a feature-length film. After encountering gravichordist Bob Grawi and flutist Pip Klein on the main concourse in Grand Central Terminal, Atlantic Airways flew the pair to England on promotional tours for the airline. And an Atlantic Records executive who heard jazz artists Zane Massey and the Foundation on the main concourse arranged for them to cut an album on the company's subsidiary label, One World Records.

More often, though, riders unconnected to the music business hire subway musicians to perform at private parties and weddings, to give music lessons, or to appear in concerts at museums, schools, restaurants, and other local cultural events. Some remarkable cross-cultural exchange results from these contacts. A rider, for instance, hired Jessel Harris to play steel drum at a bar mitzvah. Coincidentally, Harris had already bought a cassette of Jewish songs and had taught himself to play "Havah Nagilah" and "If I Were a Rich Man" (because, he says, "Hebrew tunes sound nice on pan"); he integrated them into his repertoire at the bar mitzvah. Such contacts enable musicians to expand their careers as community artists, and they allow New Yorkers to incorporate their local "stars" into significant events in their private lives.

Another example is provided by Jim Graseck, a graduate of the Juilliard School, who solos with established musical ensembles and has been a minstrel in the streets and subways since the late 1960s. Graseck has popularized Antonio Vivaldi's *Four Seasons* among a cross-section of riders who pass through Grand Central Station during morning rush hours.

In July 1990 Graseck rented Alice Tully Hall in Lincoln Center, and in March 1993 he arranged his own debut at Carnegie Hall. His street and subway audiences followed him into both establishments. I attended the Carnegie Hall concert. Tickets ranged in price from eight to twenty-five dollars, and virtually all twenty-eight hundred seats were filled. On the receiving line later that night, audience members talked to each other about the stations in which they had met Graseck and in which they regularly listened to him.

I sat next to a Latina woman and her seven-year-old daughter who was studying violin in an East Harlem music program and was scheduled to audition for Juilliard. They had encountered Graseck playing, and handing out flyers about Carnegie Hall, at the top of the "Num-

Jim Graseck plays his violin during morning rush hour at the top of the escalator for the Flushing line "Number 7" train, in Grand Central Station. Photo by Dennis Connors

ber 7" train escalator one morning in Grand Central Station. The woman hoped this concert would inspire her daughter to continue studying. She then told me that her own knowledge of the classical music tradition was limited, and said: "[Jim] gave me an entry into the music that I otherwise wouldn't have had."

After the intermission, Graseck—who had been talking to his audience throughout the evening, as he does in the subways—thanked us all for making this concert possible. After a pause, a woman's voice descended from one of the top balconies: "James, you make our hearts sing." The rest of the audience applauded in assent. That night, Graseck enabled New Yorkers to transcend cultural categories that tend to reserve "highbrow" classical music for affluent white audiences. In turn the audience members enabled Graseck to advance his career in a direction that was meaningful to him; they celebrated themselves; and they democratized one of the city's most venerated cultural institutions.

For many musicians, reaching out to people is a vital part of performing underground. Steel drummer Michael Gabriel has landed a full-time job as a musician in a restaurant on Cape Cod, but during the off-season he returns to New York's subways because he misses "making people smile." On the Citicorp platform, reggae guitarist Asheba begins Bob Marley's tune, "So Much Trouble," then addresses an extemporaneous message on the theme of reaching out to the riders around him.

Standing, as it were, on the city's economic, political, and social margins, subway musicians counteract what Stephen Baird calls New York's "individualism to the point of suicide" by promoting human contact. Some of my survey respondents affirmed that subway space gives them a unique opportunity to reach out, musically and personally. One relished "so much freedom and the joy you give to people." Another appreciated "the chance to develop communication with the public at close up." Another enjoyed "conocer a la gente, paisanos de todos los colores (meeting people of all backgrounds)."

Most of the subway musicians I interviewed were inclined to transcend racial and ethnic boundaries, and they maintained that their audiences were composed of the entire spectrum of subway riders. (One survey respondent did admit to attracting an exceptional number of "yuppies.") Yet during fieldwork I observed that their interactions with two particular populations involved different dynamics.

Musicians make especially direct, intimate connections with children. Indeed, the children are often the ones who initiate the contact. In the Times Square passageway I saw a small boy toddle over and bang on Dr. Thunder's conga drum. On the Citicorp platform a boy walked up to Asheba and strummed his guitar, and on another occasion a girl quietly stared into Jessel Harris's pan until he extended his drumsticks to her. Asheba believes that children's uninhibited responses to the music enable the adults who accompany them to "become children"—to be responsive and playful as well.

Musicians have more variable but equally striking encounters with individuals who are generally assigned to the category of "homeless," whether or not they have homes (see Appendix 1). Some drunks and junkies dance on the "stage," whisper in the musicians' ears while they are performing, and solicit donations for themselves from the audience. In these situations it is understandable that some musicians feel extremely vulnerable, as if they are on the city's "front lines." Many musicians ignore disruptive individuals until they disturb or alienate other audience members. Jalil Kifafi might integrate his unexpected guests into the scene or, at other times, sternly confront them through his microphone. Conversely, when drunks help themselves to a dollar from the money collected, the musicians and the rest of the audience may simply laugh. Because musicians and panhandlers both receive donations, they have often been linked, legally and politically. This accounts for some ambivalence and resentment between them. Yet three-quarters (fifteen) of my survey respondents affirmed that they are grateful, even "deeply moved," when homeless people give them donations. Guitarist Roger Manning calls this money "especially valuable change." Others reluctantly accept contributions from homeless fans who are more generous than many affluent riders.

Some subway musicians make a special effort to reach out to audience members with similar ethnic or racial backgrounds to their own. Andean musicians, for instance, try to uplift riders who recently immigrated from Latin America and are still adjusting to New York's highly structured routine. César Dueñas is one of these; he remembers his own first encounter with subway musicians from the Andes. In 1985 Dueñas came to New York from Peru. He worked in a pizzeria, in bakeries, and on construction sites. Then one day he encountered an Ecuadorian group underground, and their music made him homesick for his family and his country. Distance lent his cultural traditions a value he had never recognized before.[14]

Jessel Harris, a Trinidadian musician who plays steel drum, lends his pan to a young spectator on the 53rd Street and Lexington Avenue (Citicorp) platform. Photo by Dennis Connors

Dueñas had listened to Andean music in Peru but had never performed it. He promptly bought a variety of instruments—a *charango, sampoñas*—from an Otavaleño. He planned to teach himself to play, but then he met members of Grupo Charango in the subways and struck a bargain with them. They agreed to teach him, and in exchange Dueñas sold their cassette tapes while they performed. Eventually Dueñas became a member of that group, which later changed its name to Anthology. Now he earns his living, identifies with his culture, and plays *qena* and *sampoñas* for all riders in the subways.

In 1991 Angel Moreno frequently stopped on his way home from work to listen to Anthology on the Roosevelt Avenue mezzanine. Moreno was familiar with Andean music because he had performed with a folkloric group at a weekly *peña* (cultural gathering) in his home town in Ecuador. One day he approached the musicians and asked if he could accompany them. By coincidence, they needed someone to fill in for their *bombo* (traditional drum) player. Moreno, in suit and tie, strapped the *bombo* over his shoulder and played along. He was more accustomed to playing guitar, and Anthology's members encouraged him to expand his repertoire of popular Andean songs. Soon he left his job in a construction firm and joined the group. "La musica es mi vida," Moreno explained to me: music is my life.

Nilser Cortez, from Peru, met and joined Anthology in the same way as Angel Moreno. Cortez had prior musical experience, but in New York he had been working in a factory, one of the few employment options available to Latin American immigrants with limited English. He explained his decision to become a subway musician in the context of geopolitical realities. Cortez believes that the historical military intervention of the United States in Latin America contributed to the severe economic and political crises confronting Peru and other nations. He and his sisters immigrated to New York because they were no longer able to earn enough at home to support their families. Rather than be exploited as cheap labor, he has decided to earn his living by playing his culture's music. Clearly César Dueñas, Angel Moreno, and Nilser Cortez had different motivations for becoming subway musicians. Yet in all three cases, reaching out benefitted the group as well as the audience and further blurred the boundaries between the two.

Many subway musicians personify a form of individualism that combines nonconformity with a sense of social responsibility. Michael

César Dueñas, far left, who learned to play *qena* and *sampoñas* from other members of the group, performs with Anthology on the Times Square shuttle mezzanine. Photo by Dennis Connors

Anthology performs on a lower mezzanine at the Times Square station on a rainy afternoon in early 1994. *Left to right*: César Chisa, from Ecuador, on *bombo*; Angel Moreno, also Ecuadorian, on *charango*; César Dueñas, of Peru, on *qena*; and Marcial Olascuaga, also from Peru, on guitar. Photo by Dennis Connors

Christopher, for example, said: "When I'm in that station, I feel it's my station and I have a responsibility to the people listening to me." David Merk, a flutist also known as "The Wolf" because while he performs he covers his face with a lifelike wolfmask, is a soft-spoken African American man who volunteered during an interview that if he were to witness a mugging near his spot, he would jump in and stop it. Comments like these indicate that subway musicians see themselves not only as performers but as part of the informal social network of the subways, and of the city.

At the same time, some of the most dedicated subway musicians express deep ambivalence about their work. My survey respondents made the following complaints:

> "Tiring to play five to six hours in a bad, smelly environment and the money is not always good."
>
> "The noise (sometimes) and it can get a bit claustrophobic."
>
> "The steel dust."
>
> "Mean, nasty-mouthed and loud unsympathetic people! But then . . . I am like that on my *best* days."
>
> "Some people try to degrade you."
>
> "Police harassment."
>
> "Crazy people."

No survey can convey the unique stories of individual musicians, how their hopes and misgivings combine with their other characteristics. Here are a few profiles of musicians, both groups and individuals, offering a glimpse of some of the variety to be encountered.

November 17, 1990, 1:00 P.M., Roosevelt Avenue–Jackson Heights Mezzanine: Los Andinos

Los Andinos play traditional Andean ballads. Two members of the group, Jorge and Patricio Aguirre, come to New York from Cuenca, Ecuador, for short periods of time to earn money, which they send back to their families. They live and play music with their brother

Enrique, who has settled here. The Aguirres perform on weekends; on weekdays they work in a factory, making jewelry.

The fourth member of Los Andinos, Jalil Kifafi, originally from Chile, is the first subway musician I ever met. Jalil has a sixth sense about community. He introduces each song with a brief description of its origins, and he often greets riders he recognizes and says good-bye to those he has just met. Yet Jalil says that, for him, subway music is strictly an economic enterprise.

Before the group began its set, I asked Jorge why they play at this particular spot practically every Saturday.

"Para la gente latina." For the Latin American people, a large number of whom live near this station in one of the city's most international neighborhoods. For them, Jorge said, Andean music is like a voyage. It stirs up memories and helps them to relax. In fact, he added, not only Latinos and Latinas experience this sensation.

"Toda la gente." All people.

Beautiful as it sounded, I wondered about Jorge's response. We had been acquainted for two years, and I suspected he knew that was exactly what I wanted to hear. So, I asked: "¿Y el dinero?"

Jorge conceded that money is key. Los Andinos play with the MUNY program, and when they have a choice, they pick Grand Central Terminal's main concourse over Roosevelt Avenue because they receive more donations and sell more cassettes there. In his experience, Latinos and Latinas don't donate much, perhaps, he speculates, because they send money home to parents or to spouses and children, as he does.

Still, when Los Andinos play here, Jorge says he feels a "doble satisfacción," making money and giving emotional support to the Latin American members of his audience.

Summer 1991: Michael Christopher

Michael Christopher is one of the few solo musicians I know who draws a crowd in the subways. He has "circle-gathering skills," or what Michael himself calls a "carny" attitude, like a court jester. But when he sings, a very serious and thoughtful person is revealed.

Michael performs songs from the 1960s and 1970s on acoustic guitar. He's tall, and he hides his eyes under the visor of a black baseball cap inscribed with a bright pink "MTV." There's a Greenpeace sticker on his guitar case.

The first time I spoke to Michael, he was playing in the 59th Street and Lexington Avenue (Bloomingdale's) station, standing against a pillar at the edge of the BMT platform. A young blond professional woman leaned, like his alter ego, on the opposite side of the pillar. When Michael sang "Mother and Child Reunion," the woman closed her eyes and mouthed the words. When she opened them, our eyes met, and she smiled.

Two young women standing near me liked what they were hearing. One went over and asked Michael to play "Sounds of Silence." When he did, she started to cry. Her friend was bewildered by her reaction.

"He brought back the sixties," she explained.

Michael keeps up a constant patter, serving the public in the process. Sometimes he interprets the all but unintelligible public address announcements, though at other times he declares: "The TA just announced: Sni—sna—snu. . . ." In the middle of a song, still strumming, he'll warn his audience to "beware of the SLIME"—the condensation dripping over their heads at the platform edge. A few will look up, step aside, purse their lips, and smile at one another.

I introduced myself to Michael and said I'd like to interview him. He declined. He was planning to return to Paris, his adopted home, where, he said, it's easier to be a street performer. But he didn't go. Instead, I encountered him on the BMT platform almost every week for a few months, and I chatted with him whenever I could. Michael proved to be not only talented, but brilliant, especially in his own field. He was the first subway musician I'd met who identified himself as a descendant of the troubadours. He gained perspective on his own confrontations with transit police officers by recalling that troubadours had these problems centuries ago, and the penalties then were far worse. Their punishment for performing in the Middle Ages? Decapitation.

Since he was staying in New York, Michael agreed to be interviewed. In June, I found him at our appointed meeting place, sitting on a station bench with his head in his hands. He held out a yellow piece of paper—a summons for using an amplifier on a subway platform. The fine was fifty-five dollars. A moment later, though, he bounced back, as he does when he performs. "Do you know what the equivalent would have been in the tenth century?" he asked me. "Decapitation?" I'd learned my lesson. "Or flogging," he concurred.

Michael can talk about almost any subject with familiarity and ease, except himself. He convinced me that he had great dreams, then with equal intensity he told me they were illusions. But one thing was certain: being a subway musician was directly tied to Michael's struggle to define (or redefine) himself.

At our interview, Michael told me he was going to help himself out, in part by no longer being a subway musician.

"It's a sham. . . . I'm giving so many people so much happiness, while I myself am feeling so miserable. This has been like a romance. It's been so nice. So petty." All these years, he said, he's been a "ten-minute rock star."

Michael berated himself for playing music in the subways when he had the ability to be a "star."

"Do you want to be?" I asked him.

"It's not a question of whether I want to. . . . I have the ability, so maybe I have an obligation. . . . Sure, I want to." Then he doubted that he could.

What had he learned by being a subway musician?

"I've gotten smarter. Street smarts are okay. But you know what's better? Being in a situation where you don't need to develop street smarts. . . . I'd like to stay away from an urban jungle like New York. . . .

"Being with people. That's a positive offshoot of it. Mostly I've learned negative things about humanity. About twentieth-century American society. The pain is feeling the negativity, seeing people act like such suckers. . . . People on a group-consciousness level are feeling very small." They are deferring to authorities who tell them "how to think and how to feel. . . . Somebody's got to stand up and say, 'Here comes the emperor and, guess what? He's got no clothes on!' "

Did he regret his decision to be a subway musician?

"Yes. . . . *For so long*—I should qualify it." It would have been all right, he felt, to play in the subways for "a couple, maybe three years. But ten years? . . .

"I want to write an opera. . . . I want to write movies. About the absurdities of American life. I want a different way to share the gift I've been given. Not to make a difference, to put my point of view out."

Michael and I figured we wouldn't be seeing each other anymore, and we hugged good-bye. Six months later, I ran into him. He had never stopped playing on the platforms—he had never stopped being a ten-minute rock star.

October 15, 1990, 53rd Street and Lexington Avenue Mezzanine: Tutone

There is more than talent that attracts people to Tutone. John, a young African American man modestly crowned with a white crocheted skullcap, provides the backbeat on electric guitar, all the while listening to his partner Lynn on alto saxophone. Lynn, who met John when he was performing in Washington Square Park, has blond hair and blue eyes. And she knows how to play sax.

Tutone's repertoire is "feel-good music": funk, soul, and rhythm and blues. This evening, they were with their band, which includes three men whom John has known for twenty years. They played against the new glass wall framing the passageway between the IRT and IND lines. They were performing as part of Music Under New York, although they did not have their MUNY banner displayed.

Over the course of two hours, the crowd swelled. John ended the spot as if it were a nightclub act, introducing his band members. The audience, predominantly African American, applauded for each one.

As Tutone packed up, many riders came over to make contacts—to ask the members where else they would be playing or to hire them for parties. Meanwhile, I spoke with Lynn.

"Why do you play in the subways?"

"For the money. And the exposure. Somebody has to see you."

"Do people always make contact with you like this?"

"Yeah. And we usually hand out our cards. We play weddings and clubs. We just did a video—it was on Manhattan Cable this weekend."

Lynn talked defiantly about problems with the transit police, declaring, "I'm going to play anyway" and "We're not bothering anyone," though a shyness in her eyes contradicted her words. She and the band had no choice, she explained: "Otherwise, we'd have to steal." No subway musician had ever described to me the fine line between surviving as a musician and succumbing to poverty in these terms.

I asked Lynn what it was like to be a white woman playing music with African American men. How did people respond to her?

"Well, I've always felt more comfortable around black people. I don't know why." She smiled. "That's just how I am.

"Black people in general have this mistrust about white people. And I can understand why. So at first, they [the other band members] didn't trust me. But I was with John, so it was okay. They call me 'Mighty Whitey' sometimes."

And the audiences: "Sometimes they say they never heard a white woman play sax before. They say I have soul."

Later, I talked to John, a soft-spoken man whom others turn to for help and advice. He taught himself guitar and helped many of his friends learn how to play their instruments. He began playing in the subways in the late 1970s, when spontaneous performances were still banned. In those days, John said, he was ticketed a lot. "I'd say, 'Oh, I didn't know,' or I'd yes 'em to death. I avoided twenty-five to fifty tickets that way. Now, we respect the laws, you know, but when the cops aren't around, we'll play. . . . If they put me in jail, I'd say, 'I'll pay your tickets, but you've got to let me play to pay 'em. I don't know any other trade.' "

John talked about Tutone's relationship with riders and about their role in the subways.

"People do complain. They walk all the way to the other side of the platform. Then when they hear us, they come back. When we play, people are no longer mad at the conductor and the engineer for making them late, or at their boss for being mad at them for being late. . . . So many people have said to us, 'You've made my day.'

"Let's say a guy is mad at his girlfriend. Then he hears us play 'Ain't No Woman Like the One I've Got.' And he realizes: 'That's right, ain't no woman. . . .' Music helps people come back to life."

1990–1991, 42nd Street and Eighth Avenue Mezzanine: Bobby Davis

He'd sit in a corner of an alcove by a staircase, alone, and if you were in a rush you could miss him completely. He had on a wide leather cap, a bulky sweater with a sweatshirt hood poking up out the back, and tan polyester pants. His harmonica was poised at his mouth, secured with black tape to a metal halter around his neck. He held a heavy, polished electric guitar. He sat in front of an old drum with a tambourine attached to it, and when he stepped on the foot pedal, both instruments responded. Around him were his battery-powered Mouse amplifier, a small overnight bag, and a blue spittoon that he'd sometimes pull over. All of this rested on an old swatch of rug.

In 1986 Dennis Connors took this photograph of Bobby Davis, a one-man blues band, in the Times Square station.

Bobby Davis was a one-man blues band. Once I asked him:

"Is this urban blues or southern blues?"

A riff continued to flow out from under his old fingers. Then, softly:

"This is blues from the South."

I asked what distinguishes it.

"This is deeper. You gotta feel. Gotta had hard times. I had all that—hard times."

We first spoke the day before New Year's. After telling me how grateful he was to the station manager and the transit police for letting him play in this corner, he told me his name. Then he asked: "You ever heard of Sammy Davis Jr.? Yeah, he died recently. He was my cousin. Our fathers were brothers." At age twelve, he said, Sammy taught him music. "Wasn't nothin' he couldn't play."

The week after New Year's, I found Bobby packing up his things and piling them onto a dolly. A young white man was with him.

"You should've heard us," Bobby greeted me. "I had a sax player with me. I been here since 7 A.M."

Steve, the sax player, is also an actor. He'd once met Bobby playing on the platform and found their styles of music similar. "Maybe it was something spiritual," Steve said of their meeting.

"I'm tired," Bobby said. His sentences came out like delayed reactions. "Did I tell you I have cancer in my head? Yeah. I haven't been taking my medication regularly. That's not good. If I don't take it, I can die. But out here sometimes I forget. My kids tell me I got to." His kids live with him. "I tell them to bring me out here. It's hard by myself."

Two weeks later, I returned. Bobby grinned hello. A minute later he recognized me and greeted me.

Bobby said he was feeling much better. The day before had been one of his worst. Had he told me he had cancer in his brain? He'd had shooting pain yesterday.

I looked at the guitar case which sat open in front of him. There was a scattering of coins in it, lots of them pennies. He saw my glance.

"Lotta money today," he said with gentle sarcasm.

"Yeah, I see. Well, a couple of dollars."

"Guess I'll be eating soup tonight."

"Do you depend on this?" I asked.

"Yeah. I think I told you. I got my sons at home. And I raise my grandkids. Got a lot of grandkids."

He played on in silence.

"I got some money in the bank. I'll tell you how much I got." He played a few more bars. Then he told me. A couple of years ago, he said, he'd won the lottery.

"So why'd you tell me you'd be eating soup tonight?" I chastised him.

"Just joshing you, just joshing you."

Bobby then told me that his children are all successful. His sons are dancers; his daughters are teachers and doctors. They tell him not to play in the stations anymore. They offer to send him to Florida.

"Why *do* you come here at seven in the morning?"

"I gotta get up, baby! Gotta do something. If I didn't, I'd go crazy. I been doing this all my life." Bobby said he used to hold down a day job, then play in the clubs until three o'clock in the morning. He mentioned one club in particular on 145th Street in Harlem, which he said was torn down to make way for a housing project.

Bobby said he's been on his own since he was seventeen. He married twice, had four kids in each marriage. He said he raised them all and they all love him.

Bobby worked as a tailor. In fact, he said, he still makes suits. He offered to make me one.

I asked why he learned that trade.

"I always wanted to take care of my family, one way or the other. People ask me, 'How did you do all that?' Had to make an honest living. Never wanted to be a thief. Even learned to be a boxer. When I was seventeen, eighteen, I boxed in those clubs."

I have spoken to four other African American subway musicians close to Bobby's age, and all either held or continue to hold nonmusical jobs, earning low wages as cooks, clothes makers, and shoeshiners. They all invoked the American dream, and clearly as black men in this society they had worked incredibly hard to try and achieve it.

Bobby has made contacts in the subways. One person wanted to produce a video with him. Another offered to take him on tour in Europe. Bobby told them he'd listen when they "talked money. . . . We're in New York. I only work for money. I got lots of grandkids."

"I guess you don't tell too many people that you have money."

"No, no one knows. Only my children know. Most people also don't know I'm a landlord. . . . I like to work. I live to work. When I go home, it's like a dungeon. Here I see people. They compliment you. . . . No one can be happy to themselves all the time, you know? That's like a prison."

An elderly African American man came up very close to Bobby. He imitated the guitar picking until the woman he was with smiled and said, "Our train's here!"

A few people donated as they passed—a white couple, a blond woman, a few African American men. At one point a man stopped in midstride.

"How's it goin', brother? I like the way you groovin'. Keep on pushin'." Bobby thanked him.

Contributions made him feel good.

"If they give me a tip, then they enjoy my music. If they don't, I'm still happy. I know I'm not playing bad. . . .

"I'll do this till I die. When I die, I'll be finished. But I'll be happy. . . . This makes me live, doing what I want to do."

Through subway music, Bobby seemed to reinforce his lifelong self-image of a hardworking man and a fine blues musician. Whether his stories were true is unclear, but the bottom line was his music, and he could indeed play.

(Bobby hasn't been back to his spot since 1991.)

March 30, 1990, 42nd Street and Sixth Avenue IND Platform: Steven Blue

As unobtrusive as he is, Steven Blue makes people look twice. His hair is in cornrows, pulled back in a ponytail. He wears a black knit hat and reflector glasses that clip onto his nose. His mike is held in place at his mouth by a wire arc over his head.

Steven plays "easy listening" 1970s songs on an electric guitar. He has a mellow style and uses an echo effect that reminds me of John Lennon's post-Beatles recordings. As he sings, Steven breaks into a wide, contagious smile. He looks like he's enjoying himself.

On this day, he sat on a small wooden chair tucked behind a staircase on the IND platform. He kept a small bag next to him. His only other equipment was his Mouse amplifier and a donation box with a sticker on it that said "Musicians Increase World Harmony."

I joined the small circle around him, mainly made up of African American men. When I turned around, I noticed that people were watching him all along the opposite platform!

After a series of songs that flowed one into the next, I went up to Steven. He said he's been playing in the subways since the mid-1980s when it became legal. I asked him why. He answered that it's a place where he can contribute something.

"You never know if you might play a song that'll give a spark to someone and . . . help them to breathe, to relax."

What about other subway musicians? He agreed that their primary reasons for performing might be money or practice, but he said that all musicians are interested in self-expression.

"You know the sages we read about—the ones who talked about going to the mountaintop? Well, I think there's truth to that idea, but . . . I think first I need to see how much I can withstand here. . . .

"The people who stop to listen—I can't necessarily rely on them. My challenge is to see if I can generate from within myself what I need in order to play. It makes me find out who I am and what I need to survive."

This platform was exceptionally loud. I had also seen Steven on the extremely narrow platform at 72nd Street and Broadway. Did his choice of spots have anything to do with this challenge? Yes.

I told Steven that I thought I understood what he was saying. That we have to contend with something the sages didn't have: modern urban life. That we can flee to a mountaintop or confront existence here. He agreed.

Much as he talked about self-expression, Steven also indicated that that's the first step in showing concern for society.

"You know, there are people who say we are relatively free, depending on our skin color." Steven is African American. "But, we all are not free. See how everyone's constantly rushing and rushing? It does something to us."

Like other subway musicians I've met, Steven didn't see the solution emerging from one group of people or at one point in time. In fact he expressed admiration for the "old storytellers" who could conjure up images that people could see, and share stories that weren't their own. It sounded like that's what he was trying to do.

I think this sage was really saying that the subways are our modern-day mountaintops.

Riders

In December 1993 four research assistants and I surveyed forty-five riders to gauge public opinion about subway music. The sample consisted of almost equal numbers of women (twenty-two) and men (twenty-three). Of the thirty-nine who provided information about their racial or ethnic backgrounds, fourteen identified themselves as white (or more specifically as Jewish, Irish, Italian, and Norwegian), ten as black (African American, Trinidadian, and Jamaican), nine as Latin American (Dominican, Ecuadorian, Bolivian, and Mexican American), two as Asian or Asian American, two as Middle Eastern (Lebanese and Iranian), and two as biracial (black and Latin American). They represented a broad age range, the youngest under eighteen and the oldest over sixty-five. Thirteen respondents listed their occupation as "student." Other occupations included development coordinator, graphic designer, computer operator, secretary, caseworker, home health aide, teacher, recycler, building engineer, pizza man, beautician, waitress, housekeeper, and panhandler.

Over two-thirds (thirty-one) of the respondents reported taking the subways daily, weekdays and weekends, in the mornings and the evenings. Over half (twenty-four) said they encountered subway musicians almost every day, and another nineteen said "sometimes." Most of these encounters took place in the stations along 42nd Street, but they also occurred at the various stops where respondents entered or exited the system. The vast majority reported hearing musicians on subway platforms and at one other location—on mezzanines, in passageways, or in train cars.

When asked what kinds of music they enjoyed hearing in the subways, nine specified jazz and seven said Andean. Yet, just as musicians had reported playing a wide variety of genres, the largest number of respondents (nineteen) liked "any" type of music or listed unusually diverse combinations of preferences, such as: "jazz-classical," "classical or folk," "blues/classical," and "jazz, Indian music."

Respondents were asked to describe what they liked and disliked about subway music. Only five focused on quality as a critical factor, with such phrases as: "If good, a pleasant distraction"; "only if they're superb musicians"; and "they want money and they often stink."

Less than one-quarter of the sample (eleven) identified excess volume and crowding as problems, two issues that are directly related to the regulation of subway music (see Chapter 6). At the same time, practically all the respondents (forty) indicated that subway music often makes their time underground more pleasant. It is, therefore, worthwhile to explore the positive emotional benefits that subway music offers many riders.

During fieldwork, a rider named Olympia said, "It soothes." A rider named Juan Carlos said, "The soul is lighter" after hearing it. Riders and TA employees repeatedly remarked, "What do they say? Music soothes the savage beast [or breast]?"

The sense that subway music alleviates the stress of the subway routine—and of urban life—pervaded my survey sample. Over one-third (sixteen) of the respondents said subway music relaxed them, soothed them, and improved their mood. Four considered the music a diversion that made waiting for trains easier. Five defined the music as entertainment. These categories overlapped in their written responses:

> "Relaxing after a stressful day."
>
> "Entertainment—creates a more relaxed and sociable public space."
>
> "A way to spend the time waiting for the train (if they are good)."
>
> "Some sound good and make me want to dance with the music that they play."
>
> "Makes may day seem less 'ordinary.'"

Survey respondents and other riders hypothesized that musical performances increase safety in the subways by pacifying potential criminals—for example, pickpockets. Further research is needed to verify such a theory, but indeed Robert Cantwell contends that music is "essential to social and psychic life," and he cites psychological studies to suggest that music is a "foundation for the evolution of memory and the emergence of a moral sense."[15]

Subway music encourages many riders to retrieve memories on two levels. The first is individual and nostalgic. About half (twenty-three) of my survey respondents agreed that the music "brings back memories." Reminiscing seems to be a positive, pleasurable experience that releases tension and produces a sense of renewal in people. This result is consistent with Cantwell's notion that traditional music "is a kind of soul stewardship, by which [people] maintain the order, health, and wholeness of their psychic lives . . . for the music absorbs, objectifies, and in a sense redeems . . . experience, as any real art will do."[16] The second level is cultural. Over one-quarter (twelve) of the respondents acknowledged that they had heard music from their cultures in the subways, and almost the same number (eleven) reported hearing music that reminded them of their countries of origin. When this happens, riders may experience a sense of being reunited with what Cantwell calls "the dispersed 'folk' of a folk culture."[17] For instance, in Andean subway music circles many Latino and Latina riders engage in what I call pan–Latin Americanism—a distinct and quite possibly unique form of cultural encounter and solidarity.

It is important to realize that the Andean music in New York's subways is not identical to the traditional music of rural South America. As Thomas Turino explains, even in the capital of Peru, Andean music is necessarily different from its counterpart in the highlands. Migrants in Lima perform traditional Andean music to demonstrate their links with "home," but in the process they actually articulate a sense of community that is particular to their new home: "The residents' use of highland music and custom had less to do with the specific meanings of those practices in [the rural town of] Conima than with their power to draw the community together in Lima and to celebrate its special character."[18] In turn Andean music in the New York subways reflects the musicians' efforts to articulate their identities in a highly multicultural city, and to appeal commercially to a cross section of New Yorkers.

It is also worth noting that Latino and Latina subway riders identify with Andean music to different extents. Some recognize and embrace it immediately. For instance, Teresa Vélez de Carpio moved to New York temporarily to help support her family in Ecuador, leaving six children behind, including a nine-year-old daughter. The move was very difficult for her; in New York, she said, she felt incomplete. Seeing Andean musicians in the subways (and streets and parks) was "compensación." Others recognize it as indigenous music but never listened to it in their countries of origin because their societies viewed it with contempt. Still others were raised in New York City, where they may not have encountered it at all.

Subway music scenes may not be authentic in the strictest sense, but they may be equally, if not more, valuable to their participants. Collective memories such as those generated in Andean music scenes fill many riders with cultural pride and promote an awareness that each individual present has a historical dimension. As Robert Cantwell observes, "It is participation in one form or another which rewards the individual, admitting him into the community in a way that embodies its transpersonal nature in deep, personal experience."[19] These experiences also encourage social interaction and cross-cultural exchanges which transcend standard racial and ethnic identifications. Through subway music, riders recall, reclaim, and remake cultures for themselves and for the city.

July 21, 1991, 8 P.M., 59th Street and Lexington Avenue BMT Platform: Vicki

A young Polish accordionist has attached himself to this station. This evening he stood by a pillar at the edge of the platform, playing show tunes.

A middle-aged woman, rather striking with big blond curls and wearing a red power suit, donated a handful of change, then resumed reading her newspaper. After a pause, I approached her and found her willing to talk.

Her name was Vicki. I explained my study and asked why she had chosen to donate.

"It's the music he's playing. I know every piece he's played so far."

"Do you think you like them because you identify with them?" I asked her.

"I didn't think of it that way. But when I was ten years old, I studied the accordion. So maybe there's that identification also."

As we spoke, a young couple walked up to the platform edge. The woman wore a T-shirt and a madras skirt. She and her partner watched the accordionist. Then they waltzed and tangoed with exaggerated flair.

"Ahh, look at that," Vicki said. "The music has moved them too. That's cute."

The N train finally came and we converged at the door with a young professional man.

"He's good!" he said to Vicki. She agreed.

As we boarded, Vicki encouraged me to talk to him.

"Do you know him?" I asked.

"No, he just spoke to me. But I saw him donate a dollar, and he seems like an outgoing type."

The dancing couple had also boarded and I spoke to them instead.

"What do you like about subway music?" I asked.

"It's better than waiting and yelling: 'Where's the fucking train?'" the male partner exclaimed.

"It's fun," the young woman said. "There's something infatuating about it. Have you ever walked in the dark hallway in the 42nd Street station, and all you hear is the sound of a flute?"

"What kind of music do you like to find?"

"Any music you can sing to," she said. "Which is just about all music, if you have it in here." She pointed to her heart.

"What do you think the music contributes to the subways?"

She paused, then redirected the question.

"You know, there's a lot of violence in the subway. I've seen people get their necklaces snatched off their necks. . . . But when a musician's playing, people don't scream down the platform. . . . There's a calm, there's a respect."

Sunday, October 28, 1990, 10:00 A.M., Roosevelt Avenue–Jackson Heights Mezzanine

A church group, one man and six young women, sang in choir formation against a wall. One rider stood up close and watched. Some of us watched from the tops of the staircases to keep an eye on the platform below and see when our trains arrived.

A young woman holding a Bible stood on the stairs next to me, and a young man faced us. In a few moments he asked her:

"Can I see your Bible?"

"It's in Spanish."

"That's okay." He was Latino. She handed it over.

A young white man approached our staircase. He was smiling. I guess I was smiling too, because as he passed me on his way down to the platform he commented:

"That brings back memories."

September 28, 1991, 5:00 P.M., Grand Central Station, "Number 7" Platform: Olympia

Antonio Gomez, like his brother Carlos, is blind. He plays violin and has a set repertoire of short classical pieces.

A well-dressed woman dropped some change into Gomez's open violin case. We both boarded the "Number 7" train and, once inside, I approached her.

The woman, named Olympia, was very willing to talk. She told me about another violinist (Jim Graseck) who plays Vivaldi's *Four Seasons* at eight o'clock every morning in this station. She encouraged me to come hear him.

What did she think of Gomez?

"He must have been better at one time. It must be his instrument."

Why did she donate to him?

"Because he's blind. . . ." Then she elaborated on her philosophy about subway musicians.

"You can stop or pass, but I think if you stop to listen, you should donate something. These people are trying to make a buck. They're willing to do something," she said, as opposed to panhandlers.

Olympia, originally from Romania, criticized New Yorkers at length. She said they've lost their values.

"People have forgotten how to listen."

Does subway music counteract that tendency?

She thought so. Olympia had been exposed to music all her life, and she believed everyone responded to it. "Music soothes. Lullabies, the wind, the rain, all music."

She also said that music evokes personal memories and that, through them, it "engenders humanity." It takes us back to past stages of our lives, and although they may have been unhappy, when we revisit them we "forget the pain." I asked her whether the early morning version of *The Four Seasons* did that for her.

Hushed for the first time, she nodded.

Saturday, February 17, 1990,
Roosevelt Avenue–Jackson Heights Mezzanine:
Los Andinos

A large circle had formed in front of Los Andinos, and I joined it. The young man standing next to me started making comments in my direction, like: "They're good, eh?" He expressed approval every time they announced the country of origin of the next song.

After establishing that I am not Latina, he told me in English that back in Ecuador he had lots of taped music like this. He said one of the songs Andinos had played, "Lambada," is very popular now in the United States and is at the top of the record charts in many cities.

"What about in Ecuador?" I asked him.

"No, in Ecuador the people don't listen to this. To them, it's the music of the Indians, of the colored people."

"Do you consider yourself a 'colored' person?"

He nodded.

His name was Carlos. He was very handsome, dressed in sleek white pants as if he were just coming from or going to a party.

I asked him if this music made him proud of Ecuador.

"Yes."

I observed a paradox—that in his country, people don't listen to it, while here it instills pride and brings Latin American people together. He agreed. Then he defended his country.

"In Ecuador, all of the people are nice, good people. It's not like here. My father, he's in my country, he's eighty-five, he looks fifty-five. . . . Here, you eat beef, it's . . . shit. . . . Everyone I know here, I ask where they're from, they don't say here, they say Ecuador. The only problem there is the economy. . . . They're here to make money. . . . I, I have a son in Ecuador."

Many immigrants besides Carlos have come to the United States without intending to stay. But while here, they too are participating in subway music circles where Andean music is generating a pan–Latin Americanism that may not exist anywhere else.

December 21, 1991

Today my colleague from Ecuador told me about her thirteen-year-old nephew. He was raised in New York, and he has long told his parents to turn off their "silly [Andean] music." He listens to American pop.

But recently he heard a traditional Ecuadorian group in the Times Square station. "Everything came to my head," he told his family. "My grandmother dancing on the holidays, my grandfather [whom he had visited] back in Ecuador. . . . This music is in my blood!"

He bought the group's cassette, and now he warns his parents: "Don't touch my tape!"

Winter 1990: Eddy and Fernando

The subway musician is what Jane Jacobs called a "specialized public character. . . . He transmits a feeling of vicarious importance to his many friends."[20] Los Andinos transmit that feeling to two individuals in particular.

The Aguirre brothers' friend Eddy from Cuenca has settled in New York. Eddy sells the group's cassettes by walking around the circle and holding them up for prospective buyers to see. In English and in Spanish Jalil Kifafi introduces him to the audience as "Crazy Eddy," which gets a laugh in both languages.

I asked Eddy what he likes about Andean music, what it means to him. He observed that the instruments are natural, nonsynthetic, and they emit pure sounds. Their appearance and resonance capture attention. The music expresses "los sentimientos de nuestras raices"—the feelings of our people. But, he said, this complex feeling issues through a simple call that captivates everyone.

I asked Eddy why he gives up his weekends to sell cassettes.

"Me gusta ver si la gente para." He waits to see whether riders join the audience circle. The scene is exciting to him. He enjoys seeing proud Latinos and Latinas, and he observes that "la musica agrupa las comunidades." The music gathers the diverse communities of the neighborhood. He sees people asking each other: "¿Quienes son?" Who are they?

"Así es la amistad." Thus, friendship.

Fernando, another of Los Andinos' friends from Cuenca who has moved to New York, takes pictures of the group and the audience every weekend. I asked him why.

Like Eddy, Fernando is amazed by the music, by its ability to bring people together and encourage "el dialogo"—dialogue—"así." He pointed to the two of us.

Fernando plans to take his photos with him when he visits Ecuador this winter. He wants to show them to his family.

"Son mis recuerdos." They are his remembrances.

Subway music not only triggers memories, it creates them, adding to people's personal histories in this city.

Thus subway music has identifiable, meaningful causes and effects. Musicians make themselves public to earn a living while refining their art and their performance skills. The music evokes memories in riders, affording personal relief, promoting cultural identification, and facilitating moments of contact among strangers. The next chapter explores the broader implications of this contact for the experience and functions of subway space.

4

Boundaries and Bridges: Relationships in Public Space

Subway music promotes various kinds of contact between musicians, between musicians and their audiences, and among the audience members themselves. These encounters fit Erving Goffman's descriptions of "focused interactions"—public gatherings that bridge the gap between urban anonymity and private relationships, falling almost midway on a spectrum of collective behaviors. In this chapter, relying on Goffman's work, I present the formal properties of subway music scenes, to show how the participants interact.

During fieldwork I learned that an exceptional amount of cooperation and self-regulation, even feelings of community, are generated in the audience circles. Moreover, these instances of focused interaction cut across ethnic and racial lines in ways that attest to the cultural complexity and sophistication of their participants. The textures and implications of these exchanges provide interesting commentary in the ongoing debate about cultural legitimacy. In fact, subway music scenes raise a number of provocative questions. Who decides what legitimate community and culture are? Who decides where they can exist? What are the appropriate uses of public space?

Unfocused and Focused Interaction

For close to thirty years, scholars have drawn on the work of Erving Goffman to explain collective behaviors in public space.[1] In the 1950s,

Goffman, a sociologist, pioneered the study of relationships between strangers in cities. In particular, he contended that the dynamics of pedestrian traffic and spontaneous public gatherings have social meaning. Through years of field research, Goffman identified patterns of collective behavior in public, and he concluded that, however momentarily, strangers in cities behave cooperatively.

Goffman named two kinds of behavior that are especially relevant in exploring subway music. The first kind, "unfocused interaction," primarily refers to pedestrian traffic. When we walk in public thoroughfares, we exchange multiple subtle cues with people on either side of us and with those approaching from the opposite direction. By means of head tilts, eye movements, shifts in gait, even a more aggressive brush against the shoulder, we signal one another to change speed or direction. Although not always executed with the utmost grace, this coordination helps to prevent the collisions that would otherwise constantly occur.

The second kind of behavior, "focused interaction," refers to situations in which "a set of people . . . relate to one another through the medium of a common activity."[2] Amanda Dargan and Steven Zeitlin describe how focused interaction operates in the context of play: "Rules of transformation tell the players how the real world will be modified inside the encounter. With the outside world held at bay, players create a new world within. A kind of membrane forms around them. They often experience a sense of intimacy, the closeness of sharing a world apart."[3] Street performing, broadly defined, is often described in similar terms. Patricia Campbell quotes a performer who says that his act gives his audiences "permission to play."[4] Thomas Turino describes the communal fiestas in the Peruvian highlands as reflections of "people's regular need for play, communion, catharsis, for reaching further within, and getting further outside, themselves."[5]

Some instances of unfocused and focused interaction have been documented and depicted in terms of choreography. William H. Whyte calls pedestrian traffic in Grand Central Terminal "a great dance."[6] Jane Jacobs described the public life found on city sidewalks as "an intricate ballet in which the individual dancers and ensembles all have distinctive parts which miraculously reinforce each other and compose an orderly whole."[7] Subway music helps to illustrate how the dance works.

Subway music scenes involve dynamics that are more or less pronounced depending on a number of factors, including where they occur in the subway system or commuter railroad terminals. Most audience circles form on mezzanines and platforms. They provide clear examples of focused interaction (and incorporate aspects of unfocused interaction as well). Some of the largest circles display these dynamics most consistently, and they tend to appear on mezzanines.

How does an audience circle form? It begins with two or three riders, often of the same racial or ethnic background as the musicians or otherwise familiar with the music, who stop because they see the musicians setting up or hear them warming up. These first "points" on the audience circle tend to stand at a distance from one another, just as riders generally sit at opposite ends of subway benches, perhaps to maximize their sense of safety and, ironically, freedom in anonymity. Or they may separate simply to lay claim to the "elephant feet" pillars girding the mezzanine, which they use as back supports. As William H. Whyte points out, people transform street objects into street furniture.[8] Those who stop to listen to subway music frequently look for places and ways to sit down. In addition to leaning against pillars, they lean or sit on staircase bannisters and gate railings.

Some audience members assign new functions to their own belongings. Once, while watching Los Andinos on the mezzanine at Roosevelt Avenue, I saw a woman seat her young twin sons on her own feet. When Andinos played on the main concourse at Grand Central Terminal, a father and son turned their overnight bag into a front-row seat, and near them a homeless woman did the same (although first she had the resourcefulness to transform a garbage bag into an overnight bag). By creating street furniture, people make their city slightly more comfortable, more familiar. Their casual acts of transformation give them an increased sense of belonging in the spaces they temporarily inhabit.[9]

Once the music is under way, more riders join the circle. Riders seem to "see" fixed positions; when one leaves, another moves up and fills the space. Depending on how many riders stop, second and third audience tiers may ring the first. The circular structure of the scene enables riders to watch one another as well as the musicians, promoting social contact, mutual surveillance, and a greater sense of security. The circle, Sally Harrison-Pepper notes, "provides maximum visibility for the greatest number of persons, while assisting in crowd control by placing focus on the center."[10]

A multitiered, multicultural audience circle on the 34th Street and Sixth Avenue (Herald Square) mezzanine. Photo by Dennis Connors

Subway music circles possess boundaries in time and space. Riders tend to donate money at the end of a song—which on subway platforms is often hastened by the arrival of a train. Yet, an open instrument case or other receptacle enables riders to donate during a song. If one rider sets this example, others will follow suit, for as Whyte found, public behaviors are frequently copied.[11] It is more than acceptable for a child to make a donation during a performance. Audience members enjoy watching children participate in the scene and often indicate as much to others through smiles, nods, or comments. Children's responses and actions thus help to integrate the circle.

Subway music circles have maximum sizes. For instance, when recently arrived riders cannot see what is taking place inside a multitiered circle, they tend to walk away (although if the sound volume is loud, some riders may linger). Coordination extends farther out onto the mezzanine. When a circle is large, passersby generally walk around the perimeter rather than across the "stage." They do cross it when it is the most convenient route or when they are oblivious or antagonistic to the performance. Even then, they often turn their heads toward the musicians while passing, perhaps to see what has attracted so much attention. Those who walk around the perimeter sometimes applaud as they proceed on their way.

Some riders cluster at the heads of nearby staircases to keep an eye on the platform below while they watch the performance. When their train comes, "staircase spectators" stream down as those who have just arrived in the station stream up, thus minimizing the possibility of bottlenecks. Such accommodations between the subway music circle and passersby are constantly replicated.

In addition to forms of tidy coordination, subway music scenes are shaped by a range of behaviors, reflecting riders' intense curiosity, casual interest, indifference, annoyance, or hostility. One of the most striking aspects of these scenes is the proximity of audience members to musicians. Riders can study the performance and feel completely engaged. Stephen Castro, a young Puerto Rican man, was watching César Dueñas play *qena* with Anthology one afternoon on the 42nd Street and Eighth Avenue mezzanine. "You could watch him all day," he said to me. "Imagine what he's thinking. . . . My hair's standing up! You too?"

Some riders make themselves more public than the rest of the audience by positioning themselves directly in front of the musicians. This practice is more common, and less conspicuous, on subway platforms, where space limits often bring musician and audience closer together or otherwise distort the shape of the circle. For instance, on platforms riders regularly stand behind a steel drummer to watch his technique over his shoulders. Conversely, in express stations the audience circle includes riders on the opposite platform, who cannot donate money but can provide some of the loudest applause.

If a musician is positioned near a bench on a platform, it is not unusual to find one seated rider watching the performance and the next one reading a newspaper, dozing, or staring into space. Couples standing at the platform edge who seem completely engrossed in their own affairs may suddenly do a dance step. Riders peering into the tunnel for the next train may tap their feet in time with the music. In passageways, most riders rush past the musician, but some donate money, nod, or exchange a few words while on their way. When a musician performs in a subway car, the most impervious riders may donate money; others may sing along, smile, or laugh with strangers seated nearby. Ironically, subway music would fail if it met with unanimous support. It works because it allows people to make different degrees of commitment to the scenes in which they find themselves.

Goffman called instances of focused interaction "little societies." He believed that an investigation of their rules would shed light on behavioral processes in larger social units.[12] He did not equate focused interactions with communities, but he did identify attributes common to both, such as attachment of the individual to the collective and solidarity with it. He believed, however, that focused interactions have an effect on people which more permanent group activities do not. It is an "attachment . . . of a very special kind. [Focused interactions] are things going on at the moment, from moment to moment. . . . [They do] not involve the committing of such things as one's financial resources or promises to work in the future, but rather one's attention, interest, and orientation—in short, one's capacity for involvement."[13]

Many contemporary sociologists and urban anthropologists agree that focused interactions possess social meaning. The question remains, however, whether it is appropriate to call these temporary social units communities. In *The Hidden Musicians*, Ruth Finnegan withholds the term "community" from the local music rehearsals and performances she studies, because she feels that the traditional connotations do not relate to the process of local music making. Instead, Finnegan creates a new term, "pathways," which, like focused interaction, describes the places and activities through which urban people

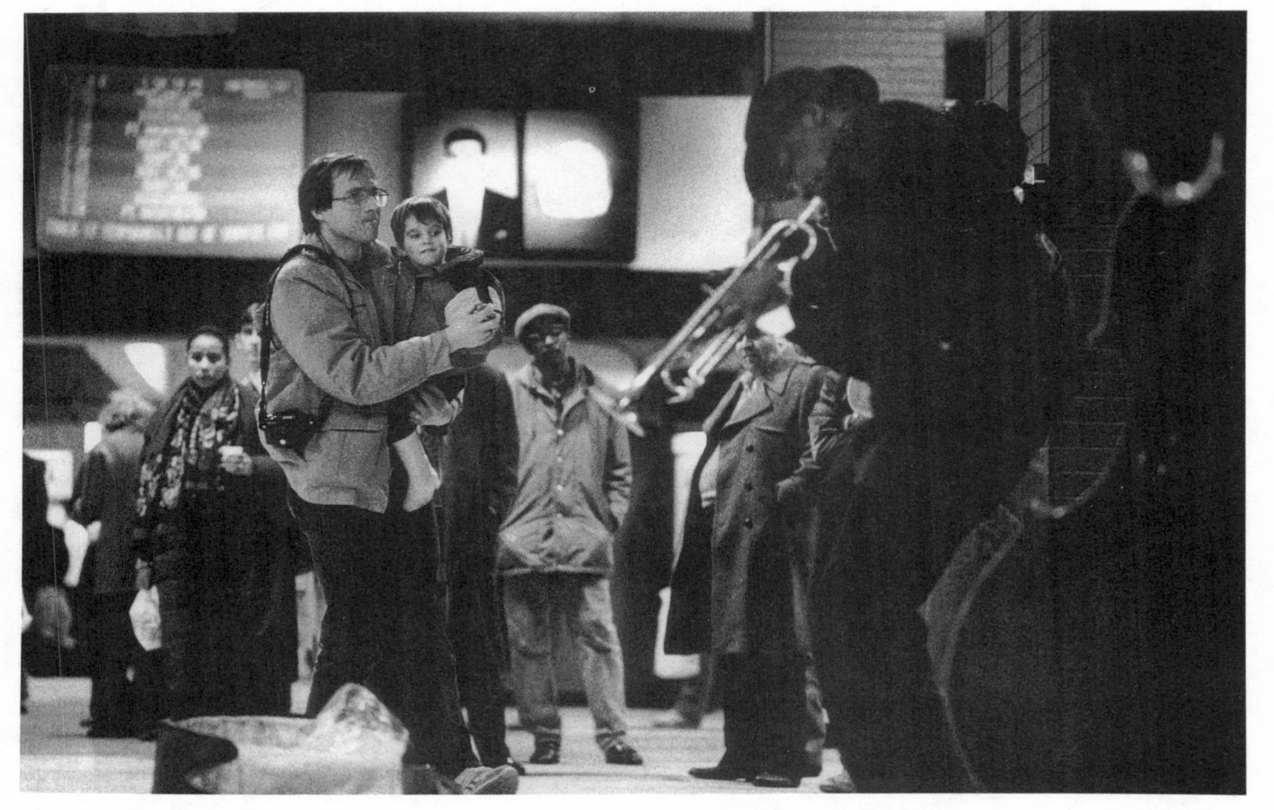

Father and son watching the Roy Campbell Sextet in the Long Island Rail Road waiting area of Penn Station. The scene allows spectators to watch the musicians up close. Photo by Dennis Connors

A rider dances to David Gaskin's calypso band performing as part of MUNY on the 34th Street and Sixth Avenue (Herald Square) mezzanine. Subway music encourages freedom of expression among the audience members, who make various degrees of commitment to the scenes in which they find themselves. Photo by Dennis Connors

engage in meaningful but limited relationships, "routes through what might otherwise have been the impersonal wilderness of urban life, paths which people shared with others in a predictable yet personal fashion."[14] Yet, later she adds: "If we follow an emergent definition of 'community,' then it could be argued that periodic musical festivals can indeed play a part in how . . . people can experience a sense of 'community.' "[15]

I would agree. Already in the late nineteenth and early twentieth centuries, urban theorists reinterpreted the meaning of community to reflect the new organization of social life in the modern industrialized city.[16] Presently, I believe, its meaning needs to be reinterpreted once more to include instances of momentary, shared experience in a multicultural city. A redefinition of community might also encourage much-needed policy review by calling attention to public space activities that local government has traditionally devalued or suppressed.

Subway music scenes can be thought of as "transitory communities." The pun is welcome, for it reinforces the notion that moments *in transit* have meaning, both symbolic and real, for the cross section of New Yorkers who gather spontaneously in subway music scenes and make human contact.

Thursday, February 14, 1991:
Roosevelt Avenue–Jackson Heights Mezzanine

Los Andinos have begun to play here every Thursday afternoon. They returned today, as did the two curly-haired Peruvian men who sell cologne in the audience circle and start their weekend early with a few beers. Other people were also beginning to look familiar to me. The Chilean woman was back with her two-year-old son, whose name is Michael. And the large African American man in the mackinaw shirt was again talking to someone in the shadows of a nearby staircase.

Michael had his red plastic guitar with him. Clutching it, he scampered over to face Los Andinos, and as he danced and played it seemed as if the group was looking through a mirror at the next generation of subway musicians.

Michael cemented relationships in the circle, even on this dimmest of mezzanines. An old man wearing dark glasses tapped one of the Peruvians and pointed. Others laughed. Two older women donated coins to Michael, which made his mother laugh!

When Michael ran around the circle, people extended their arms to prevent him from escaping out into the dangerous station. There was safety in the inner circle. Michael had become everyone's charge.

Suddenly, he fell and dropped his guitar. Then, as if out of nowhere, the man in the mackinaw shirt appeared. He picked it up, handed it to Michael, and strummed an imaginary guitar of his own to get Michael to play again.

In recent decades, as sociologists have expanded their definition of social life in cities, anthropologists have changed their approach to interpreting cultural life. Whereas in the past anthropologists studied cultures primarily as discrete sets of customs, values, and beliefs, many now study world cultures, described in terms of the relationships, or "flows," between ethnic and racial groups living in a single area. Rather than focus on supposedly bounded rural areas, as was traditional, those who study world cultures often identify cities as prime areas of study. I introduced the term "fusion" to describe the cultural flows between New York subway musicians who jam together. Now I would like to identify other cross-cultural exchanges that characterize the city's subway music scenes.

New York has long been known as a gateway to America. Only in the 1980s, however, was the term "minority majority city" applied to it. During that decade, unprecedented numbers of Asian, Latin American, and African immigrants replaced New Yorkers of European ancestry who had already moved to outlying areas. As a result of these shifts, no one group dominates demographically. In fact, a representative of the New York City Planning Department calls it "the most ethnically and racially diverse city in the world."[17]

The subway system is perhaps the most heterogeneous public space in New York. It is also an enclosed space where people are forced into such close proximity for such significant lengths of time that, however surreptitiously, they study each other's faces, dress, language, and behavior. Indeed, not all New Yorkers are equally represented underground. Elderly and more affluent residents, for example, seem to use the trains less frequently than others. But the great range of racial, ethnic, and cultural groups, generations, and socioeconomic classes in the subways creates the possibility for encounters and exchanges between people from distant parts of the city, if not the world.

During my fieldwork, a number of musicians and riders declared that "music is universal." The truth of this cliché is evident when participants use subway music as a vehicle of communication. Belying the old melting-pot theory ("we are all the same"), in which the political Right has such vested interest, and also the Left's politics of difference, subway music audience members exchange information about their separate cultural identities in the context of an experience they collectively create. In Thomas Turino's words, "These artistic practices open the possibility for transcending 'rationalist' discourse and unifying *difference*; the various fusions and creative visions become real insofar as they can be seen, heard, danced to, and enjoyed."[18]

Moreover, subway music scenes reveal that New Yorkers' cultural knowledge defies conventional expectations.[19] On the one hand, people are presumed to possess identities and cultural affinities that may in fact be alien to them. As I have noted, some immigrants from South America are unfamiliar with Andean music either because the cultural authorities in their countries of origin devalued it or because they were raised elsewhere. Indeed, they may identify with Andean subway music more directly than other riders because they understand it linguistically or associate it with cultural conventions that are familiar to them. Yet in fact, they too may be experiencing it for the first time.

On the other hand, some people have developed strong identification with cultural traditions originating in groups different from their own. Thus, for example, bluesman Elijah "Carolina Slim" Staley was performing one evening on the 68th Street and Lexington Avenue (Hunter College) mezzanine, when a young white professional man in the audience quietly pulled a harmonica out of his trenchcoat pocket. Clearly familiar with the song and the musical style, the man provided accompaniment. Since then, Elijah Staley has apprenticed a talented white teenager named (appropriately enough) Jeremiah, who plays electric guitar and has learned to perform and dress, in Staley's words, "like a traditional bluesman."

In other situations, imagination combines with knowledge to increase cultural understanding. On the mezzanine at Roosevelt Avenue, a Jamaican woman named Beverly explained to me that she knew how to dance to traditional Andean music because it reminded her of calypso—music from her country of origin. When Los Andinos played in Grand Central Terminal, I spoke to a homeless woman who articulated a reaction shared by others (myself included) when she said: "I don't understand the lyrics, but I like the sound." Conversely, Trinidadian subway musicians often play pop tunes or television theme songs on the steel drum because, in Michael Gabriel's words, "You got to

Traditional bluesman Elijah "Carolina Slim" Staley and his partner Jeremiah perform in the MUNY spot at the Grand Central end of the 42nd Street Shuttle. Photo by Dennis Connors

play what the people know." Subway music either introduces us to or blends familiar with unfamiliar cultural conventions; we may begin to identify with and integrate these new aural and visual textures into our personal cultural repertoires. In the words of one of my subway rider survey respondents: "It's beautiful because we hear music we never hear before."

Culture is a source of knowledge, and subway music circles abound with teachers. Ricardo Silva of Antara del Barrio motions to his audience to clap with him, and some riders learn a new rhythm. During Evelyn Blakey's "Cafe Subway," some riders learn to applaud in the middle of a piece. Riders ask each other questions, including: "What country are they from?" and: "What is that instrument made of?" One evening, while Andinos played on Grand Central Terminal's main concourse, an Ecuadorian man named César traced the origins of Andean music for an elderly white couple in the audience. He began by describing the sound of the wind above the Andean mountains and explaining that it is replicated by the *sampoñas*. In addition to being cross-cultural, the lesson became intergenerational when César called his young daughter over to help him with his English.

Subway music circles sometimes witness symbolic enactments of the racial tensions that exist in this city. A few times while conducting fieldwork for this study, I observed African American teenagers caricaturing Andean musicians at the periphery of the circle. In most instances, the audience integrated the teenagers into the scene by watching and smiling at their performances. Simply by paying attention to these reactions, the audience promoted safe expression of racial difference.

The mere presence of subway musicians may have positive effects on race relations in New York City. For instance, our society often stereotypes young African American men as dangerous or criminal. When riders with these biases encounter an African American man in the subways playing a saxophone, a drum, a flute, or a violin, they must question, if not dismiss, their preconceptions. African American subway musicians who play blues, jazz, Caribbean, Afro-Andean, or European classical music also implicitly teach riders that people of African descent identify with diverse cultural traditions. Indeed, many subway jazz ensembles include black, white, and Asian members. They provide models of coexistence.

Gina Higginbotham, coordinator of the MUNY program, witnessed a compelling example of how subway music participants mediate and transcend racial conflict. In 1991 MUNY sponsored a special event in honor of Hispanic Heritage Month. Part of it took place in the Atlantic Avenue subway station in Brooklyn, shortly after the first widely publicized racial incident in nearby Crown Heights had occurred. Higginbotham, who went to oversee the Atlantic Avenue event, saw two black-hatted Hasidic Jewish men stop to listen to Trinidadian steel drummer David Gaskin, who was then performing. After one of the men told the other to proceed to their destination, he stayed to listen. Soon he was dancing in place. "He couldn't control himself," Higginbotham recalled.

Two African American boys watched the Hasid and laughed. Then they started to dance, and they said to him:

"Hit it, Daddy!" To which the Hasid replied:

"Yeah!"

A spectator turned to Higginbotham. She says there were tears in his eyes. He said to her:

"In a neighborhood with so much tension—look at this."

While the news media reported on continued racial violence in the city and local government tried to defuse the crisis through new peacemaking slogans and "reservation only" ceremonies,[20] New Yorkers of various backgrounds conducted their own form of conflict mediation by watching and enjoying exchanges with one another in subway music circles.

Legitimacy, Authenticity, and Access

Musicians, cultural institutions, and government agencies often disagree about what constitutes meaningful and legitimate cultural activity. In recent years scholars have criticized all three for oversimplifying the discussion. I want to review some of the main arguments and examine the scholarly critiques in an effort to situate subway music in this discussion and, ultimately, identify what makes subway music unique.

The Arts for Transit Office of the MTA maintains that the MUNY program brings musical events to a "nontraditional audience," alluding to nonaffluent and nonwhite subway riders.[21] The statement implicitly raises a larger issue, namely, that much cultural entertainment in American society has been rendered virtually inaccessible to a significant portion of the population.

This was not always the case, nor did it simply result from the commodification of culture. In *Highbrow Lowbrow: The Emergence of Cultural Hierarchy in America*, Lawrence Levine claims that until the twentieth century, Shakespearean plays as well as opera and the symphony were "part and parcel of popular culture" (p. 22). Boundaries between performers, spectators, and original texts were highly permeable. Actors and conductors mixed genres and routinely adapted what today would be called "classic" plays and compositions. Audience members assumed the role of participants "who feel a sense of immediacy and at times even of control, who articulate their opinions and feelings vocally and unmistakably" (p. 26). Above all, the theater and the concert hall were "microcosm[s] of American society" (p. 25). The social elite and the poor attended the same cultural events in the same cultural spaces. Indeed, Levine notes the limits to that democracy: "Various classes saw the same plays in the same theaters—though not necessarily from the same vantage point. . . . Seating arrangements," he says, "dovetail[ed] with class and economic divisions" (p. 24).

The climate changed significantly in the mid- to late nineteenth century when members of the social elite attempted to make sense of what they considered an increasingly disorderly world—and to compensate for their loss of social and political power—by establishing their hegemony in the cultural sphere. They endowed Shakespeare, opera, and the symphony with sacred aesthetic properties that only "the experts" and "the educated" could appreciate. They established new codes of conduct in cultural spaces, requiring audience members to experience culture passively, silently, and individually. Ultimately they appropriated culture itself, calling theirs "high culture" and equating the lower classes' "popular culture" with poor-quality entertainment (pp. 6–7).

In recent decades, these class-bound distinctions have lost a good deal of their force. Subway musicians certainly do their share to confound the cultural hierarchy. For instance, Jim Graseck popularizes Vivaldi's *Four Seasons* by bringing it into the vernacular setting of Grand Central Station. Nor are cultural activities being brought to "nontraditional audiences"; on the contrary, most subway musicians actually represent the cultures of those audiences. As the examples in this chapter have demonstrated, it is often *traditional* audience members who are being exposed to unfamiliar cultural conventions and who request information from their nontraditional counterparts in

Riders encounter Jim Graseck playing classical violin in Grand Cental Station. Photo by Dennis Connors

subway music circles. Nevertheless, cultural categories persist. As will be seen, they continue to inform the decision making of those individuals who are paid to identify legitimate culture in our society.

Meanwhile, within the universe of popular culture, a similar debate has centered on the notion of authenticity. Starting with folk revivalism at the turn of the century, continuing through the populist movement of the 1930s, and resuming with the counterculture of the 1960s, folk musicians and enthusiasts held that their music was a more authentic genre of popular culture than such commercial counterparts as Tin Pan Alley. Folk music was said to possess certain "essentialist" qualities: its lyrics had the power to articulate the experiences of both performer and audience; its songs originated either in antiquity or in close-knit rural communities; and its performers rejected commercialism and new technological processes. Thus, in the early 1960s some musicians scorned electric amplification of their instruments, creating a conflict that came to a head at the 1965 Newport Folk Festival when Bob Dylan appeared on stage with an electric guitar and a four-piece rock band.[22]

Critics now challenge the assumption that folk music's content literally bound performer and audience together or reflected either one's life experiences. In *No Respect*, a radical deconstruction of popular culture, Andrew Ross contends that the folk music played in the 1930s was "anachronistically based upon romantic, preindustrial notions of the 'folk-popular.'"[23] In *Sound Effects*, Simon Frith praises folk as a major source of inspiration for rock music. Nevertheless, he maintains that "the radical tradition of American folk music was primarily the 1930s creation of this group of metropolitan, left-wing bohemians. Their account of 'the people' was as rooted in myth . . . as that of their more respectable, bourgeois, folk predecessors." By the late 1960s, Frith explains, such artists as Bob Dylan were writing thoughtful, political, but individual expressions virtually divorced from any notion of a folk community.[24] These critics imply that while the folk musicians of both the Old and New Left responded to real social conditions and needs, they did not directly confront assumptions about their music's authenticity. They never fully acknowledged that their articulation of folk traditions amounted to musical innovation.

Musical authenticity is often implicitly defined as the preservation of "ancient," original compositions. But ironically, overemphasis on "the original" tends to constrain originality. Thomas Turino discusses this paradox in *Moving away from Silence* when he compares and contrasts the practices, values, and goals of recently formed musical ensembles in Lima with traditional groups in the highlands of Peru. Limeño ensembles can theoretically draw musical ideas from the city's cosmopolitan soundscape, but instead they aim to "sound like [rural] Conima" (p. 206). Consequently, the urban ensembles' members are expected to demonstrate a high degree of competency before participating in public festivals where competitions are won through strict imitation of the highland "canon" (pp. 204–5). Meanwhile, music making in the highlands is a collective activity (for men) in which all participants help to produce compositions for upcoming fiestas. Moreover, highland musical competitions are won through innovation. Groups emphasize subtle distinctions in an effort to sound unique (pp. 76–79). Thus the urban migrants' musical performances actually run counter to the values at the source of the canon, and conversely, rural practices would thwart musical achievements within urban performance frames (p. 225). The urban and rural musicians' respective notions of authenticity correlate with their particular social, cultural, and political realities.

These various reinterpretations of authentic culture help to clarify the meanings and value of subway music. As I have noted, subway music rarely fits the strict definition of authenticity. Indeed, a considerable number of the musicians underground learned to sing or play in communal settings from older people. But more often than not, they do not literally articulate their audience members' life experiences. Indeed, some people are disturbed by the results. During fieldwork, two ardent defenders of tradition—one a Latino musician, the other a Latino audience member—called the Andean fusion music heard in New York's streets and subways "corrupted" or "prostituted" versions of the original. And Elijah Staley feels strongly that transforming musical tradition has its limits. One evening during a subway performance he compared the process to adulterating "Grandma's pound cake. If you add milk, it's not Grandma's anymore. It's somebody else's." Yet, right after sharing this thought with his audience, Staley and his young white partner, Jeremiah, played blues versions of "Old MacDonald" for a little girl in the circle and a Beatles tune. Subway music depends on musicians and audience members who combine their varying amounts of traditional knowledge with imagination, constructing cross-cultural experiences that are authentic precisely because they transform culture to articulate the richness and originality of particular urban moments.

Is local music making nevertheless more authentic than music that is commercially produced and distributed from remote sources? Both Simon Frith and Andrew Ross reject this notion. They argue that commercial processes can actually increase access to cultural experiences. According to Frith, the rock music of the 1960s and 1970s was the expression of a newly emerged youth culture, and young consumers influenced the decisions of the music business whenever they listened to particular radio stations, bought particular albums, or attended particular concerts. "Music is never just a product," Frith says; "artistic value . . . has an unavoidable complicating effect on . . . production."[25]

Ross maintains that commercial processes are democratizing insofar as they facilitate musical and other forms of cultural and political discourse and transformation:

> In short, this demonizing of commercial music closes off any discussion of the way in which popular musical taste—with its shifting definitions of "black" and "white" meanings—is actually negotiated in the space between the industrial logic of mass distribution and local forms of consumption. Demonizing is all the more purblind if we consider that it is in that very space that the voice of popular persuasion about social change in a multiracial culture is always likely to have its broadest audience and therefore its best chance of making a breakthrough in the process of winning active popular consent.[26]

Clearly, Frith and Ross advance the discussion on cultural authenticity. But while they identify the positive transformational potential of commercial culture, they downplay its negative impact on people's very experience of culture, particularly in urban settings. For instance, consumers who can afford to pay may be able to choose from a wider array of entertainment forms than ever before, but that entertainment is being produced, and controlled, by an increasingly small number of private corporations.[27] And by reinforcing the notion that leisure is "naturally" a commodity to be purchased and enjoyed privately, mass culture promotes social disengagement. Amanda Dargan and Steven Zeitlin elaborate on this point:

> The media can't replace the real experiences of growing up and getting to know a city street; it can't create a sense of place. Even drugs, which have ravaged urban communities in ways far more destructive than television, are a way out of neighborhoods and locales; in the television-soaked America of today, young people become frustrated with communities and relationships which have none of the glamour of the world depicted on television; advertisements remind them constantly of what they do not have. Ironically, the fear of drugs and crime keeps city residents locked in their apartments, allowing nothing in except television and feeding the vicious cycle. Local communities have been devalued in contemporary American life, which emphasizes success stories and celebrities in the constant barrage of the media.[28]

While folk, and more broadly local, culture may not have "essentialist" qualities that make it more authentic than commercial culture, there is nevertheless something *essential* about it, namely, the opportunity it affords people to participate, to engage in what Turino describes as "a special relationship based on 'being there.'"[29] Indeed, Frith in the end singles out local music making, in particular punk rock, as especially meaningful cultural activity.[30] In his more recent work, *Art into Pop*, he in effect provides a definition of authentic culture which emphasizes the value of local, participatory experience:

> For 1960s nostalgics, post-punk/postmodern culture clearly represents the triumphs of artifice over art. . . . For 1980s optimists, by contrast, postmodern culture is actually speaking the "truth" of capitalist experience for the first time. . . . Artifice isn't the issue here . . . but, rather, the old Romantic search in a new commercial setting for expressive directness, feelings untrammeled. . . . What's most striking about contemporary culture, then, is not the impossibility of Romantic art but people's continuing belief in it, their determination to express themselves anyway.[31]

Ultimately, subway music eludes the cultural studies critiques. By choice or by circumstance, the musicians are generally independent of the culture industries. Every day, they promote direct expression without relying on commercial processes that might alienate audiences from their own experiences. They also challenge conventional notions about the role of commercial relations in our lives when they sell us their cassettes and CDs, and we listen at home to the music of those we smile at and offer feedback to regularly. The scenes they produce in and of themselves reject prepackaged entertainment as well as enclaves of style. Above all, subway musicians maintain what is most essential to the folk tradition: they democratize leisure by inviting everyone to join in the creative process.

January 8, 1991, 5:30 P.M.,
Roosevelt Avenue–Jackson Heights Mezzanine

Cuzco, an Andean trio with a driving rhythm, had attracted a crowd of around a hundred people. A black woman standing about twenty people away from me was swaying in place. Our eyes met. She smiled at me and said something about the music. I moved over to her.

"Makes you want to dance," I said.

"It does," she agreed. "That's why I am dancing here."

Her speech had a Caribbean lilt. Her name was Beverly. She was from Jamaica.

"What do you like about this music?" I asked.

"Music is like love," she said. "Where there's music, there's love!"

Beverly became more courageous, moving farther into the "stage" area.

"I don't understand the words, but I like the music. . . . It sounds like calypso, in my country. That's why I know how to dance to it." She invited me to join her. I declined.

"If everyone weren't so afraid," I said, "we'd probably all be dancing." A Latino man was also stepping in place.

"I'm not afraid. Only if a church friend came, I'd be careful. But there's nothing wrong with what I'm doing. I'm not committing a crime."

"Would you ask others to dance?" I asked.

Beverly was a step ahead of me.

"Yes, but they declined."

"You asked?"

"Yes, twice. But people are too shy. They [fold their arms] and [shake their heads]."

"Do you ever feel afraid to ask?"

"No, because people's around."

"You feel safe."

"Yes."

Beverly expertly whirled her hips and made her way clear around the inside of the circle. Riders laughed. She had given them a common focus and she was enjoying herself.

Beverly had taken off her coat and left it with a shopping bag by my side. She was wearing a red sweatshirt, a red knit hat, and earmuffs. The outfit, the dancing, and the setting certainly clashed with the expected subway routine. I laughed too.

Then a young white man who seemed to be emotionally disabled approached Beverly.

"Hey, I want to dance just one dance with you. Here, give me your hands." He took Beverly's hands and swung arms with her, but when he swiveled his hips Elvis-style, she turned away and he ran off. The audience howled.

"I was afraid when he started moving his hips," she said. "But others are around."

Beverly danced some more.

"Last time," she said, "I was so tired, I went straight to bed! This is my exercise."

Beverly worked as a home attendant for an elderly man. She loved to sing and dance. She sometimes went to the Apollo Theater in Harlem, but otherwise she didn't go out. Why not? I asked her.

"I don't got the money."

It was important to Beverly to become brave enough to dance on this "stage," because then she would be able to "get up in public" anywhere.

The Politics of Public Space

The social interaction and cross-cultural exchange I observed in subway music scenes derive their form and meaning from the public space in which they occur. In turn they transform that space into a broad-based meeting place. Not everyone agrees, however, that the subways should have multiple functions. There are two distinct theories about the purpose of public space. That both have been incorporated into American city planning helps to account for the frequent ambiguity in public space regulations.[32]

The first theory upholds what Paul Chevigny calls the controlled community ideal, the assumption that "neighborhoods are made more livable and safe if they are quiet and nearly deserted" and that "contact with strangers . . . is something to be avoided, something that interferes with the controlled environment" (p. 92). This premise is evident in George Kelling's article "The Contagion of Public Disorder." Inasmuch as Kelling personally advised the New York City Transit Police in the early 1990s on how to revise their crime-fighting strategy, it is worthwhile to review his argument.

Kelling contends that social disorder causes fear and leads people to abandon their public spaces, which in turn allows real crime to occur. He defines disorder in human terms: "youths hanging out on the corner; panhandlers, hustlers, and suggestively dressed prostitutes on the street; public drunkenness and rowdiness." The solution, he says, is to reinstate "moral reliability," a code of conduct supported by community residents and enforced by local police.[33]

Kelling thus revives the rhetorical strategy identified and criticized in the 1960s of "blaming the victim"—of ignoring the larger social, economic, and political crises that landed many of these populations in public space in the first place. His use of the word *disorder* compares to what Chevigny and other political theorists describe as government's tendency to make rules that encode "powerful unspoken judgments expressing some of society's attitudes about respectability and status as well as race" (p. 175).[34]

By contrast, Chevigny says, the second theory upholds the urban diversity ideal (pp. 93–94). Jane Jacobs is associated with this view, which she articulated in the 1960s in *The Death and Life of Great American Cities*. Jacobs found that busy streets are interesting and enjoyable because they accommodate loads of strangers in a range of activities. They are also safer, she discovered, because their regular users monitor the goings-on. Moreover, Jacobs observed, busy streets are not disorderly; in fact, social order is kept "by an intricate, almost unconscious, network of voluntary controls and standards among the people themselves, and enforced by the people themselves." She concluded: "No amount of police can enforce civilization where the normal, casual enforcement of it has broken down."[35]

In the 1980s, transit executives began to recognize the usefulness of the urban diversity ideal, although still in the shadow of a controlled community. David Gunn, who became TA president in 1984, was known for his obsession with cleanliness and was praised for eliminating graffiti from subway cars.[36] His penchant for order, and his belief that the subways should function only as a transit facility, also led him to shut down most of the system's newsstands.[37] When the stands closed, riders protested. Not only did they miss making purchases, but they missed the additional human presence. In *Subway Lives*, Jim Dwyer quotes a straphanger named Kevin Hayes, who compares the newsstands to "a campfire on the prairie when no one else is around." Dwyer himself editorializes: "The newsstands made the stations feel safer."[38] Gunn continued his crusade almost until the end of his tenure in 1990. Subsequently, many stands were remodeled and reopened.[39]

In 1989 the TA advanced arguments about disorder once again when it proposed regulations that would have banned subway music from platforms. At public hearings, musicians and riders testified that, in Jane Jacobs's words, an "almost unconscious network" exists underground and musicians are an important part of it. As a result of this testimony and in an effort to avert legal action, the TA and MTA passed a modified set of regulations (see Part II). Yet, as the politics of subway music demonstrate, the authorities continue to vacillate between the two public space models, tending toward controlled community.

In the past, even those researchers who supported the urban diversity ideal saw the need to maintain clear boundaries between public and private spaces. For instance, Jacobs stated: "The sum of such casual, public contact . . . is a feeling for the public identity of people, a web of public respect and trust. . . . And above all, *it implies no private commitments*."[40] Now scholars are more inclined to identify a flow between the two domains. Ulf Hannerz, an anthropologist, sees urban public space as a "pool of potential interaction partners," rendering people of very different social and cultural worlds accessible to one another. Depending on the degree of commitment chosen by the individuals involved, public acquaintances can turn into private friends, and thus public space may contribute even more permanently to urban people's lives.[41] This kind of flow characterizes those friendships between subway musicians and riders which extend outside the stations. Some examples are especially compelling. During my field research, I met four subway musicians who had married members of their audiences, and one who considered naming his next child after his two closest friends—members of his group whom he had originally met in the subways.

I do not mean to deny that notions of proper conduct and safety are being seriously challenged in New York's public spaces. Public institutions and government agencies have reacted primarily by encoding the controlled community model, revising and posting rules and regulations in transportation terminals and parks, as well as in libraries and post offices. To avoid being accused of discriminating against homeless people or other members of the underclass, they design rules that implicate everyone. Thus, for instance, the New York Public Library now reserves the right to remove patrons who smell bad.[42]

By contrast, urban ecologists are encouraging government to fight alienation, rather than people, by identifying and supporting those instances of "purposeful behavior" in which people are already engaged,[43] instances such as subway music. Michael Walzer, an urban planner, contends that cities do not need more single-minded spaces with narrowly defined, instrumental functions. Instead, they need more open-minded spaces that encourage positive social activities and attitudes such as lingering, receptivity, and "tolerance for diversity."[44] Subway music, I believe, helps to transform the single-minded subway system into an open-minded transit facility and meeting place. The political implications of this transformation are the subject of the second part of this book.

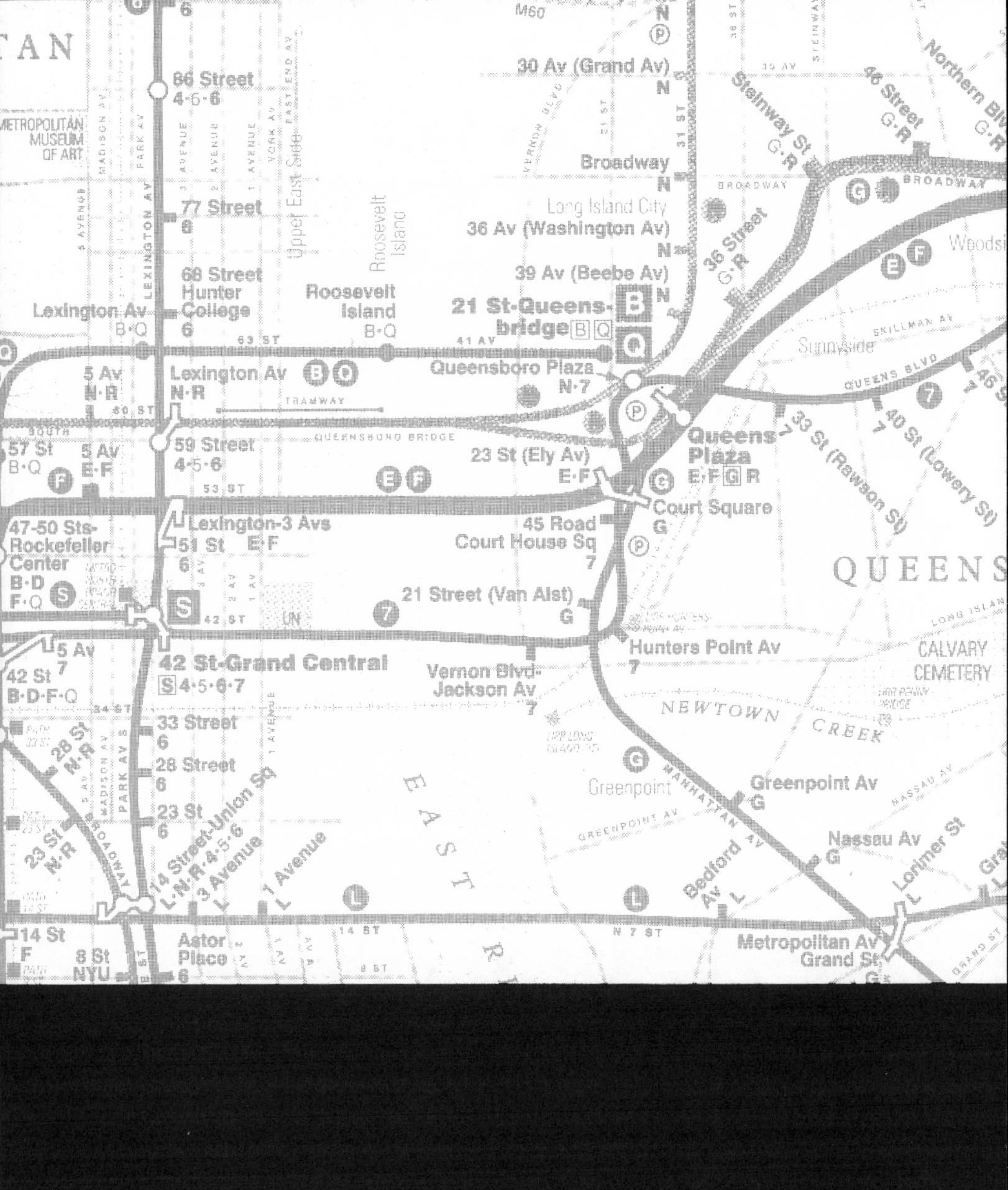

PART II

SEEKING HARMONY UNDERGROUND

5

Music Under New York: Official Sponsorship

In the first part of this book, I described New York City subway music in terms of spontaneous interactions between musicians and riders. Actually, however, musical performances are framed by the MTA Music Under New York program and by TA regulations governing "non-transit use of transit facilities."

Thomas Turino describes frames as "metacommunicative devices that define how social action that takes place within them should be interpreted." When government establishes official performance frames for public spaces and when performers accept those frames as "natural," they are likely to be "as much mechanisms of control as they are liberating."[1] MUNY is an example of this complex process. Part of the MTA's beautification efforts, it marks perhaps the first time in the history of mass transit that government has managed to both embrace subway musicians and impose notions of cultural legitimacy on them.

At the same time, since MUNY bestows special status on its members, it produces tensions, especially in conjunction with the TA rules that frame the entire subway music scene. Transit police officers who are uncertain about the TA rules, for example, often rely on MUNY's extra legitimating force to contain the activities of freelancers. Meanwhile, the populations that encounter musicians daily—lower-level transit employees and concession stand workers—have opinions that are hardly accounted for in the MTA program and the TA policies. In the following chapters I analyze the official performance frames and present a range of views from within the informal social network of the subways, with the aim of identifying ways in which the transforming experiences of subway music scenes might in turn transform subway politics.

The MUNY program schedules musicians (as well as a smaller number of other entertainers) to perform, amplified if they wish, in twenty-three designated spots on subway mezzanines, in commuter railroad terminals, and seasonally at Yankee and Shea stadiums. They are not scheduled on platforms at least in part because the TA has argued that performances on the lower level can compromise public safety (see Chapter 6). Since 1991 an additional MUNY spot has been located above ground at Duffy Square, a traffic triangle currently leased by the city to the Times Square Business Improvement District. Most of these spots are in midtown Manhattan, one of the city's major centers of business and commerce, where underground pedestrian traffic is heavy and, consequently, donations are ample. Musicians consider a number of MUNY spots to be "prime" performance spaces.

MUNY is selective. An audition is held annually, and successful candidates are permanently added to the roster. Members receive free tokens to enter the stations for their scheduled performances and are paid a small stipend when they participate in MUNY special events (in 1994 the rate was twenty-five dollars per person at events where the musicians were allowed to collect donations and fifty dollars per person where they were not). But aside from a banner that members must display during their scheduled sets, MUNY performances are identical in form to freelancing, and MUNY members depend on donations just as freelancers do. Indeed, a number of members "double" as freelancers at times when they are not scheduled to perform.

MUNY is one of many programs administered by the MTA Arts for Transit Office, whose primary task is to arrange visual displays in the stations. Through its permanent art program, the office commissions established artists to design and produce public works. Temporary exhibits feature works by community groups and "unestablished artists," according to Wendy Feuer, who has served as director since the office opened in 1985. The goal, Feuer explains, is to represent different levels of the art world in the subways.

The initiatives that led to the establishment of Arts for Transit date back to 1975.[2] In that year, the Municipal Arts Society, an organization founded in the late nineteenth century to support preservation and beautification efforts in New York City, secured sponsorship from the Exxon Corporation to develop a visual arts project for the MTA called "Platforms for Design."[3] Subsequently, the society obtained matching grants from the federal Urban Mass Transportation Administration and introduced "Adopt-a-Station," which promoted public-private partnerships in the subways. By the early 1980s, artists on the MTA Board of Directors and in its Government Relations Office were searching for additional sponsors to fund more visual arts projects. In 1981 MTA chair Richard Ravitch secured 7.7 billion dollars in state funds to launch a five-year capital improvement program; once the overhaul of tracks and trains was well under way, the MTA turned its attention to aesthetic considerations. Ravitch's successor, Robert Kiley, obtained another 8.5 billion dollars for capital projects, at which point Arts for Transit was formed to consolidate and expand the recent public art initiatives.[4]

The Arts for Transit promotional brochure states that the office is "recapturing the lapsed tradition of integrating aesthetic elements with the fundamental needs of quality design and progressive engineering."[5] The allusion is to "City Beautiful," a turn-of-the-century urban design movement whose proponents held that fine architecture had positive effects on public behavior. There was more than a hint of elitism to the Victorian belief that beautiful surroundings could elevate "common people" and persuade them to contribute to the "public good." Nevertheless, City Beautiful inspired some exceptional public architecture in, and under, New York. When the first IRT line was built, Brian Cudahy writes, "the construction contract was most explicit: 'The railway and its equipment as contemplated by the contract constitute a great public work. All parts of the structure where exposed to public sight shall therefore be designed, constructed, and maintained with a view to the beauty of their appearance, as well as to their efficiency.'"[6] Between 1900 and 1904, IRT financier August Belmont spent $500,000 decorating his stations with bas reliefs and mosaic murals, some of which the MTA has recently restored.[7]

What is generally unknown, however, is that Depression-era artists attempted to introduce a politically radical form of art into the subways. According to Helen A. Harrison, the WPA Federal Art Project envisioned public art as a way to employ artists and benefit society simultaneously. The Public Use of Arts Committee, composed of members of the Artists' Union who would be working on the project, took the idea one step farther, Harrison says, and asserted that the accessibility of art was "not separate from the achievement of social equality." Ironically, the PUAC expressed solidarity with the public in their works by depicting the toils of transit workers and riders, whereas a survey revealed that riders preferred to be presented with images of natural landscapes. The project ultimately foundered because the WPA cut back on funding and the city Board of Transportation never extended official support.[8] Yet even if not entirely successful (some of the less overtly political works were in fact exhibited), the WPA project constitutes another vital part of the subway art tradition in New York.

Official interest in subway art revived in the 1970s once the federal government began to recognize the costs of its postwar decision to build highways and bridges for suburban commuters while allowing urban mass transit systems to fall into disrepair. Through matching grants, the Urban Mass Transportation Administration revived the City Beautiful tradition—without the explicit class bias—by encouraging local transit authorities "to enhance the physical quality of the subway environment."[9] The MTA has echoed these and even stronger environmental principles in recent years,[10] but its beautification efforts are also consistent with the UMTA's sense that art makes a good promotional tool. For instance, in 1988 MTA Marketing Research Director Peter Harris conducted a customer survey and concluded that "spruced-up stations might go a long way towards reducing anxiety about the subway."[11]

The MTA created the Marketing Research Division in the 1980s when it adopted private-sector strategies to improve the subways' image. This administrative shift is largely attributed to Robert Kiley, who succeeded Richard Ravitch as MTA chair in 1983. A former Central Intelligence Agency official and deputy mayor of Boston, Kiley had headed the Massachusetts Bay Transportation Authority from 1975 to 1979, overseeing the inauguration of the first subway art program in the nation, Arts on the Line, as well as Music Under Boston, the first government-sponsored subway music program. Transit executives in Boston and New York credit Kiley with introducing Music Under Boston and transplanting the program to New York. What in fact was Kiley's innovation?

True to Boston's populist and intellectual traditions, the MBTA introduced Arts on the Line as a public service with the potential to promote radical social change. In the introduction to the program's promotional brochure, a professor at Tufts University predicted: "All of these works will cause citizens to address the meaning and purpose of public spaces, to interact with and be challenged by their environment rather than simply enduring it. Art serves here not as decor, but as a means of shaping consciousness."[12] But these assertions referred to the visual arts, not to live musical performances. In fact, as early promotions clearly stated, Music Under Boston was created only after freelance musicians had already established a presence: "In the past, musicians, acting on their own, have come into the stations to play with and without permission. In general, our passengers were delighted, although there were occasional problems. . . . Some music students were persistent, and we wanted to figure out a way to make it possible to have music in the stations."[13]

The MBTA claimed to be responding exclusively to music students, as if to assure riders that the performances were somehow linked to the cultural establishment. But Stephen Baird recalls that the MBTA contacted him through the Street Artists' Guild, a self-help organization of street performers and subway musicians based in Boston and Cambridge, for names of freelancers to perform at the Music Under Boston opening ceremony.

MBTA executives looked for a community-based or grass-roots arts institution to run the program because they felt the administrator should understand the musicians' needs and also because they wanted their consultant to work for free in exchange for the publicity generated. They asked the New England Conservatory of Music if its students would assume this responsibility. The conservatory declined, but the Cambridge Multicultural Arts Center accepted the offer. When in 1986 the center still had not located corporate funding and could no longer absorb the program's operating costs, Music Under Boston was terminated. Freelancers have continued to perform, however, in accordance with an unofficial agreement between the MBTA and the Street Artists' Guild.

Although it is not readily apparent from MTA promotional materials, freelance subway musicians also provided the impetus for the creation of MUNY. By the late 1970s, freelancers had begun to proliferate underground in New York. In fact Wendy Feuer says that when other MTA executives approached her about the possibility of running MUNY, her initial response was: "There are [already] street musicians in the subway; why are we doing this?" At a press conference, Kiley provided a partial answer when he talked about the MTA's beautification efforts. "My hope," he said, "is that our musician friends and their art will help us to be soothed." He anticipated that MUNY would become "a permanent part of the culture of New York."[14]

In 1985 MUNY began as a pilot program in eight designated spots. As in Boston, freelancers provided the talent. Steve Witt recalls that he was freelancing on the main concourse at Grand Central Terminal when an MTA employee dropped a card into his open guitar case, inviting him to join. During that initial phase of the program, there were no auditions.

In 1986 Wendy Feuer secured a $75,000 grant from the General Electric Corporation with which to operate MUNY. The grant enabled Arts for Transit to hire Symphony Space, which Feuer describes as a "well-established arts organization," as creative consultant. Symphony Space designed and administered many aspects of the MUNY program which have been retained by more recent consulting agencies. It helped to identify prime performance spaces (by watching and talking to MUNY members who also freelanced), which were then inspected by TA officials and designated as MUNY spots. It also introduced the call-in system, whereby MUNY musicians request two weeks' worth of spots two weeks in advance of their performances. Together with Arts for Transit, Symphony Space developed promotional items, including the banner that members display when they perform with MUNY, which features the program logo, along with individual members' names and telephone numbers. Feuer explains that these items gave MUNY "its own identity," distinguishing it from freelancing. Auditions, instituted during that period, were meant to "professionalize" the program. Symphony Space publicized the auditions in such cultural institutions as the Juilliard School. A MUNY source was quoted in a newspaper article explaining: "We want to ensure high standards so we don't get any dogs."[15]

In 1987, with the General Electric start-up grant finished, Wendy Feuer approached Robert Kiley and proposed that MUNY become a permanent part of the MTA's overall budget. Kiley liked the idea. The positive response of riders had proven that MUNY could be good publicity for the MTA. Feuer agreed: "You can't buy advertising at that rate."

In 1988 the contract with Symphony Space was not renewed, at least in part because the two agencies had divergent views on who should receive the publicity generated by the program. Arts for Transit then contracted with MPL Productions, a performing arts agency. In 1993 a new consulting firm, Performing in Public Spaces, was hired. MUNY's estimated 1994 budget, itemized in Table 1, amounted to $127,000.

Table 1. MUNY Budget, 1994

Tokens	$26,500
Special Events	14,000
Car cards	7,000[a]
Banners	4,000
Arts for Transit events (musicians' fees)	1,000
T-shirts	1,000
Miscellaneous	1,000
MUNY consultant	72,500

Source: Metropolitan Transportation Authority, Policy and Planning Department, Arts for Transit Division, *1994 Budget: Explanation of Professional Services Expenses* and *Explanation of Variances in Other-Than-Employee-Compensation Costs* (furnished by the MTA freedom of information officer).

[a]These are advertisments posted along the walls of subway cars, to publicize selected special events.

Wendy Feuer calls MUNY a "win-win situation" because it benefits both member musicians and the MTA. Indeed, there are MUNY members who appreciate the program because they believe it has created performance spaces for them. Other members only half jokingly refer to the arrangement as "mutual exploitation." Some also question the logic of hiring administrators to schedule musicians who are not paid a salary.

These contrasting views call to mind the question posed earlier: Does MUNY signify that the MTA has accepted freelance subway music or appropriated it? The answer, in effect, is both. The MTA supports the survival of this public art form to the extent that the art form in turn promotes the MTA. However closely related they have become, there are still two classes of music in the subways—official (MUNY) and freelance. The MUNY frame establishes a power structure that often severely constrains musicians' patterns of use of subway space and complicates their relationships with one another. The following analysis of MUNY's structure and procedures presents a perspective that on the whole contrasts with the MTA's.

There are two key figures in the MUNY administration. The first is the program manager, who since 1991 has been Erica Behrens. Behrens is responsible for monitoring the consultant's activities, which she does through daily telephone conversations, weekly special events meetings, and monthly budgetary evaluations. She represents MUNY before MTA executives, and she attends to interagency relations, particularly when problems arise between MUNY members and the transit police.

The second key figure is the MUNY consultant, Gina Higginbotham. From 1989 to 1992, Higginbotham assumed this role as an employee of MPL Productions, and in 1993 her own organization, Performing in Public Spaces, won the MUNY contract in an independent bid. Higginbotham manages operations on a daily basis. She handles the bi-monthly call-in system, assigning two weeks' worth of spots to the members who request them. She types these schedules onto permits which members must show, when asked, to the transit police, station managers, and terminal masters. She sends copies of the schedules to the station managers and terminal masters who oversee the locations where MUNY performances take place. She prepares narratives and budgets for her meetings with Erica Behrens, writes a newsletter for and about MUNY members, and organizes the special events. Finally, she answers telephone inquiries about the program, and she makes herself available to members who stop by her office to discuss problems or to chat about their latest experiences underground. Higginbotham herself was a busker in the late 1950s and early 1960s; she has a special sensitivity to MUNY members' needs. Behrens believes that Higginbotham's relative informality is a good counterbalance to the Madison Avenue image members encounter when they visit the MUNY office at the MTA.

With her considerable involvement in the program, Higginbotham was quick to confirm that musicians have three main incentives for joining MUNY: access, protection from police, and promotions. MUNY musicians have exclusive access to spots in the commuter railroad terminals, namely, Grand Central and the Long Island Rail Road in Penn Station, and they have priority over freelancers in MUNY spots located on subway mezzanines. MUNY legitimates its members in the eyes of the transit police, station managers, and terminal masters; in the musicians' words, MUNY reduces police harassment. And MUNY provides members with promotional items such as the banner, T-shirts, biographical sketches, and special events literature, which are intended to help them attract riders and make contacts. Higginbotham also acts as an "agent" for members when she arranges media coverage of special events and provides referrals to private companies and cultural organizations that call and express interest in hiring performers. As a result of these calls, an advertising agency included MUNY members in a promotional video for the Coca-Cola Company, and MUNY members have performed in outdoor festivals from New York's Lincoln Center to Venice, Italy. According to Higginbotham, in the time that she has worked with the program, thousands of contacts have been made through her office.

Fourteen of the twenty musicians I surveyed in 1993 were MUNY members. When asked what they liked about the program, a number of them mentioned access. They valued the "fair allocation of spots" and "the chance to perform at Grand Central, Penn, and other choice 'sanctioned' spots." One said, "MUNY made it possible to play on a regular basis."

It is not entirely accurate, however, to say that MUNY provides access. In June 1985 the TA nullified its total ban on spontaneous performances, notably, at the same time that freelancer Roger Manning was challenging its constitutionality in court (see Chapter 6). That September, the same month that Manning won his case, the MUNY pilot program was launched. This sequence of events and the recollections of some of my sources strongly suggest that, originally, the MTA created MUNY with more than beautification in mind. MUNY, it seems, was meant to displace and, thus, suppress freelance subway music. It follows that once freelancers' First Amendment rights were upheld in court, MUNY assumed the modified role of regulating access to prime spots. Some MUNY administrators believe this arrangement is a service to all subway musicians because, they say, it eliminates territorial disputes. In reality, it eliminates competition for MUNY members. As one member who doubles as a freelancer put it, "MUNY legitimates 20 percent of the subway musicians and delegitimates 80 percent."

MUNY has exclusive access to the prime spots in the commuter railroad terminals. Before the program existed, freelancers performed, albeit unauthorized, on the main concourse at Grand Central Terminal. By 1988, an official source told me, they were routinely ejected from the terminal even if MUNY members were not scheduled at that time or had not shown up to perform. Some subway musicians and civil liberties attorneys question the constitutionality of this policy since, they contend, it restricts free expression in a public forum. Indeed, Metro-North Commuter Railroad, the MTA agency that oversees Grand Central Terminal, has since addressed this issue by making separate "freedom of expression" permits available to freelancers, authorizing them to play in three other spots. But those spots have neither the aesthetics nor the pedestrian traffic of the main concourse. Moreover, the availability of the freedom of expression permit is not widely publicized. Consequently, most freelancers assume that Grand Central Terminal is off limits to them.

Many members appreciate the priority status MUNY confers in designated stations, since it saves them the time they would otherwise spend searching for performance spaces. When members find freelancers in their spots, they can simply present their MUNY permits and tell the others to leave. Normally, the process works smoothly; the freelancers comply. Sometimes, however, freelancers object to the two-tiered system, and tensions surface.

December 28, 1991, Noon, Times Square Shuttle Mezzanine

An Andean group had been playing against the old steel gates opposite the shuttle since ten thirty in the morning. One of the musicians, who identified himself as indigenous, had set his open guitar case in front of the group. The top of the case was lined with a poster declaring: "500 Years of Indian Resistance." The musicians played dark, haunting music on panpipes and drums. César Dueñas joined the audience and explained to me that this was Altiplano music, from the highlands of Bolivia.

At noon, Zane Massey and his jazz band arrived with a MUNY permit to play in the same spot. Zane is a superb tenor saxophonist. Every year at a MUNY special event he assembles a band that performs a piece composed by his renowned father, Cal Massey. We had spoken before and here we greeted each other.

Zane leaned his instrument and equipment against the wall by the Andean musicians, at the same time telling them that they needed to

Zane Massey, a tenor saxophonist, performs with the Roy Campbell Sextet below an escalator in Penn Station. Notice the "staircase spectators" behind the group. Photo by Dennis Connors

pack up. The leader of the Andean group refused to go, and told Zane to call the police over if he liked.

In a few moments, Zane returned with four officers, one of whom began to talk with the Andean group leader. When Zane spoke up this officer said: "You came to us, and we're doing it, so keep quiet."

The Andean group leader argued that Times Square is a public space, implying that a permit could not determine rights. The officer turned diplomatic.

"Look," he said. "This permit just says Times Square, but I know this is where all the MUNY musicians play." He then called Gina Higginbotham and confirmed that this was a MUNY spot. The Andean group packed up.

Zane looked visibly upset by the confrontation; he felt bad for the other group. He told them that he was scheduled to perform until three o'clock and that they could return then. "I want to be harmonious," he added.

About twenty of the riders who had been listening to the music stayed to watch the incident. Others came over to see what was going on. A woman in a tattered coat and knit hat assumed that the police officers were trying to eject all the musicians from the station, and she began to chant, "Let them play! Let them play!" Other riders thought the same, and they chimed in.

A young West Indian man was leaning against a pillar, and I walked over to him. He was angry. "Indians have more right to be here than any of us. They're harassing him because he's Indian." It would be difficult, though not impossible, to charge discrimination, since Zane's jazz band was composed of two African American men and two Japanese men.

A white man with a grizzly beard walked up, looked around, and focused on the Andean instruments. Our eyes met. "Beautiful music, isn't it? Blows your mind," he said. I told him about the conflict, and he saw no problem. "They [the Andean group] can find another spot in the system." And off he went.

I explained the incident to a middle-aged man who had watched it unravel. He thought the permit system was unfair, and in turn he decided to explain it to me. "Let's say I have permit for your coat, and I say, 'Give it back.' Does that fair? Does that fair? Something not right. The public can see."

After going over this analogy many times, we were joined by an

African American man who broke the cycle. "Yes, it's fair. The permit eliminates the confusion."

The middle-aged man finally conceded the point, but he insisted that there should be "one rule for everybody"—that every subway musician should have a permit.

I asked the African American man, who produces a music program on cable television, how he thinks the permit system ought to work. He said subway musicians should have to meet certain qualifications. "Should the permit depend upon how well they play?" I asked. "No," he said emphatically. "Who's to judge how good or not good you are?"

This scene illustrates how the MUNY access policy divides musicians. MUNY administrators report that these incidents are on the decline, and that non-MUNY freelancers are expressing less resentment toward the program's members. Even if such a change is occurring, no one has tried to find out whether freelancers are pleased with their lot or have simply resigned themselves to their inferior status. It is also unclear whether MUNY eliminates or creates confusion by regulating access to spots. Moreover, it is debatable whether the procedures for gaining access to the program in the first place are democratic.

MUNY holds its annual audition on a balcony in Grand Central Terminal. The all-day affair is open to the public, although the public stands and watches from behind a velvet-covered chain. Chairs and lunch are provided for the panel of judges and the news media, and Gina Higginbotham offers sandwiches to homeless people who pass by. The judges sit at a long table and candidates come before them to present samples of their performances.

Until 1993 performers called Higginbotham or the program manager and were scheduled to audition in the same sequence as their calls. Higginbotham advertised the audition through "a huge mailing" to community groups and arts organizations. She and Erica Behrens report that in 1993 they received a combined total of over three hundred requests for auditions.

Freelancers learn about the audition procedures primarily by talking to MUNY members they meet in the subways. Some find out from transit police officers or station managers, and some receive informational flyers from MUNY staff members who encounter them and consider them good candidates.

Guitarist James Warren auditions on the second-floor balcony of Grand Central Terminal before a panel of judges for the MUNY program. Photo by Dennis Connors

The vast majority of MUNY members (as many as 95 percent) began as freelancers. MUNY administrators recognize that these performers often possess a unique combination of talent and street skills. Yet MUNY has no democratic mechanism established for publicizing the audition to all the city's freelancers, and consequently a number of them are left out of the selection process. Although language barriers exist, Spanish-speaking musicians tend to inform one another about the audition. It is, instead, some of the older African American musicians who struggle with the system and fail to navigate it. Bobby Davis had never heard of MUNY until we discussed it, and he asked me to help him make an appointment. JC, a jazz clarinetist and saxophonist whom Steve Witt described in his newspaper column as "truly a master," told me that he had tried to schedule an appointment but was informed that he had missed the deadline.[16]

Even freelancers who succeed in making appointments may have difficulty attending an audition that takes place only once a year. When MUNY first started to receive funding, the administrators decided to audition the original roster. Steve Witt could not attend because the date conflicted with the schedule of his part-time job at *Downtown*. He was dropped from the program (and wrote scathing articles until he auditioned and was reaccepted in 1991). Although the auditions last only five minutes, they play a major role in determining a musician's prospects of economic survival. By regulating access to some of the most lucrative spots, MUNY affects musicians in and outside its framework.

Arranging an appointment is only the first step. Candidates must meet the audition criteria in order to be selected. The criteria, however, are not necessarily obvious. Judges are instructed to consider whether the music is acoustically suited to the subways, will not "aggravate" riders, reflects the city's cultural diversity, and is performed at a reasonable volume level. These criteria are broad enough to be interpreted in multiple, even contradictory, ways by the various judges. For their part, none of the candidates or the MUNY members I interviewed knew what standards were being applied to them. When asked what the judges were looking for, three of the MUNY members in my 1993 survey sample ventured an answer. One said "good music" and two said talent, uniqueness, and adaptability to the stations—reasonable responses, but not exactly the criteria that the judges were given.

MUNY looks for "impressive," "high-quality" candidates—in other words, "professional" musicians.[17] "Professionalism" is another term

Saxophonist JC, described as "truly a master," performs incognito on a Times Square platform. Photo © Alex Lopez

with multiple cultural and political meanings. Ruth Finnegan contends that the professional/amateur distinction is irrelevant in discussions about local music making since the musicians represent an exceptionally wide range of backgrounds and goals. In more established contexts, professional artists are often defined as those who work full-time at their craft. What is full-time music making in the subways? One of Wendy Feuer's favorite subway musicians doubles as a surgeon. Feuer concludes that professionalism in the context of the MUNY auditions is "something you just know." Indeed, faced with ambiguous selection criteria, the judges are likely to base their decisions on established urban aesthetic notions about what a professional musician is, and even about what a musical performance is. These notions might be appropriate for private venues that appeal primarily to the affluent middle class,[18] but they are too narrow to take into account the many cultural and class values represented in the city's subway music audiences.

One source added that MUNY groups are more "organized." This term implies that professionalism depends in part on stable membership within groups. Stability does make certain kinds of advancement possible, but it is not a realistic goal for many subway musicians, MUNY or freelance, nor is it a very reliable standard of judgment. For instance, virtually all jazz ensembles in MUNY rotate members because of scheduling conflicts. Turnover in Andean groups may reflect differences in style, clashes of culture, class, or personality, or transitory patterns of residence. A Bolivian *charango* player reports that he left Anthology in order to tour Japan with singer-songwriter Paul Simon.

Over the years, the panel of judges has come to represent an increasingly narrow cultural perspective. The MUNY consultant chooses the panel, which has included Arts for Transit staffers, Transit Authority officials, transit police supervisors and officers, a representative from the Office of the Mayor, MUNY members, and such musical guests as Odetta and Dave Van Ronk. Since 1991, however, this last category has been at least partially replaced by administrators of other government- or corporate-sponsored music programs, including SummerStage in Central Park and Lincoln Center Out-of-Doors. While it would be unfair to presume that these administrators uphold elitist cultural values or that the folk musicians do not, the shift in the panel has political meaning. It reinforces the bureaucratic nature of MUNY.

Ironically, the program may have reached its bureaucratic limit. In

1993, three hundred performers called to schedule auditions; one hundred were in fact scheduled, and twenty-four performers were selected. MUNY administrators readily admit that talent was not lacking. The problem is to a great extent administrative: MUNY does not have the funds to hire more staffers to schedule more musicians. And Erica Behrens's time is limited, since she also manages the Arts for Transit permanent art program. MUNY has reached the point where preserving its own frame is as much of an immediate concern as extending benefits to additional musicians.

MUNY administrators also say that they cannot accept many more members because the prime spots have reached their "saturation points." Even current members have less frequent access to them than they did in the past. During fieldwork, however, at least one member told me that some of his colleagues do not show up as scheduled, and transit police officers often refuse to allow others to perform in those spots without permits. Gina Higginbotham asks members to call in their cancellations, and she arranges official replacements. Nevertheless, MUNY may actually be depriving musicians and riders of musical spaces.

The MUNY members I interviewed identified some of the program's other structural limitations. Four members, each of whom plays a different genre of music, criticized the subjective nature of the procedures. They feel that MUNY administrators favor certain members by scheduling them more frequently at the prime spots and repeatedly inviting them to participate in the paid special events. Another regrets that he was never asked to be a judge at the annual audition. One complains that a program administrator has advised the MTA and TA to pay MUNY members no more than fifty dollars when they are hired to perform at events internal to the agency. One MUNY group was temporarily banned from the program for "bad behavior," and there was no independent adjudication process through which it might present its position.

In turn, some members "work the system." They "pool" permits, fusing groups in order to play at prime spots, although this practice is generally against program procedures. A few have unfurled their banners on subway platforms—non-MUNY territory—counting on uninformed transit police officers and freelance musicians to believe that MUNY members have special legitimacy there as well. MUNY administrators report that its members are pleased with the program, and perhaps the majority are. But there is no official record of those who are dissatisfied, since they have decided that it is "safer" not to speak up. It is precisely because the situation is politically sensitive that I am not naming the MUNY musicians among my sources in this chapter.

In 1991 ten of the twelve candidates I interviewed at the annual audition said they wanted to join MUNY at least in part to escape the police harassment that is directed against freelancers. In 1992 all the candidates I spoke to said the same. In 1993 nine of my fourteen MUNY survey respondents indicated that access to MUNY spots provides protection from police harassment—that the two issues are linked.

Nevertheless, some MUNY members report that the program does not adequately protect them. In fact, they are subjected to their own forms of police harassment. One MUNY group was ordered to leave its spot because of a typographical error on its permit. Another group was ticketed for playing half an hour longer than scheduled. Like freelancers, some MUNY members are told to lower their volume, or to move, without explanation. They resent this treatment because, when performing under the MUNY banner, they feel that they are providing the MTA with a service at no cost.

MUNY members have the option of reporting their confrontations with the transit police to Erica Behrens or Gina Higginbotham, who follow up in an effort to prevent these incidents from recurring. Over the years Higginbotham has worked to improve relations between MUNY and individual officers, and she has invited transit police platoons to special events. As a result, she says, officers have become more supportive of the program. Yet, as important as these instances of mediation are, they do not address persistent systemwide communication problems between MUNY and the transit police. Moreover, MUNY administrators advise members to comply with transit police orders, and they banned the group mentioned earlier because of station managers' complaints. Ultimately the MUNY program defers to TA employees in order to protect itself.

Members receive no protection in one of their most frequent confrontations with officers, over the sale of cassette tape and compact disc recordings. These sales are prohibited in all but the commuter railroad spots; thanks to the efforts of Wendy Feuer, MUNY members may sell them there. Meanwhile, the TA maintains that it does not allow unlicensed commercial activity, but it has not acknowledged the possibility of making commercial licenses available to musicians. Despite the ban, MUNY members and freelancers continue to sell cassettes and CDs in the stations. One MUNY member reported to me that an officer confiscated his group's cassettes and issued him a summons to appear in criminal court. "I'm a criminal," he said reproachfully. Another feels very strongly that MUNY administrators should be advocating on members' behalf for the right to sell their work.

The reality is that to join MUNY, musicians must give up a number of rights. They sign a contract prohibiting the use of visual devices other than the MTA banner. Apparently this clause is not strictly enforced; many of the program's traditional bluesmen bring various household objects (silverware trays, jars, and rugs) as well as handmade signs with them, giving their presentations a cultural context and making their stark performance spaces feel more like home. The contract also requires members to waive their right to sue the MTA for injuries they suffer, and to accept responsibility for accidents in their vicinity, during MUNY performances.[19]

Most ironic of all, when MUNY members freelance, they are not protected by the program. They are subject to the police harassment directed at freelancers even though they are performing the same music, possibly even in the same spots, as when they are with MUNY. This situation reinforces the impression that MUNY exists not so much to assist its members as to promote the MTA.

Each year, a number of candidates at the MUNY auditions expressed excitement about having their musical careers boosted by the program. Indeed, Gina Higginbotham has managed to arrange coverage in *Backstage* magazine and the *Daily News*, and on local radio stations and network television. She reports that the publicity generates calls from private outfits looking to hire musicians and from non-street or subway performers interested in auditioning. It appears MUNY has awakened the cultural establishment to a reality that riders have long recognized—that the subways are a vital performance space.

In these respects MUNY candidates and members may consider the program a stepping stone in their careers. But when asked to define "success" in the subways, the members among my 1993 survey respondents still answered in terms of the individual bonds that form between musicians and audience members in both MUNY and freelance subway music scenes:

"When a person stays to listen."

"Feeling like you really add something positive to people's lives."

"When I can see the joy I give to people."

"Making good money and reaching people."

Some respondents have resolved to continue performing in the subways (here referred to as part of "the street") even after launching more established musical careers. One explained: "There was a time when I had to street perform—and it accounted for up to 90 percent of my work. But as I've grown, so have the places I perform. So now I play once a week [in the subways] because I want to. There is an energy on the street that you can't find on any [other] stage or performance space. I feel if I think I'm too good or big to play on the street, then I'll quit the business. The street can be a great high and a humbling experience."

Indeed, MUNY has attracted some exceptional musicians underground with strong connections to the established arts world. Alto saxophonist Sayyd Abdul al-Khabyyr formerly played with Dizzy Gillespie, and vocalist Evelyn Blakey learned some of her craft from her father, the jazz legend Art Blakey. Both doubt that they would perform underground without an "organized" program like MUNY on the scene. The subways would be much poorer for their absence.

But is it possible that MUNY is simply filling a void that a subway-musician-run organization could fill? MUNY is a program; it is not an organization. It promotes a sense of camaraderie among its members but enables them to perform without learning much of the etiquette that freelancers practice. Virtually the only time nonfreelance MUNY members interact is at special events. In 1991 at a Women's History Month event, a member remarked to Gina Higginbotham: "I don't know anyone here."

Indeed, Higginbotham promotes contact among MUNY musicians. Her newsletter creates a "virtual" community by updating members on each other's achievements. She asks Zane Massey to organize a band out of various MUNY musicians to play his father's *Liberation Suite* at special events. But her position limits her ability to advocate for members or to promote activism. In 1991 when members complained to her about the program, she admonished them: "Go organize yourselves!"

MUNY is the first government-sponsored and funded subway music program to draw the interest of the cultural establishment underground. It has captured the attention of administrators in other major subway systems, including Los Angeles and Tokyo. But the transit executives and art "professionals" who invented MUNY did not invent subway music. Rather, they adapted freelancing to promote the MTA, and unfortunately in the process they introduced exclusion into an activity that is ideologically based on inclusion.

MUNY administrators face the challenge of accommodating increasing numbers of musicians, both freelancers and performing artists from the cultural establishment. Prior to the 1994 audition they introduced a prescreening process, requiring candidates to submit audio or video cassettes in order to be considered. Although Higginbotham assured those who called that a "living room tape" would be sufficient, only 107 out of over 300 sent in samples of their work. Of those 107, 40 were invited to audition, and in the end 10 were added to the MUNY roster. To make the roster reflect more of the diversity of the riders, the administrators have also set an implicit "quota" on certain genres of music. Surely both procedures are susceptible to charges of class and cultural bias.

The increased requests for auditions are not necessarily intended as a compliment to the program. They are at least in part a consequence of the police harassment that freelancers frequently experience, which makes it more difficult for them to earn a living. The most effective way for MUNY to limit requests for auditions is to advocate for all subway musicians.

MUNY administrators are aware of many of the issues raised in this chapter and are beginning to address them. Above all, they need to review the main purpose of the program. Is it to regulate freelance subway musicians indirectly, to enhance the subway music scene, or to provide a different form of entertainment underground? It might appear that MUNY would want to increase its links with established urban performance frames, but it is worth recalling that the New York subway system possesses a diverse, at times even radical, public art tradition. The radical strand includes the MTA's decision in 1985 to invite freelance subway musicians to join the MUNY pilot program.

Whichever direction is chosen, MUNY should be restructured to support positive relationships among musicians. Of course any changes will necessarily be gradual, but the following steps might be considered:

1. Rework MUNY's access policy so that it avoids provoking conflict between MUNY members and freelancers.

2. If auditions must be held, develop inclusive criteria for choosing musicians and judges. Involve all the populations interested in and affected by subway music, particularly riders. Consider setting a time limit on membership. Rotation would enable more freelancers to belong to MUNY, and it could make former MUNY members more aware of the need to organize and defend the rights of all subway musicians.

3. Enable MUNY musicians to form an oversight body to hear and adjudicate grievances among members as well as between members and the program. This body should also help to reorder MUNY's priorities.

4. Attract MUNY members to less popular stations, especially in the outer boroughs of Brooklyn, Queens, and the Bronx, through public-private partnerships modeled on "Adopt-a-Station." Instead of relying on corporate grants, make MUNY more community-based by arranging to have area businesses provide members with stipends for performing in local stations, perhaps in exchange for publicity. Reallocate MUNY's promotional budget to fund more special events and help members obtain services they say they need, including access to recording facilities, health insurance, and a credit union.

5. Encourage the formation of an independent self-help organization to promote cooperation and community among subway musicians. The organization could share, if not assume, some of MUNY's responsibilities, particularly with regard to scheduling performances in prime spots.

The public has already given the MTA reason to reduce MUNY's control. In 1988 Peter Harris reported his finding that freelance subway music helped the MTA's image as much as MUNY did: "Less than one in five (22%) have noticed that some musicians are MTA-sponsored. . . . There is no mandate currently for greater government control over music in the subways. Our customers like the musicians regardless of whether they have been officially sanctioned by the MTA."[20]

6

Sounds and Silence: Regulating Subway Music

Let me present two statements. The first is an excerpt from the TA regulations:

> Non-transit uses are non-commercial activities that are not directly related to the use of a facility or conveyance for transportation. The following non-transit uses are authorized and permitted by the Authority, provided they do not impede transit activities . . . : public speaking; distribution of written non-commercial materials; artistic performances, including the acceptance of donations; solicitation for charitable, religious or political causes.[1]

The second is from testimony delivered at the public hearings held before these regulations were adopted:

> The issue is not safety, nor is it obstruction of pedestrian traffic, nor is it noise. It is merely a matter of accepting a reality of New York's wonderfully creative and enterprising spirit.[2]

The legal status of freelance subway music became a point of contention in the 1980s, embedded in a larger debate about the status of free expression in public space. This chapter traces the debate, focusing on the major turning points: the *People v. Manning* case in 1985, the TA Experimental Guidelines in 1987, the TA proposal of new rules together with the remarkable public hearings on them in 1989, and

Carew-Reid v. Metropolitan Transportation Authority in 1990, the first federal case to uphold the constitutional rights of subway musicians. Legal issues that surfaced in previous chapters are discussed, including the captive audience principle and the public forum doctrine.

The outcome of the debate is difficult to gauge unless viewed in its political and cultural context. Laurence Tribe explains that First Amendment decisions tend to be influenced by the national political climate,[3] and the musicians' defeat in the appeal of *Carew-Reid v. MTA* certainly reflected the tilt in the higher courts of the 1980s in favor of the rights of the affluent. Ultimately, this saga is about people with varying amounts of power who attempted to define the purpose of subway space.

Spontaneous music making was prohibited in the New York subways from the time the first line opened in 1904, but the explicit ban in the IRT's original rule book signals that musicians were already singing and playing in transit facilities. During the LaGuardia mayoralty (1934–1945), freelance street and subway musicians were equated with beggars, and they shared the status of "undesirables." Although LaGuardia fought for the rights of African Americans, new immigrants, and the poor, he also supported prevailing notions about modernization and maintaining social order, which encoded subtle discrimination against these three populations when they engaged in itinerant activity in public space.

At the same time, however, LaGuardia was one of the strongest advocates of New Deal reform, which was helping to liberalize the nation's political mood. Reflecting this shift, the Supreme Court extended First Amendment protections to various populations, including union activists, Communists, and Jehovah's Witnesses.[4] Moreover, in 1939 the Court articulated the concept of the public forum for the first time. *Hague v. CIO* established that activities deemed to be speech-related uses of city streets and parks could be neither banned nor subjected to discretionary licensing. This doctrine marked a departure from the previous view that government, much like a private owner, could control speech and assembly in urban public space.[5]

The public forum doctrine was further developed in the 1960s and 1970s as social attitudes became more supportive of popular culture and street life. In an effort to turn New York into "Fun City," the Lindsay administration permitted sidewalk cafes to open and affirmed street music and poetry readings in city parks. Also during that period, says Paul Chevigny, a "'public law' consciousness" emerged in the federal courts, and judges were upholding the First Amendment rights of people fighting for civil rights and civil liberties.[6]

In 1968 the courts made the significant decision that First Amendment protections extended to certain activities in transportation terminals. The United States Court of Appeals for the Second Circuit ruled in *Wolin v. Port of New York Authority* that the Port Authority ban on antiwar leafleting in its bus terminal without prior permission was unconstitutional.[7] Subsequently, in *People v. St. Clair*, the Manhattan Criminal Court found unconstitutional a TA rule that provided: "No person shall distribute any hand-bill or display any flag, banner, sign or marker on or within the New York City Transit System." Above all, *Wolin* and *St. Clair* established that the subways are not merely a public space, traversed by the general public, but a public forum, such that "no distinction can be wrung for First Amendment purposes between a subway platform and a public street."[8]

The courts had long considered various forms of entertainment to be protected under the First Amendment.[9] Nevertheless, in the 1960s the TA elaborated its ban on spontaneous music making and decided to fine, even jail, rule violators. Thus, in the late 1970s and early 1980s, when musicians began to venture underground in greater numbers and with more regularity, they were issued summonses for "begging and soliciting" or for "entertaining passengers."[10] They were also ticketed for such rule violations as "obstructing traffic," "disorderly conduct," and making "unnecessary noise." James Humphrey recalls that, already in those days, riders "booed" transit police officers who tried to stop his performances.

In 1985 the MTA introduced MUNY as part of its overall campaign to use art to draw New Yorkers back into the subways. A few of the sources I interviewed, however, believe that MUNY's original aims were to displace freelancers and avert litigation: MUNY made it impossible for freelancers to argue that the MTA and TA prohibited subway music performances of any kind. Indeed, one case was already pending.

People v. Manning became the test case. On February 6, 1985, Roger Manning, an acoustic guitarist, was playing on the Lexington Avenue and 59th Street BMT platform when a transit police officer issued him a summons for "disorderly conduct" based on the TA prohibition against "entertaining passengers." The summons required Manning to appear in Manhattan Criminal Court. Originally, Manning said in a recent interview, he planned to represent himself, but the presiding judge postponed the proceedings until he sought legal counsel. (Manning believes the judge gave him these instructions because she recognized the merits of his case.) He returned with the legal director of the New York Civil Liberties Union, Arthur Eisenberg, who argued that the TA total ban on spontaneous performances violated Manning's First Amendment right to express himself freely.

When the court issued its decision in September 1985, it observed that the TA had eliminated the total ban in June to allow the MUNY program into the subways and held that this policy change invalidated the charges against Manning. It also ruled retroactively that the total ban had been unconstitutional, establishing for the first time that acoustic freelance music is constitutionally protected on TA property.[11]

Some musicians continued to dispute their tickets and engaged in other forms of political activism, and from all indications they prompted the TA to rework its policy. Already, however, their gains were being accompanied by losses. Veteran musicians recall with more than a touch of sarcasm that while music making was banned they were issued ten dollar summonses; ever since the ban was lifted, they have been fined over fifty dollars for other rule violations.

After the *Manning* decision, police officers tried to stop performances by ticketing musicians for soliciting donations without prior permission, although apparently the TA had never made permits available to them. Lloyd Carew-Reid, a classical guitarist originally from Australia, received a number of these summonses. With Art Eisenberg as his counsel, Carew-Reid appeared before the newly formed Transit Adjudication Bureau to challenge the constitutionality of the charge. The bureau withdrew the summonses.[12] Subsequently, Carew-Reid and Robert T. Perry, a civil liberties attorney, planned to challenge the "unnecessary noise" charge on one of his tickets before the city Environmental Review Board. Carew-Reid and Eisenberg also arranged meetings with TA officials in an effort to draw up an agreement between the authority and freelance musicians. These projects were never completed, partly because of TA policy changes. Meanwhile, Carew-Reid was becoming a politically active and outspoken subway musician.

Thus, in the mid-1980s lower courts upheld the constitutionality of freelance subway music and the TA could no longer ban it outright. But government has a right to regulate the time, place, and manner in which First Amendment activity is presented, so long as the regulations do not discriminate against its content, for that could be construed as censorship. Free expression may be circumscribed in this way to advance a substantial government interest, such as public safety or reliable operations. With these possibilities in mind, the TA proceeded to design new regulations—three versions.

In 1987, the MTA board (which is also the TA board) authorized an interdepartmental committee to design and promulgate experimental guidelines. Although they did not replace existing regulations, the guidelines marked the first time the TA explicitly permitted what it called "expressive activity," subject only to time, place, and manner restrictions. TA staff summary sheets stated that this policy shift was undertaken because various "religious, political or charitable causes" were soliciting funds in the system without applying for permits and, moreover, because the MUNY program had attracted "ad hoc" musicians underground (though it seems the reverse was true).[13] The experimental guidelines suspended the requirement to obtain a permit to solicit donations. They also permitted musicians to use amplifiers at a sound level of up to ninety decibels.

Many musicians use a small battery-powered amplifier commonly known by its trade name, "Maxi Mouse," or simply as a "Mouse" or an "amp." It is no coincidence that the appearance of the Mouse on the market in 1978 immediately preceded the proliferation of subway music. It offered mobility to electrically amplified instruments, and it enabled musicians to make themselves heard in an extremely noisy environment.[14] The guidelines required them to obtain a sound amplification permit from the transit police, although the amplified musicians I interviewed who performed underground at that time do not recall such a permit system ever being implemented. Compared to the previous total ban, the experimental guidelines were extremely permissive. David Goldstein, the attorney who later counseled the musicians in the *Carew-Reid* case, believes there were "no problems" during that period.

Some TA officials disagree. For instance, Lieutenant Eugene Roach of the transit police recalls that the "novelty" of performances drew large audiences. He says that some riders and some cleaners who worked for the TA complained about the crowds, and some token booth clerks were disturbed by the musicians' volume. Meanwhile, in 1988 MTA marketing research director Peter Harris conducted his customer survey and discovered that 70 percent of the respondents liked subway music on both mezzanines and platforms. In an internal memo, Harris concluded: "It is difficult to imagine a way to prohibit music on platforms without some adverse public reaction."[15] Implicit in his conclusion was a policy change that TA officials were about to make public.

In early 1989, the TA released a document titled *Proposed Rules for Non-Transit Use of Transit Facilities*. It consisted of a staff summary sheet explaining why the interdepartmental committee monitoring expressive activity considered it necessary to revise the experimental guidelines; the proposed rules themselves; and a copy of the state environmental quality review assessment, which had been completed and sent to the appropriate agency.

If adopted, the proposed rules would make the experimental authorization of expressive activity permanent, although subject to broader time, place, and manner restrictions. People engaged in such activity would have to stay fifteen feet away from turnstiles and concession stands, twenty feet from token booths, staircases, escalators, and elevators, twenty-five feet from MUNY performances, and fifty feet from TA offices—the same requirements stated in the experimental guidelines, only at greater distances. The ninety-decibel volume limit would be changed to eighty-five decibels measured at a distance of five feet. Permits would have to be obtained for activity in high-density "critical stations." And there would be one major new restriction: all expressive activity would be banned from subway platforms.[16] With this provision, the proposal set off a heated public debate.

It would seem that freelance musicians were the target of a government conspiracy. First the MTA had created MUNY to monopolize mezzanines, and next the TA was proposing to eliminate freelancers from platforms. Evidently the authorities were neither considering freelancers' interests nor concerning themselves with the political effects of these policy decisions on the subway music scene as a whole. But a conspiracy theory cannot fully explain what happened; conflicting government priorities complicated the matter. The top executives of the MTA and TA articulated their divergent positions. Robert Kiley, MTA chair, "strongly opposed such a blanket rule," the *New York Times* reported, "not only because it would almost certainly be struck down by the courts as a violation of free speech, but also because the public would not stand for it."[17] TA president David Gunn, by contrast, had just shut down most of the system's newsstands and signed the staff summary sheet in the proposed rules. He considered any activity that did not make subway cars run to be a form of "disorder." Kiley's and Gunn's divergent positions reflected their personalities and also the roles of their respective agencies. The MTA was prepared to acknowledge the importance of free speech activity in the campaign to improve the aesthetics and public relations of the transit system, whereas the TA viewed the issue through the lens of daily operations. In time, the two men, longtime friends, would reach a compromise.

To solicit public comment, the TA and MTA held public hearings on the proposed rules in Manhattan, Brooklyn, Queens, and the Bronx in April and May 1989. Close to eighty people attended the four hearings; a handful testified at two or three of the locations. Some of the speakers were affiliated with the New York Public Interest Research Group, a grass-roots consumer advocacy organization, which sponsors the Straphangers' Campaign, a watchdog group that evaluates subway service. Some musicians identified themselves as members of STAR, Subway Troubadours Against Repression, an organization of subway musicians which Lloyd Carew-Reid founded when he learned about the proposed rules. NYPIRG and STAR formed an ad hoc coalition when the proposal was released.

The largest, and most entertaining, hearing was held in the MTA boardroom on Madison Avenue. Political and religious activists, subway performers, and riders spoke, sang, played, and juggled before board members in almost unanimous opposition to the proposed rules. Only one speaker complained that subway musicians were "fulfilling the prophecy of my father and decent parents of yesteryear and today regarding show biz people."[18] As they did in the subways, performers transformed a formal process into an intimate encounter. Riders explained why experiences like these are so valuable to them.

The Manhattan hearing began with a videotape prepared by the TA Stations Department, lending visual support to the authority's argument that expressive activity compromises public safety. Interestingly, whereas the proposed rules applied to all expressive activity, the video featured only artistic performances. Steve Witt, who attended this hearing, enumerated his objections in his newspaper column:

> The fact that the videos were made at major subway stations, and most of them during the rush hour, was not mentioned as a cause of the crowding. Among the performers were break dancers and tumblers, who in the spectrum of performers always need a larger space

> for their efforts than single musicians. . . . The video didn't even show the awestruck and smiling faces of children and adults enjoying a performance nor did it mention that in the board's own study, 70 percent of the subway riders were in favor of subway performers.[19]

Art Eisenberg of NYCLU testified that the proposed rules were "unconstitutional as a matter of law, and unwise as a matter of public policy" (hearing transcripts, p. 18). He affirmed subway music along with other free expression when he concluded: "These rules, unfortunately, stand in stark contrast with that long-standing city tradition of commitment to artistic and political and cultural pluralism" (p. 21). Like many speakers after him, Gene Russianoff, staff attorney at NYPIRG, charged that the ban on leafleting on platforms together with the distance requirements throughout the system amounted to an attempt to censor groups such as the Straphangers' Campaign which are sometimes critical of subway service: "So where does this leave the First Amendment? Down the block from the subway station" (p. 15). These two speakers were followed by Neal Rosenstein, a NYPIRG staff member and subway performer, who used juggling pins as a metaphor for service on various subway lines, and by Laurence Kobak, better known as Sailorman Jack, who led the board in a chorus of an original tune: "Dirty old train, you're driving me insane" (pp. 41–45, 60–63).

At all four hearings, speakers expressed support for musicians who performed on subway platforms. In the process they refuted arguments the TA had presented in its staff summary sheet as justification for the proposed rules. First was the contention that music created safety hazards on platforms by drawing crowds.[20] Jim Maisano, a rider, testified: "The Transit Authority seems to believe that subway performers attract crowds. They do not. It is the subways themselves which attract crowds. The crowds and safety hazards will be present with or without these restrictions" (p. 52). LiAnne Kratzer, another rider, added: "A crowded platform is inherently unsafe, but it's not because people flock through the turnstiles to crowd around a musician, but because service is not sufficient to accommodate rush hour crowds" (p. 81). James Howard, a musician, said: "An MTA employee working on a platform of one of the busiest stations in the city told me the other day that music soothes the savage beast and that he feels musicians help, not obstruct the managing of crowds of commuters" (pp. 56–57).

Second, the TA had implied that musical performances had caused accidents on the platforms, citing irrelevant statistics as evidence: "In 1987, 533 persons were pushed, fell, jumped or otherwise landed on the trackbed with resulting fatalities and catastrophic injuries." It had also contended that the music endangers track workers by interfering with the warning signals of oncoming trains.[21] A musician named Migdalia Cortes painted a different picture: "Most performers perform inwardly, not on the tracks, not on the platforms. They perform inwardly underneath the stairwells. So the people come to us, you know, we don't get in their way" (p. 141).[22] Faith Alfieri, a law student in Robert T. Perry's class at New York Law School, testified:

> I spoke personally with a track worker and asked him whether, in all the years he had been working there, a musical performance had ever drowned out the noise of an oncoming train. He stated that this was never the case, further remarking that each car of the subway train weighs several thousand tons and to drown out the volume of a whole train would take considerably more than any noise he had ever heard coming from a subway platform. "At those levels, it would take a full orchestra to drown out the noise of a train. Yeah, more than that, you're right." (p. 115)

Third, the TA had contended that the platform ban was necessary in order to meet a state legislative mandate to reduce noise levels in the subways. The actual purpose of the mandate was to pressure the TA to reduce the noise generated by subway trains and station construction projects.[23] Anita Lerman testified:

> It's very clear to me as a rider that whoever it is that runs the subways never rides them, because if they did, the subways could not be what they are. The noise, you are quite right, is excruciating, but that has nothing to do with any of the people that you're trying to ban. It has to do with primarily at this point, the poor way that the announcements have been regulated, ear-drilling bing-bongs, . . . every time the doors open and close. (Queens hearing, p. 37)

Musician Casey McDonald stated his objections: "It seems that if volume, noise—first off, being a musician and having what I do referred to as noise is like calling by blood liquid and calling by body, what you see, as merely like something that is, something that has no emotional content or no conscious value. That's noise. That's noise" (Bronx hearing, pp. 22–23). Two speakers did support the idea of regulating amplifiers, and another advocated an amp ban throughout the subway system. A number of musicians offered to collaborate with the TA and MTA on a station-by-station survey, to tailor the regulations and address concerns about particular stations.

Fourth, the TA had argued that expressive activity violates riders' "privacy rights."[24] Although the charge might sound ridiculous in the context of the subway system, it does raise the issue of the captive audience. While free expression takes precedence over many other interests, the First Amendment does not guarantee people the right to express themselves when their audience is captive—when listeners have no opportunity to escape. During the Manhattan and Brooklyn hearings MTA board member Daniel Scannell frequently invoked the captive audience argument. He cited *Lehman v. Shaker Heights*, in which the Supreme Court upheld a municipal government's right to allow commercial advertisements and at the same time ban political ones from city-owned buses to minimize the imposition on captive bus riders.[25] Scannell drew a parallel between that case and music on subway platforms. Speakers rejected the argument along strictly legal, as well as creatively cultural, lines. Art Eisenberg explained:

> Understand that that captive audience principle was a principle endorsed only by one Justice in the *Shaker Heights* case. It is not, in fact, a principle that the Court has widely accepted, and in its application, I think we have to be very careful about narrowing it to the circumstances before the Court in that case, which were in fact riding in a bus, by analogy, perhaps, riding in a subway car. Once you start extending the captive audience principle well beyond that, I think you trench upon serious First Amendment problems. (Manhattan hearing, p. 24)

Nick Schorr, a rider, said that "as long as people have the freedom to move away and say, Oh, my God, not 'Misty' again, or, you know, they're singing Carpenter songs—whatever your, wherever your musical standards are. As long as we have that cultural freedom to say, Oh, boy, I'd rather hear the screech, . . . then there is no way that they should be banned" (pp. 107–8). Another rider, Donald Walth, testified: "If I don't care for the music, I leave. . . . Some are a little rough around the edges. Some are precious gems. . . . But I enjoy them all. I even enjoy the poorly played music, because I like to get the reactions of other people" (p. 151).

In the state environmental quality review assessment, the TA had declared that these rule changes would have no negative impact on the subway environment. But the assessment was tailored for outdoor rural areas, and consequently, the TA had been able to disregard most of the questions. While reading the proposed rules document, Eric Strangeways, a rider, had noticed that the assessment was in effect a rubber stamp: "We're not talking about topsoil here, so no wonder those forms were pretty irrelevant. There was not a balancing of First Amendment values involved in that document, and I don't think in the consideration of these things so far" (Queens hearing, p. 46).

In addition to refuting the TA's arguments, speakers identified ways in which freelance subway music benefits the authorities and riders. Steve Witt described his colleagues and himself as

> a liaison between the MTA, you people, and the public. For instance, when the D train was running on the N line for two and a half years, many times I was playing and I had to say, "Well the D's on the N line but only from 34th up. From 34th down, it's running on the regular D line, unless you take the Shuttle where you go uptown to the Number 1 train." . . . If you think about it, dear members, we want to work with you. We really do, you know. (Manhattan hearing, pp. 87–88)

Stella Cerruti, a rider, depicted freelance musicians as allies of the transit police. "Independent subway musicians do not need policing," she said. "Muggers, rapists, and drug dealers need policing. In fact, I would venture to guess that the very presence of the independent subway musician on a platform or in a dimly-lit passageway actually serves as a crime deterrent and has probably discouraged many a would-be mugger" (p. 109). James Howard and other musicians observed that they provide diversion for riders, reduce stress, and even promote a sense of community:

> It has become quite clear to me that people in the subways are not just moved by good music, but people need it. Especially because at times the subways can seem so inhumane and antagonistic, music brings a piece of happiness and even feelings of community to the passers-by. . . .

> Many times when a train pulls in, people who have been listening to me say "Thank you" as they get on the train. Dozens of people have told me that music makes the subways bearable. Often, people choose to miss a train or two and to listen, as if they were relieved to find a place of happiness, or a haven, in an otherwise unappealing and scary place. (pp. 55–56)

Speakers also noted that subway music promotes complex cross-cultural and cross-class exchange. Lynn O'Hare, a teacher, testified:

> One little boy [in her class] said . . . music in the subway lets people who can't afford to go to live concerts hear music. He said you don't have to be rich to listen to music.
>
> And I think it's important to note that this—these are upper middle-class children who—this really opens their mind to people of other races and social and economic groups, and they live in a very enclosed world sometimes. And it's as much opening for them as it is for people who can't afford to . . . pay for concerts. (p. 163/a)

Others described the positive effects of subway music on people's lives and its meaning for urban life. Donald Walth explained: "I even find myself occasionally going out of the way to hear musicians, because I know if the musician will be there that day, that I will go that way around, because it's something that, it's different. It adds something to my life, I think, in a positive way" (p. 153). Then there was Peter Barkman, a musician: "I can't really speak for other musicians, but—I think I'll get really emotional up here. This is really weird. . . . I'm sorry. . . . We've been doing this about eight months. I don't know why on earth I'm crying. But there's a lot of love down there, and I don't want to lose that, I guess, is what it is" (p. 93). The final speaker, musician Paul Clark, exposed the antihuman impulse behind the proposed rules:

> Oh, it's fun. Another opportunity to perform. Life is filled with opportunities to perform. Street musicians remind us that all the world is in fact a stage, and all you have to do is declare yourself and there you are.
>
> I think we should all congratulate ourselves on the process, public forums, getting up there, trying to nudge our institutions along so that they can keep up with the individuals. Kind of lumber behind the times. But so it is. . . .

> This is the Twilight Zone aspect of the show. Even as we speak, we're in transit. More and more evidence suggests that the earth is a transit system. And that each and every organism present is in transit to destinations unknown. Yes?
>
> We might ask now, what are the proposed rules for non-transit use of this earth facility, and what constitutes a violation of the rules? . . .
>
> Now, putting the problems in context, if we want less congested platforms, we should have lobbied against zoning loopholes, against greedy developers who crowd the neighborhood. Why did we neglect Planned Parenthood and sexual education to reduce unwanted births, all these little babies everywhere. . . .
>
> I suggest we ban or restrict the *Wall Street Journal.* I see guys every morning—they walk right to the threatening edge of that—I think we should restrict conversation. Conversation that captures the heart and liberates the mind.
>
> Now, if silence prevailed on a platform, and everyone turned their head to greet the inherently dangerous train as it came into the platform, think how much safer it would be. . . .
>
> I have a serious thing to end on, though. . . . We know how deeply we continue to violate the earth facility. I think we've got to remind ourselves of that because this transit facility, I mean we do exist in a greater context. (pp. 165–72)

Many speakers, both musicians and riders, explicitly supported "independent," "spontaneous," freelance subway music, and criticized MUNY's bureaucratic structure. They perceived government-controlled performance frames as political, and often politically discriminatory. Lloyd Carew-Reid stated: "Music Under New York performers . . . are unfortunately taken advantage of and forced into a position of regimentation. . . . Spontaneous music is in fact, I contend, a therapy, an essential therapy for society. Without spontaneous musical performances and artistic performances of all kinds in public places, I believe that you end up with a sick society" (pp. 64–66). Rider Don Cohen testified that, outraged over the proposed rules, he had formed an organization called FEST (Friends Established to Support Subway Talent), a group of business executives who were arranging a weekly concert series at the Lone Star Roadhouse featuring freelance subway musicians. FEST shared some of MUNY's problematical features—it auditioned musicians and offered them no more than donations—but it established a forum that validated freelancers and pressured the TA and MTA to do the same (Bronx hearing, p. 41).

Although the topic of subway music dominated the hearings, speakers were at least as outraged by the notion that the authorities might abrogate their fundamental free speech rights, in particular their right to engage in formal political activity. Members of the New York City Council and the New York State Legislature attended or sent representatives to deliver messages, evoking populist images and also confessing their personal interest in maintaining the subways as a channel of communication for their own reelection campaigns. Some threatened that if the proposed rules were adopted, their constitutionality would be challenged in court. State Assemblywoman Catherine Nolan reported that the legislature had drawn up a bill in response to this proposal which would restore a clause to the State Rapid Transit Law explicitly stating that the subways are an extension of the streets (Queens hearing, pp. 7–23). In a spontaneous colloquy at the Brooklyn hearing (where he was the only board member in attendance), Robert Kiley assured the public that the MTA was not "in the business of trying to regulate pamphleteering. . . . Pamphlets will continue to go forward" (Brooklyn hearing, p. 62).

The MTA board had the option of either adopting the rules as proposed or sending them back to committee for revisions. As Kiley had promised, the rules were revised.

In October 1989 the MTA adopted the *Rules on Non-Transit Use of Transit Facilities*, which apply only to TA property. Differing considerably from the proposed rules, they abandoned the "critical stations" idea and authorized expressive activity on subway platforms. Thus political, religious, and charitable organizations could drop their threats of litigation and resume their activities underground. During a recent informal interview, Gene Russianoff explained that NYPIRG forms ad hoc coalitions in crisis situations and disbands them when a battle is won or a compromise is reached. In 1989 NYPIRG made a political decision about the extent to which it could challenge the TA and MTA. "We did the best we could," Russianoff said, "to fight back terrible, terrible [proposed] rules."

The rules that were adopted retained the distance requirements of the proposed rules, except that leafleters and political campaigners were exempted from the prohibitions against standing near token booths and TA offices. The most important restriction from the point of view of musicians, however, was a total ban on the use of amplification devices on platforms. In practice, the effects of this provision for many freelancers were no different from those of the proposed rules. The restrictions in the new rules targeted freelance musicians.

Members of STAR filed a lawsuit in federal district court challenging the constitutionality of the rules. They sought a preliminary injunction to restrain the MTA and TA from enforcing the amp ban, arguing that it caused them "irreparable harm" by preventing them from performing. They also requested an injunction on a section of the rules which prohibited unlicensed commercial activity such as cassette and CD sales. And they challenged the exclusionary structure of the MUNY program, which restricted freelancers' access to mezzanines and barred all but MUNY members from Grand Central Terminal.[26]

As plaintiffs, the musicians argued that the rules were not reasonable time-place-manner restrictions on their First Amendment right to free expression. Valid time-place-manner restrictions have to meet three criteria. First, they must be "content neutral"—they must not suppress a particular viewpoint or form of communication. The musicians charged that the rules discriminated against "electric music," a twentieth-century phenomenon including radio, records, and any music involving microphones, amplifiers, or other technological devices. In his affidavit, Michael Lydon, a subway musician and rock author, explained that while amplifiers can increase volume, their primary function is to change the quality of sound, and therefore the use of amplification is a creative choice.[27] Plaintiff Peter Barkman, who played rockabilly in the subways, confirmed that his electric guitar made no sound at all without an amplifier.[28]

Second, restrictions must be "narrowly tailored" to serve a substantial government interest. In this case, that interest was public safety, which the MTA and TA said would be advanced by eliminating the "evil" of musicians' "excessive noise."[29] As defendants, the authorities maintained that amplified platform music interfered with transit police radio communications, with track workers' signals, and with riders' ability to hear public address announcements. TA officials stated in affidavits that, using decibel meters, they had conducted safety studies and found that subway musicians routinely exceeded the volume limit

Rules of Conduct
For the safety and comfort of all customers, everyone must obey the rules. They're the law. Failure to pay the fare or violation of any other rule can result in arrest, fine and/or ejection.
— No destroying subway property
— No littering or creating unsanitary conditions
— No smoking
— No drinking alcoholic beverages
— No panhandling or begging
— No amplification devices on platforms
— No more than one seat per person
— No blocking free movement
— No lying down
— No unauthorized commercial activities
— No entering tracks, tunnels and non-public areas
— No bulky items likely to inconvenience others
— No radio playing audible to others
New York City Transit Authority

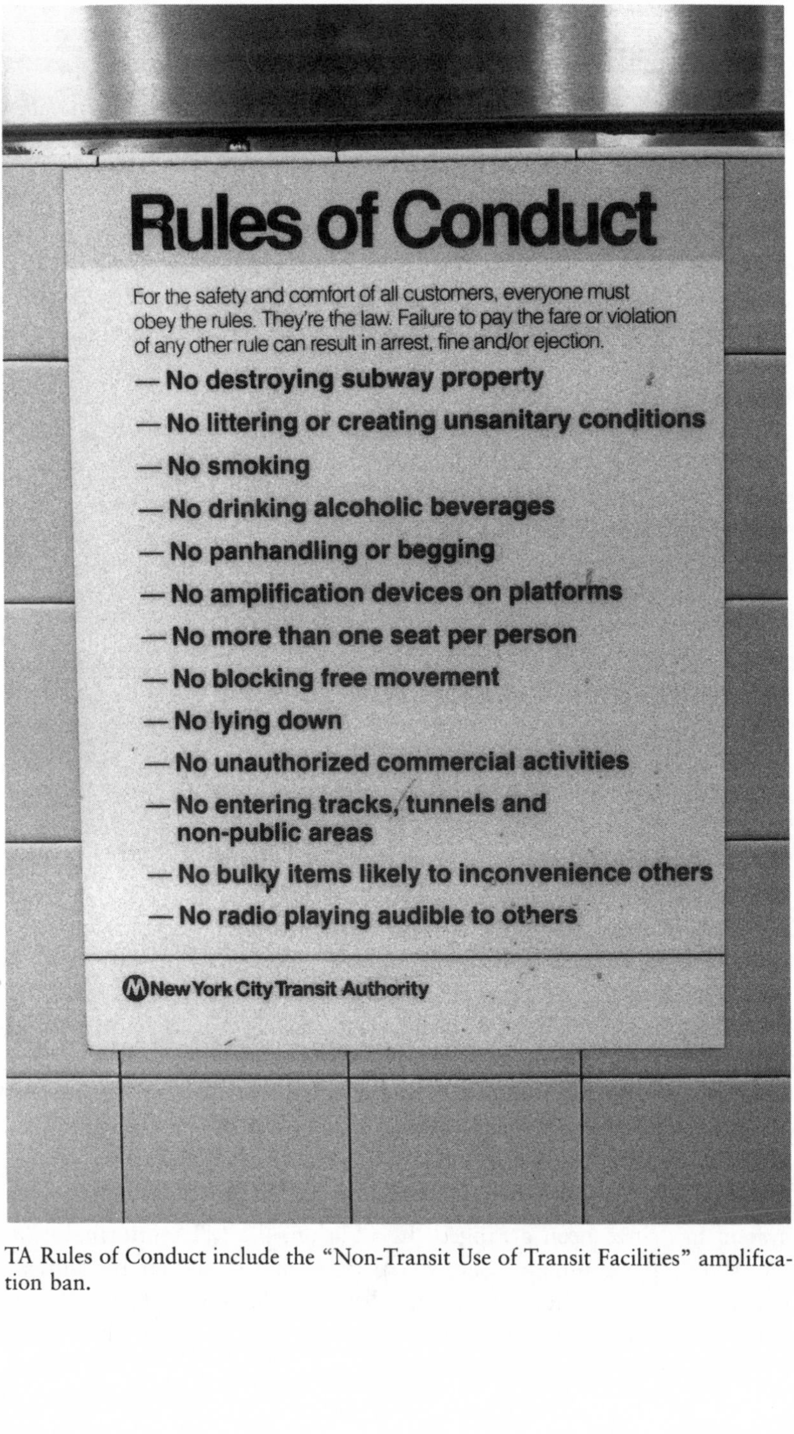

TA Rules of Conduct include the "Non-Transit Use of Transit Facilities" amplification ban.

of eighty-five decibels measured at a distance of five feet specified in the rules.[30]

Lloyd Carew-Reid and Peter Barkman conducted their own safety studies and reported that they could play comfortably below the decibel ceiling. They also discovered that the sounds produced when a token booth clerk emptied coins from the turnstiles, when conductors made announcements inside train cars, and when a homeless man crumpled a paper bag all measured just below or above the decibel ceiling.[31] Since the TA had not succeeded in showing that all amplified platform musicians produced excessive noise, they argued, the amp ban eliminated more than the specific "evil" it was intended to target. Therefore, they concluded, the regulation was not narrowly tailored. They recommended the less-restrictive alternative of providing transit police officers with decibel meters to verify that all musicians, amplified and acoustic, played below the decibel ceiling on subway platforms. Indeed, the rules required the officers to monitor the volume of all musicians.[32]

Third, time-place-manner restrictions must leave alternative channels of communication open for the affected activity. The musicians contended that MUNY virtually eliminated their alternatives in the subways and that inclement weather often precluded performances in streets and parks.[33]

The court agreed with the musicians that the amp ban was overbroad and thus violated their First Amendment rights. Judge Louis L. Stanton granted their motion for a preliminary injunction, enjoining the MTA and TA from imposing the amp ban. He did not grant the musicians an injunction on the ban on selling cassettes and CDs, rejecting the argument that these sales are an extension of their creative activity.[34] The judge's decision did not even mention the challenge to the MUNY program. David Goldstein, the plaintiffs' counsel in the *Carew-Reid* case, acknowledges that the musicians had lived with MUNY for four years without challenging its existence; a more elaborate suit would have had to be filed to merit review.

At the end of this hearing, Goldstein recalls, an MTA representative offered to arrange to issue "freedom of expression" permits, allowing freelancers to perform in parts of Grand Central Terminal. This permit system has since been arranged. In addition, the MTA informally offered to design commercial activity permits that would enable subway musicians to sell their recordings legally. The follow-through was never completed, partly because it involved lengthy paperwork. Nevertheless, the offer suggests that cassette and CD sales can be made legal in the subways.

The MTA and TA arranged for a temporary stay on the preliminary injunction. In February 1990 they appealed the district court decision in the United States Court of Appeals for the Second Circuit. One member of the three-judge panel that heard the case was Frank X. Altimari. In that same month Judge Altimari wrote the majority opinion for the court of appeals upholding the right of the MTA and TA to ban panhandling. He concluded that panhandlers' speech is not entitled to constitutional protection because their activity is a form of assault and the prior court decision upholding subway panhandling had failed to consider "the common good" (see Appendix 1).

As defendants-appellants, the MTA and TA described the complexity of their responsibility "to balance several, sometimes competing interests . . .: the interests of musicians and other individuals engaged in expressive conduct; the interests of subway riders who hold divergent views on the desirability of music in the transit system; the TA's interest in the safe and efficient operation of the system; and the interests of the TA and the public in effective enforcement of rules preventing safety hazards."[35] The brief did not mention the recent proposal to eliminate virtually all expressive activity from the subways.

To show that the amp ban was a reasonable time-place-manner restriction, the MTA and TA cited arguments in *Ward v. Rock against Racism*, a recent Supreme Court case with serious, albeit ambiguous, implications for street performing.[36] The case upheld the right of Central Park to regulate the volume of independent concerts in its bandshell by requiring musical groups to use the park's sound system and audio technician. Thus, on the one hand, the Supreme Court ruled that music making is a constitutionally protected form of expression. On the other hand, the Court sanctioned increased government control. To support their claim that the amp ban was content neutral, the MTA and TA cited *Rock against Racism:* "A regulation that serves purposes unrelated to the content of expression is deemed neutral, even if it has an incidental effect on some speakers or messages but not others" (*Carew-Reid v. MTA* 903 F.2d 914, at 916).

Rock against Racism also eliminated the requirement that the regulation be the most narrowly tailored means of serving a substantial government interest. Thus, in the *Carew-Reid* appeal, the authorities argued that banning amplifiers was a more convenient method of achieving their goal than equipping transit police officers with decibel meters (at 918). The court of appeals agreed: "The regulation is not invalid simply because a court, second-guessing the decisions of the governmental body, discerns some less-restrictive alternative to the regulation" (at 917). The court also affirmed the defendants' contention that mezzanines, streets, and parks were available to the musicians as alternative communication channels, that the First Amendment "does not guarantee . . . access to every or even the best channels or locations for . . . expression" (at 919).

In May 1990 the court of appeals ruled that the amp ban was a reasonable time-place-manner regulation. It reversed the district court decision, and the ban officially went into effect.

Since the court of appeals agreed that the amp ban was a reasonable restriction, it did not see any need to conduct a public forum analysis, which would have led to closer scrutiny of the ban's effects on the content of electric music. But in their legal brief the MTA and TA invoked the public forum doctrine and revealed their position on the legal and political status of subway space. It is, therefore, worthwhile to review this part of their argument.

In the 1980s the Supreme Court established three categories of public forums: "traditional," "designated" or "limited purpose," and "nonpublic." These are defined in the *Brief of Plaintiffs-Appellees* in the *Carew-Reid* appeal: "Traditional public forums are 'places which by long tradition or government fiat have been devoted to assembly or debate,' such as 'streets and parks.' . . . Designated public forums are places 'which the state has opened for use by the public as a place for expressive activity.' . . . Finally, a nonpublic forum is '[p]ublic property which is not by tradition or designation a forum for public communication.'"[37] The MTA, described in state law as "a public benefit corporation created to operate the commuter transportation system in New York City and the surrounding counties,"[38] and its subsidiary, the TA, stated in their brief that the subways are a nonpublic forum. In their words, "The government has the same right as a private property owner 'to preserve' non-public forum property 'for the use to which it is lawfully dedicated.'"[39] The authorities claimed they had not opened up the subways to First Amendment activity. Perhaps this helps to explain their decision to use the less committal term "expressive activity" in official documents.

Laurence Tribe sees danger in the current reliance on this argument.

He says that in recent years "the Court has . . . restricted the protection offered to speech under the public forum doctrine by greatly expanding the third category . . .—that of nonpublic forums. . . . Carried to its logical conclusion, it would make nearly all restrictions on speech self-justifying, since the very fact that the government had denied the plaintiff access could be invoked to prove that the government never intended to create a public forum. . . . Where so much discretion is vested in the government, the forum itself can be defined in terms of viewpoint."[40] David Goldstein attempted to make a similar point. In his legal brief, he argued that the TA and MTA had designated the subways as a public forum in 1989 when they adopted the rules, and consequently, it was unconstitutional for them to decide to admit acoustic freelance musicians and restrict amplified ones. Ultimately, Goldstein believes the amp ban is political, an attempt at social control. "The bureaucrats," he said, "figured that most subway musicians use amps. 'If we get rid of the amps, we get rid of two-thirds of the subway musicians.' They didn't care who they got rid of. [The ban is] arbitrary and irrational." A look at which subway musicians use amplifiers and which do not tends to confirm this assessment. The amp ban targets classical, folk, and electric guitarists, keyboardists, and vocalists with microphones. It allows trumpeters, drummers, and saxophonists to remain even though their volume can equal, if not exceed, that of their amplified counterparts.

My own experiences lend additional support. While conducting research for this book, I requested copies of the TA safety studies cited by the defendants in the *Carew-Reid* case. Instead, I received two decibel ceiling studies involving taped, not live, music. In 1992, moreover, one of the TA officials who had supplied information for the defense declined to be interviewed, claiming to have limited recall. These responses suggest that the amp ban rests on data that are at best inconclusive and quite possibly nonexistent.

Laurence Tribe observes that communication channels have increasingly come under private control and that government is steadily restricting individuals' access to the remaining forums in which speech is, indeed, free. He warns of the negative consequences that may be expected.

> These changes in access to and control over the forms of public communication have eaten away at the average citizen's rights of expression and, thus, at the prospects for realizing free speech values. Inas-

> much as those values are essential to the character of our constitutional order, it is not exaggerating to say that that order could be seriously threatened by a continued failure of the Court to take account of background institutions of power and the costs of participation in public dialogue.[41]

The conservative panel of judges who decided the appeal in the *Carew-Reid* case chose not to consider these issues. Their decision effectively silenced the musicians in STAR, who had neither the affluence nor the political power to pursue the case further. David Goldstein had donated his services, and he and the musicians could not afford to continue. Furthermore, although they were pleased that a federal court had affirmed their constitutional right to perform in the subways, some musicians considered the appeals court ruling a defeat. STAR disbanded, mainly because it lost the energy and determination of Lloyd Carew-Reid, who left the subway music scene shortly thereafter.

But surely the court of appeals decision does not fully reflect the TA and MTA positions on subway music. What of the TA's decision to introduce experimental guidelines in 1987 and to authorize expressive activity in 1989? What of Robert Kiley's decision to distance himself from the proposed rules? And what of the public hearings, where board members concluded by thanking musicians for their "good humor" and "good spirit," and where Kiley declared: "I think the musicians are terrific"?[42]

In a recent informal interview, Art Eisenberg shed light on the ambiguity by explaining the "slippery slope" of jurisprudence. The Supreme Court has said that the First Amendment protects a broad range of expressive forms, including music, film, theater, books, even topless dancing. It has ruled in this fashion to prevent government from making policy decisions favoring the content of one form of speech over another. The Court, however, does not know where to draw the line. If musicians and book vendors have a constitutional right to express themselves and receive money in public thoroughfares, why not visual artists, T-shirt vendors, and others? The slippery slope helps to account for the ambiguities in public policy on street performing and subway music.

Ultimately, the explanation is political and cultural. Although the TA and MTA have authorized free expression, they still seem to distrust spontaneity. The TA wants to maximize the predictability of goings-on in the subways, just as Metro-North wants to in the commuter railroad terminals, out of legitimate concern over public safety and reliable operations but also out of a sense that government is mandated to control the public's activities. The problem with this perspective is that it prevents the TA and MTA from recognizing the positive cultural effects of spontaneous performances—the extent to which freelance subway music informally regulates subway space. As a result, the rules tend to be ineffective, if not counterproductive.

The TA officials I interviewed are of the opinion that the rules both accommodate expressive activity and regulate subway music. They believe that the amp ban is being uniformly applied and that, in combination with the "common sense" of everyone involved, it is proving adequate and effective. In reality, the ban is enforced quite unevenly. If no problems are being reported, then, it is because "common sense" is regulating subway space regardless of the ban.

A number of musicians still use Mouse amps and microphones on subway platforms. They violate the rules, and they risk receiving tickets or even more severe penalties. How the transit police enforce the amp ban and other subway music regulations is the subject of the next chapter.

7

Walking the Beat: Transit Police

The New York City Transit Police Department represents the TA on the "front lines." Transit police officers are responsible for enforcing TA regulations, including the rules on "non-transit use of transit facilities," such as the ban on amplifiers on subway platforms. And yet the enforcement of these rules often bears minimal relation to what is actually stated in the regulatory code. Some officers invent broad restrictions that delegitimate all freelancers. Some issue summonses based on dubious discretionary decisions. Conversely, some choose not to enforce the rules, and they allow amplified musicians to stay on the platforms.

What accounts for this uneven application? To understand the ideology that frames enforcement, I begin this chapter with a look at the reorganization of the Transit Police Department, which was undertaken in 1990, and at the patrol strategy that accompanied it. I then examine the officers' actual enforcement practices with respect to subway music, and I conclude with a consideration of the complex ways in which officers and musicians affect one another's status in the informal social network of the subways.

The information in this chapter is drawn primarily from interviews I conducted with Lieutenant Eugene J. Roach and Inspector Ronald R. Rowland in the Office of the Chief of Transit Police; with Lieutenant Jeffrey McGunnigle, who at the time of the interview was an executive officer in Queens District 20 (he has since been promoted to the department's Special Services Bureau); and with nine patrol officers. Two of the officers were African American men and the rest of the sources were white men of various ethnic backgrounds. Although my sample did not fully reflect the profile of the transit police, it did reflect the relative percentage of white men (57 percent) to black men (16 percent).[1] Responses differed significantly not by race but by rank. The three higher officials tended to focus on broad policy objectives and were optimistic about the status of operations. Patrol officers were more inclined to describe problems with the daily enforcement of regulations.

I interviewed the officials in their own offices. Since Lieutenant Roach and Inspector Rowland worked together, I met with them at the same time. One of my interviews with the patrol officers took place at his district headquarters, and the remainder were held spontaneously on subway mezzanines while they were on duty. I recorded five of these interviews. Toward the end of my fieldwork, two officers with seniority informed me that members of their rank are not authorized to grant interviews without advance permission from their supervisors. I have decided to use the ones that had already been granted, but to protect the individuals involved, I refer to them by letter code only.

The transit police is one of many departments in the Transit Authority. Its highest ranking official, the chief of police, has the same status as senior vice president in the other departments. But, as the title of chief indicates, the transit police, like other police forces, is a semimilitary organization. It uses the titles found in organizations of war, such as officer, sergeant, lieutenant, and captain, and the military chain of command. In fact the Transit Police Department employs a number of Vietnam War veterans, including Inspector Rowland and Lieutenant Roach, whose military skills dovetail with the department's structure and goals.

In the 1960s, serious crime proliferated in American urban centers and began to occur more frequently in the New York subways. To address the problem, the transit police force was expanded in 1965 to twenty-nine hundred officers.[2] By 1992 the department employed four thousand officers, making it one of the ten largest police forces in the nation.

Yet, through the 1980s, transit police officers suffered from low morale. They worked under extremely harsh environmental conditions out of substandard station facilities, which were not renovated as part of the MTA capital improvements program. Their antiquated radio system left them without backup support in crisis situations. Decision making in the department was highly centralized. And the officers had no sense of identity or mission to distinguish them from the more prestigious New York City Police Department. In early 1990, over half the transit police officers wanted either to merge with or to transfer to the NYPD.[3]

In March 1990, Alan Kiepper was appointed president of the TA, and in April he appointed William J. Bratton as transit police chief. The officials I interviewed credit Bratton with reviving the department. From 1990 to 1992, Bratton reduced and clarified the chain of command. He assigned district commanders the responsibility of establishing problem-solving teams, drawing members from all ranks to assess departmental needs and operational strategies. After receiving broad input, Bratton arranged to improve the design of uniforms, equip officers with more accurate nine-millimeter handguns, make a new fleet of surface vehicles available for backup support, reconstruct the radio system, and renovate and expand station facilities.[4] In late 1990 new recruits began to receive transit-specific training apart from candidates for the NYPD or the New York Housing Police. In 1991 the transit police became one of the few forces in the nation to receive accreditation. The officials I interviewed believe that these various aspects of reorganization accounted for the record number of applicants who took the transit police entrance exam beginning in 1991.

Like Robert Kiley and Alan Kiepper, Bratton made use of marketing techniques to improve the department's image and step up recruitment efforts. The "old-timers" who had joined in the 1960s were starting to retire and needed to be replaced. Lieutenant Roach estimates that the "new kids" have reduced the average age on the force from thirty-five to twenty-eight. He does not believe that the age reduction or loss of experienced officers has had a negative effect on job performance.

The new officers are subway musicians' peers. Whether or not this symmetry has any real effect on enforcement practices, it is striking at a symbolic level. Two groups of young adults are attempting to improve the subway environment—one with a strategy that demands conformity, the other with a philosophy of individuality; one through elaborate institutional controls, the other through an elaborate network of informal controls.

When the department undertook reorganization, it also adopted a "community-based" or "problem-oriented" policing model. Bratton consulted George Kelling, a professor of criminal justice, and concluded that ridership had dropped by 1990 because people were afraid of venturing underground, feeling the subways were "out of control." (The national recession and a recent fare hike were acknowledged but seen as only secondary causes of the decline.) Robbery, farebeating, and "disorder" were identified as the major problems. This assessment was informed by Kelling's "broken windows" theory, which is based on the analogy that "just as an unrepaired broken window in a building signals that no one cares about the structure and may lead to additional vandalism, so unsuppressed disorderly behavior sends a message that no one is in control." Thus, the transit police patrol strategy aims to "fix the windows" (pursue minor rule violations) while "fixing the house" (fighting more serious crime). The broken windows theory also holds that "people who break minor rules are often prone to commit more serious and harmful crimes." In an effort to prove this point, the department reported that in 1991, 1,754 of those stopped for farebeating were wanted on warrants and 136 possessed illegal weapons.[5]

Having accepted Kelling's sweeping definition of disorder, Bratton initiated an aggressive campaign against rule violators, broadly identified as "panhandlers, unauthorized merchants, . . . people sleeping in corridors," and anyone "obstructing free movement or transit operations." Between 1990 and 1991 the number of summonses issued for such rule violations increased by 35 percent, or fifty-three thousand, and ejections from the subway system increased by 473 percent.[6]

This patrol strategy, in actuality, is not all that new. Michael K. Brown, a sociologist, explains that major efforts were made after World War II to professionalize the nation's police forces by shifting officers' attention to the prevention and elimination of "crime and disorder." According to Brown, the reform effort has succeeded in making police forces more efficient, but it has also created a permanent conflict for officers. On the one hand, they must adhere to the rationalized, image-conscious standards of their departments; on the other hand, they must decide how to use their coercive power when confronting unpredictable situations on the streets. Moreover, Brown says, the officers' role is plagued with ambiguity because society has reached far less moral consensus than is often claimed on how to define "disorder."[7]

Enforcement of the TA rules helps to illustrate this ambiguity. Ironically, the MUNY program aims to improve the subway environment by promoting musicians, while the transit police strives to do the same by, in effect, criminalizing them.

The survey I gave to subway musicians in December 1993 asked respondents whether transit police officers had stopped them or issued them summonses for rule violations. Thirteen out of twenty had been stopped for using an amplifier, twelve for producing "unnecessary noise," eleven for performing without a MUNY permit, ten for blocking traffic or creating crowd conditions, nine for selling cassettes or CDs, two for "disorderly conduct," and eleven for no specific reason. Officers had issued summonses to five for using an amp, four for producing "unnecessary noise," four for selling cassettes or CDs, three for performing without a MUNY permit, three for blocking traffic or creating crowd conditions, two for "disorderly conduct," and seven for no specific reason.

Lieutenant Roach was a patrol officer in the mid-1980s when subway music proliferated. He recalls that the novelty of the performances drew huge crowds. He became a mediator, directing traffic and appeasing inconvenienced riders. The lieutenant believes that the current rules clarify the officers' role in relation to musicians and establish a framework that prevents musicians from interfering with transit operations.

In fact, however, problems persist, and to a great extent they have to do with enforcement. Some officers are inventing regulations that are far more restrictive than the rules actually in effect. One of the most common and disconcerting inventions is the claim that only MUNY musicians may set up in the subways. Officers tell freelancers that they need permits to perform. All six of the freelancers in my sample reported being stopped for not having a MUNY permit, even though the courts have upheld their constitutional right to perform in the subway system. As a TA official observed during the 1989 public hearings, many officers need uniform rules to follow. Unfortunately, the MTA and TA do not have uniform rules. Since MUNY members have permits, officers assume that other musicians must have them as well. Thus, they invent consistency. Officer V explained: "It's a cut and dry issue. Either he [the musician] is supposed to have a permit and he does have it, or he's supposed to have a permit and he doesn't have it. One way he has to go, one way he can stay." The invented rule signals that administrators have not yet managed to clarify the relationship between MUNY and freelancing for the transit police. As long as officers restrict subway space in this manner, MUNY can be challenged for censoring freelance musicians.

The inventions and confusion continue when the musicians bring their summonses to the TA Transit Adjudication Bureau. Robert T. Perry, who counseled Lloyd Carew-Reid in the mid-1980s and since then has been representing hip hoppers and other musicians, reports that many of the bureau hearing officers who decide these cases are unfamiliar with the rules. Thus, uninformed musicians with no legal counsel end up paying penalties for invalid charges. For example, an Otavaleño musician told me his Andean group paid seventy-five dollars for an overdue summons that charged them with performing without a MUNY permit.

Over the years, officers have also invoked obsolete arguments to restrict musical performances. Officer M revived one of the safety charges refuted during the 1989 public hearings when he explained to me that he does not allow any musicians to play on subway platforms because "people might fall on the tracks." Officer H maintains that it is illegal to collect (in his words, "solicit") donations. When he warns musicians, "You're going to build up your violations," he said, "they close their [instrument] case."

During our interview, the officials in the Office of the Chief offered explanations for such misinterpretations and misapplication of the rules. Some patrol officers are assigned to shifts on which they rarely encounter subway music. They have volumes of other rules to absorb. The rules on expressive activity changed many times between 1987 and 1990, and officers learn rules during their initial training; reviews are conducted only when rules are amended. In other words, apart from the new recruits, officers have not reviewed the subway music regulations since 1990.

Officer H confessed, with more than a touch of sarcasm, that he cannot rely on those higher up for correct information. Instead, he must base his decisions on a general understanding of his duties: "You get conflicting orders from different people. One boss tells you one thing, one something else. . . . So you pick the brains of those in the know. You call the Legal Bureau. They don't have a clue. 'Oh, we'll get back to you, we gotta research that.' So what do you do in the meantime? . . . I just try to maintain order."

In 1990 the transit police command staff adopted a "walk-around" style of supervision to increase their familiarity with current enforcement problems and to respond more immediately to officers' questions.[8] Nevertheless, as Michael K. Brown observes, large police departments have limited ability to provide adequate information to, or impose formal controls on, their patrols.[9] Transit police officers work alone and without supervision far more often than their counterparts above ground. Relying on themselves, they develop their own enforcement styles, which sometimes include forms of harassment.

Clearly the term "harassment" has variable definitions. From subway musicians' perspective, it may refer to the excessive use of authority or the inappropriate use of force. Misapplication of the rules, as I have described, is one example. Threatening language is another. A musician I interviewed reported that one patrol officer warned: "I'm gonna give you a hard time whenever I see you." Musicians also report that officers have confiscated their cassettes and equipment. One freelancer was physically escorted out of a station even when he had agreed to leave. Other freelancers report that plainclothes officers stop their performances and ticket them without warning. A subway singer who is successfully working his way out of homelessness and drug addition says that he has been jailed a few times for making music.

In March 1991 I witnessed and experienced an extreme example of police harassment directed against musicians and riders. Larry Wright and a friend, both teenagers, were drumming on plastic buckets on the 42nd Street and Eighth Avenue (Port Authority) mezzanine, surrounded by a large audience circle. When a young white officer walked across the "stage" with a German Shepherd, the drummers stopped immediately. The canine officer then directed the musicians to a corner of the mezzanine. Many of us promptly formed a circle around the officer, the dog, and the musicians. Riders called out questions about constitutional and civil rights in subway space, including "What are you going to do to them?" "Since when is music illegal?" and "Isn't this a public space?" Apparently, the canine officer was intimidated by this collective reaction. He tried to gain control of the situation by asking, "Are you trying to incite a riot?" and by giving the dog slack to bark and lunge at us.

When we did not leave, the canine officer called for backup support. Six more officers arrived, including two white women and one African American man. In a matter of minutes the canine officer and his African American colleague pulled two young African American men out of our circle, then frisked and arrested them. "This is not fair!" a Caribbean woman called out. "If you arrest them, you should arrest all of us!" Instead, the officers physically disbanded us. When I asked a female officer a question, she shoved me. The African American officer dragged one man off by his collar. As they walked away, other riders wondered how police could deny teenagers a social outlet that might keep them out of the kinds of trouble that, ironically, require police intervention.

I filed a formal complaint with the transit police Civilian Complaint Unit, and I received a written reply that stated: "An investigation has been conducted. Based on the information you and the other witnesses provided, it has been determined that the [canine] officer's conduct was not improper."[10] The determination was especially disturbing since the incident had occurred just as Los Angeles was beginning to look into reports of widespread police brutality.

From the patrol officers' point of view, many of the tactics that musicians experience as harassing are simply enforcement tools used with all rule violators in an effort to maintain order. The tools include warnings, fines, ejection, and in extreme cases, arrest. Officers said they are trained to follow cues—that any escalation of conflict is determined by the musicians. Michael K. Brown refers to this aspect of police behavior as an "attitude test." The officers' course of action is influenced by the extent to which civilians are willing to defer to police authority.[11]

Yet, the preceding examples show that officers' decisions are far from neutral and objective. In the Larry Wright incident, it would appear that the canine officer acted out of a personal sense that he had lost control of the situation. Moreover, officers may be motivated to issue summonses to musicians by an informal quota system. During one interview an officer explained to me that while he is not instructed to write a specific number of tickets, his standing might be called into question if he consistently brought in fewer than the rest of his platoon. An informal quota would help to explain the sharp increase in summonses issued to various populations and in ejections when the new patrol strategy was introduced. Thus, confrontations between musicians and officers are shaped at least in part by officers' interpretations of events and by their discretionary decisions.

Both the officials and the officers I interviewed acknowledged that discretion is a major part of rule enforcement. Inspector Rowland described discretion as a combination of "personal judgment, past experience, and the conditions at the moment." The officials conceded that it is impossible for officers to confront every rule violation occurring in the subways. Officers recognize that they cannot, the officials said, and over time they develop their own system of priorities.

Far from signaling the limits of officers' authority, however, discretionary decisions often reflect the extent to which their authority supersedes TA rules. Thus, musicians reported that officers had told them to stop or had ticketed them without explanation. Moreover, officers have broad latitude to decide whether musicians are blocking traffic or producing crowd conditions. District commands may even issue directives advising them to watch for these problems during rush hours. It is only when officers claim the directives are "new rules" that they overstep the official bounds of their authority.

Discretion can also work in the opposite direction. Some officers I interviewed all but ignore the regulations, or they use discretion in ways that appear lenient, flexible, and generous. Officer H, for example, lets musicians play with amplifiers on platforms. Officer Z lets them perform on mezzanines even when his supervisor has told him to "get them out." Officer G recognizes that subway musicians can be cooperative and self-regulating. He tells them to turn down their amplifiers just until a crowd condition subsides. He also lets them handle their territorial disputes alone. Officers M and Z are musicians themselves and therefore, they believe, they are more sensitive to subway musicians' needs.

Michael K. Brown explains that leniency—or, more precisely, nonenforcement of minor violations—hearkens back to a traditional model of police work that combined compassion with coercion. Brown says that officers use discretion in this way to gain public support and also to resolve conflicts between official policy and their personal insights—in this case, perhaps, their sense that musical performances have a legitimate place in the subway system.[12]

One overall goal of the rules and their enforcement is to enhance public safety, which in the subways can refer either to accident prevention or to crime deterrence. The TA has long argued that subway musicians make accidents more likely by interfering with transit operations and obstructing traffic. During the 1989 public hearings, however, some speakers rebutted that argument by contending that musicians actually promote crowd control. Many more testified that musicians prevent crime on deserted platforms by drawing riders together—consistent with Jane Jacobs's "eyes on the street" theory—and by maintaining a presence in parts of the subway system where officers can only offer "limit[ed] police surveillance."[13]

At the 1989 hearings, Steve Witt suggested that subway music circles function in much the same way as the off-hour waiting areas that the TA has designated on subway platforms.[14] During interviews I asked officers whether they agreed with this comparison. Most did not. They believed that the waiting areas are safe because token booth clerks supervise them by means of video monitors (though in fact only some are equipped with monitors). From their perspective, safety is achieved not through numbers but, rather, when lower-level TA employees, backed by transit police officers, supervise and control subway space. Some officers contended, furthermore, that large audiences invite such "crimes of opportunity" as pickpocketing and chain snatching. They added, though, that in this respect all crowds in the subways are a liability.

The officials and two of the officers I interviewed asserted that the subways would be safer in both respects if the TA eliminated all subway music, MUNY and freelance. On the other hand, Officer H felt that some of the public safety arguments the TA had advanced in the late 1980s were invalid. For instance, the TA had claimed that subway music interferes with the public address system, but Officer H admitted: "The public announcement system is horrible. You can't hear 'em [the messages] anyway. But something's coming out of 'em; that's all that matters. [The TA] will argue: 'Yes, we made an announcement, yes, people heard them.' Even though nobody understood what they meant. . . . As far as they're concerned, people are getting a public announcement. There's no interfering with that scratch."

Indeed, both lieutenants conceded that subway music reduces riders' fear by increasing their *perception* of safety. In the early 1990s an MTA survey revealed that riders believed 25 percent of the city's crime occurred in the subways, whereas in fact 3 percent did.[15] Lieutenant McGunnigle explained that improving perceptions of the subways is half the battle in the campaign to increase ridership and he decided that subway music should be supported for this reason. "Some things are worth a few problems," he said. In fact, in its promotional brochure the transit police asserts that "a confident riding public . . .

becomes a strong police ally."[16] If this is the case, then surely subway musicians, as confidence builders, are exceptionally strong police allies.

During our interviews, officers asserted that they carried out their official duties and did not build relationships on the job. Yet, the same officers who rigidly enforced rules (real or invented) indicated that musical performances positively transformed their own experience of the subways.

I asked Officer V, who had called the regulation of subway music "a cut and dry issue," whether he had ever seen musicians interfere with TA work.

> *Officer V*: Not really, not really. I've seen TA cleaners sing with the guy.
>
> *ST*: Have you?
>
> *Officer V*: Yeah. 103rd and Broadway. Here he wasn't playing an instrument He was just singing. You let him stay? He's not bothering nobody. He was singing songs about religion. Freedom of religion, right? Therefore, he has to stay. . . . And the TA cleaner, who's along singing—as he was working, he was singing next to him—singing his response, or whatever.
>
> *ST*: Does subway music ever make your job easier?
>
> *Officer V*: Not really easier, just more pleasant. Sometimes you'll hear it, and it is nice music, the guy's really talented. You have a violinist, I don't know his name but he's played in Carnegie Hall [Jim Graseck], and he's known throughout the system. . . . He's great! The guy is really good. He plays good music, he's very, very talented, so it's really a professional show you're getting over there. . . . I would walk over there to tell him to play a song for me and he would pack up, ready to go. I'd say, "No, no. You're doing the right thing here, you're making people happy." Who's gonna stop him? The guy's great.

Officer V clarifies more than, perhaps, he realizes. Although at first he is only prepared to say the music makes the subways more pleasant for him, he ends by observing that it does the same for riders. More than that, he calls it "doing the right thing," indicating that it is a positive, meaningful contribution to subway space. His response suggests that the questions "Does the music make your job more pleasant?" and "Does it make your job easier?" are in fact related, for Jim Graseck improved the atmosphere and, thus, helped him to achieve order and control. Indeed, Officer V might not respond as positively to all styles of music, but his earlier description of the a capella singer proves that the Graseck incident was not unique.

In responses like this, Officer V and his colleagues implicitly acknowledged that they are part of a broad, informal social network underground. Michael K. Brown explains that police officers act within "informal patterns of social control to maintain order" in the hope that the public will affirm their legitimacy and obey them when it is truly necessary.[17] Yet this behavior reflects a role conflict. Officers V and R said they dislike telling musicians to pack up because when they do audience members label them as the "heavies." Officer V believes that a TA department other than the transit police could regulate subway music.

Over the last decade, many kinds of activity proliferated in subway space, raising important questions about the role of the transit police. Officers were instructed to eject various populations from the subways, provided that First Amendment rights (for those whose rights had been acknowledged) were respected. But they quickly learned, in Officer H's words, that "it's like the tide's rolling in and you're trying to shovel it out. . . . They're gonna keep coming back. They're gonna come back." City politicians expected officers to be middle managers; riders wanted them to be social workers; and the subways' other populations needed them to be friends. Ultimately, the heavy demands of these various expectations and the contradictions among court decisions, TA regulations, and personal insights into broader social realities have left some officers extraordinarily frustrated. They simplify matters by denying that itinerant activity such as musical performance can improve the subway environment and by doubting that it can be accommodated at all. Officer H said: "Subway music is like a flower in a vase on the platform. Makes the subways better. It's two contrasting items. But this First Amendment stuff has got to end. People have rights and rights, but as they express themselves, they're shirking the rights of someone using the system for what it was built for. . . . You're not supposed to generate good will in the subways. That's not what the subway's for."

The transit police promotional brochure states that "the subway is not a community" because "it is not a place where most people live or work." Yet, it recognizes that "Transit Police patrol officers have more daily face-to-face interactions with the public than most of their city counterparts."[18] Whether or not the transit police is willing to call the subways a "community" (Inspector Rowland was), there is good reason for them to acknowledge the existence of an informal social network underground in which both authorized and unauthorized people work, live, and establish a range of relationships. In short, the department could apply the highly democratic principles of its recent internal reorganization to its interactions with other populations in the subways, to identify forms of collaboration that could, or already do, make policing less burdensome. Subway music, I am suggesting, helps to produce a more elaborate, acceptable, and enduring order underground.

When asked how transit police officers treat them, the majority of the musicians I surveyed offered positive responses, such as: "Nice—some of them give you donations." Almost half, however, added their qualifications. "Pretty well—at worst they tolerate—sometimes they've been a bit nasty," one said. Another responded, "Some are very prejudiced and mean and threaten you."

During interviews, musicians explained that it is often the new recruits who treat them poorly. Michael Gabriel said: "I've had supervisors come and tell me they like my music, then a few minutes later a couple of rookies tell me I have to leave." A few Latino and African American musicians felt that some harassment is motivated by racism on the part of white officers. Conversely, another African American musician said that some black officers are even less sympathetic because they are trying to prove that they are part of "one blue family." Some musicians believe that crackdowns are related to officers' musical tastes and moods. One, however, said an officer had confided that district commands periodically instruct his rank to harass musicians. And in early 1994 some musicians reported increased police harassment coinciding with the TA's latest campaign against panhandlers.

When asked how they reacted in confrontations with officers, most of my survey respondents said (perhaps not surprisingly) that they complied with police orders:

> "Express why if for no reason, but pretty much keep quiet and move if I have to!"

"Angry but level-headed."

"It wasn't fun—was upset."

"Miedo—no hemos experimentado así [scared—we had never experienced this]!"

"Very politely—have to—it's my character."

"Let them have their way. Can't do nothing about it. Pack my bags. Don't want sticks upside my head."

"Went home."

Musicians understand that officers equate silence with compliance and assertion of rights with confrontation. Most remain silent in order to avoid summonses or other problems. Lloyd Carew-Reid was more inclined to "confront" officers by asserting his rights, and one of his colleagues believes this is why officers were not inclined to make discretionary decisions in his favor.

Musicians rationalize their compliance in various ways, reflecting differences in their political status and survival strategies underground. MUNY members generally defer to officers and let the program administrators mediate, as they have been advised to do. Two veteran white musicians consider occasional tickets to be the "rent" for their use of subway space. Some hip hop drummers wait until officers who have told them to stop are out of the area, then they resume playing. For the most part, musicians play the cat-and-mouse game: when told to desist, they find another spot.

One story reveals the complexity of the musician-officer relationship. A veteran subway musician admits that he preferred the days when playing music was illegal underground and officers relied solely on their discretion to regulate subway space. He explains that after the right to perform in the subways was upheld in the courts and the TA and MTA authorized the activity, the number of freelancers steadily increased. Now others are playing in his favorite spots. Moreover, some of them either do not know the "unspoken law" or are too financially desperate to care about etiquette, and they set up on him. "I've been displaced," he laments. "I miss my old patrons."

Herein lie the limits of litigation. Court decisions can expand musicians' civil liberties, but they do not guarantee that musicians will act like a community. Nevertheless, court protection is an important first step; basic organizational mechanisms can then eliminate the need for musicians to ally with officers against other musicians or to wax nostalgic for the days when the authorities could deny their rights completely.

Contrary to official TA belief, the amplification ban is not being uniformly applied. Subway music, primarily freelance, is being regulated and eliminated by the transit police patrol strategy and by erroneous enforcement. Yet at the same time, some officers are using their discretion to allow the music to continue, not only because they tolerate or enjoy it but because they see the ways in which it improves interactions in subway space. The next chapter considers the officer-musician relationship within the broader web of the subways' informal social network.

8

Music on the Job: Subway Workers

The subways serve as the work setting for a considerable number of people. In addition to musicians and the transit police, TA station managers and lower-level employees establish a regular presence in subway space, as do concession stand workers who lease property from the MTA. (Panhandlers, itinerant vendors, homeless advocates, and representatives of religious groups and charitable organizations are not discussed directly in this chapter but might also be considered regular subway workers.)

During interviews and in survey responses, members of these groups indicated that they were very aware of the presence of musicians underground. Their reactions varied according to their personal tastes, their opinions on the appropriate use of subway space, and their power relative to that of the musicians. Station managers, for instance, are responsible for monitoring rule enforcement in the stations under their charge. This chapter begins with interviews I conducted with the managers in three of the busiest stations, revealing the various ways in which they attempt both to abide by TA regulations and to accommodate musicians.

Next, I present the results of the survey I distributed in December 1993 to station supervisors, platform conductors, assistant train dispatchers, and hourly employees. In 1989 the TA cited employee complaints when it proposed new rules and the MTA did the same when it adopted the rules banning amplification devices from subway platforms. According to my survey results, employees continue to have complaints about the music, which suggests that the rules, or at least enforcement practices, are not addressing their concerns. My respondents also expressed considerable support for musicians, however, and recognized the music's positive effects on some "customers."

This chapter concludes with profiles of five concession stand workers in various multicomplex stations, based on interviews I conducted with them in the winter of 1993. Their responses reveal how they negotiate and share subway space with musicians. Some of their strategies are negative and raise questions about the role of race and class in the subway music scene, which will be addressed further in the concluding chapter. But most of the strategies are very creative, challenging the assumption that significant and enduring social relationships cannot, or do not already, exist in the subways.

Station Managers

As president of the TA, Alan Kiepper has advanced a public relations strategy similar to the MTA's. He has shifted the focus at the TA to improving the subways' image through aesthetics (the "Poetry in Motion" billboards inside train cars were Kiepper's own idea) and customer service. Thus, in 1990 Kiepper introduced the station manager program, expanding it from a station superintendent program that his predecessor, David Gunn, had begun in 1985 when the Stations Department was reorganized. Station managers oversee fewer stations than superintendents did and thus maintain greater control of their areas. By 1994, fifty managers were handling two hundred stations.

Station managers have two principal spheres of responsibility. They are in charge of maintaining the physical condition of their stations, monitoring cleaning operations and arranging any necessary repairs. They are also expected to answer riders' questions and help them navigate the system. Station managers are generally longtime TA employees who have risen through the ranks. They must be exceptionally dedicated, for they work ten- to twelve-hour days (without overtime pay) and are on call around the clock. Because their photographs and office telephone numbers are prominently posted in their stations, they are some of the most visible public figures in the subways. In terms of public relations, the station manager program seems to be very successful. In fact, in 1993 the TA received an award from the Ford Foundation for this innovation in public management.

But the program does not benefit subway musicians. A number of station managers are misinformed about the regulations authorizing acoustic music on platforms and acoustic or amplified music, MUNY or freelance, on mezzanines, and those who have asked for clarification have discovered that their superiors are also uncertain. At worst, station managers believe that only MUNY members have a right to perform in the subways; at best, they think the TA rules are simply guidelines for their own discretionary decisions about the musicians who perform in their stations.

To the extent that they know them, station managers strongly support the official performance frames. Yet, they also recognize the musicians' needs, and they appreciate the music's positive effects on the subway environment. Consequently, when they implement the rules they tend either to deny or to compromise their own insights. Two of the managers I interviewed indicated that they consider this process reasonable, but a third described the frustration awaiting a middle manager who tries to regulate subway music on such ambiguous terms.

I conducted interviews with three station managers. One was Dennis Cherry, who oversees several elevated platforms, local subway stops, and the Roosevelt Avenue–Jackson Heights station in Queens. The others were Robert Gorvetzian in Grand Central Station and Jerry Owens, who manages the 42nd Street and Eighth Avenue (Port Authority) station as well as the local 50th Street stop on the Eighth Avenue line. Cherry worked as a typist, railroad (token booth) clerk, and station supervisor before he became the first manager of his stations. Gorvetzian began ten years ago as a railroad clerk, was subsequently promoted to station supervisor, then worked as manager of the 14th Street and Seventh Avenue stop, after which he assumed the same position in Grand Central Station. Like his two colleagues, Owens was a station supervisor until he was promoted to station manager in the summer of 1993.

All three managers explain that they are responsible for maintaining the "quality of life" in their stations, which they do by taking care of the physical environment and addressing customer concerns. Each one, however, describes challenges particular to his stations. Cherry is determined to eliminate graffiti from his elevated platforms through the TA Graffiti Free program, which fights taggers in much the same way as the transit police battles other rule violators.[1] Gorvetzian is collaborating with community service workers to implement the latest

TA antipanhandling campaign. Owens makes sure that his 42nd Street station is clean and has adequate lighting and signage and that the employees use their "customer service skills." He wants to change the reputation the station has developed because of its proximity to the lively, chaotic Times Square area.

On the topic of subway music, Cherry says that only MUNY members are allowed to play in his multicomplex station. If they do not display their banner, he asks to see their permit. If they have no permit—if they are freelancers—he considers their performance "illegal" and does not allow them to stay. Cherry also reports that he cannot accommodate platform musicians. Unlike midtown Manhattan stations in the city's commercial center, Roosevelt Avenue is located in a neighborhood where people both work and live. Consequently, the station experiences "rush hour all day" and Cherry believes that platform musicians impede traffic flow.

There are two MUNY spots in Grand Central Station. One is at the foot of the 42nd Street shuttle, and the other is at the opposite end of the shuttle passageway, where riders transfer to East Side trains or exit through Grand Central Terminal. In addition, freelancers regularly perform in the middle of the passageway, right by the door of Gorvetzian's office.

According to Gorvetzian, TA rules prohibit the use of amplification, even by MUNY musicians. He is aware that some MUNY members use amps, but he is "not strict." He simply asks them to "tone down" in order that riders can hear the public address announcements.

In late 1993 Gorvetzian attended a meeting about the MUNY program. He and other station managers asked about the legal status of freelancers (because the issue was not raised during the formal presentation). MUNY administrators explained that music is a "form of art" and that it would not be consistent with transit policy to automatically "throw them off the stations." Consequently, Gorvetzian allows freelancers to perform on mezzanines during nonrush hours, provided they are not amplified and they are not blocking traffic. He says that freelancers are not allowed on platforms at Grand Central Station. These platforms, he explains, are constantly crowded and "people tend to congregate" around the musicians, producing unsafe conditions. Gorvetzian realizes that platforms may be more lucrative spots, but he concludes that in this case what is "common sense" for the musicians is "not best for the TA."

Owens believes that only MUNY members are authorized to perform. "Anyone else is not allowed," he says, "regardless of the instrument they're playing." On his own initiative, Owens asked his department for the subway music "guidelines," and he asked MUNY administrators for the "guidelines and policy of their organization" because he wanted to know the conditions under which he could ask for police assistance in regulating the music. Yet he found that the TA policy is "somewhat vague" and subject to individual interpretation. For instance, some sources told him that amplification is "fine," but others said "definitely not on platforms." Owens is most concerned about the mezzanine at the mouth of the passageway connecting his area to the Times Square station. "If the music is good," he observes, "quite a few people stop," causing traffic congestion. By contrast, platform musicians have not caused problems, which is why Owens concludes, "I guess I will allow them to continue."

Station managers can advise musicians to move or to leave. Otherwise they have no power to actually enforce the rules. Rather, they serve as "another pair of eyes" for the transit police. In Cherry's view, enforcement of subway music regulations is a simple matter. If musicians do not have a MUNY permit and do not follow his instructions, he calls an officer over to "evict" them. Occasionally, musicians have protested or pleaded with Cherry to let them stay and he has responded: "I understand that, but in the meantime you need to get in contact with the [MUNY] program." Until we spoke, apparently, he was not aware of MUNY's bureaucratic limits. He had heard about a court case involving freelancers, but he had not sought out the decision and the TA had never furnished it. Indeed, relatively little music is played in his multicomplex station, and excessively strict enforcement is one of the reasons. Anthology, for instance, stopped freelancing there in 1991 and did not try again until 1993.

When musicians perform on a platform at Grand Central Station, Gorvetzian asks them to move. "I'm just telling you what the rules are here," he says to them, "and right now you're disobeying them." Only when they disregard his instructions does the situation become a "police matter." Gorvetzian says that problems occur very rarely. Once, for instance, freelance Andean musicians were playing on one of the IRT platforms, not realizing that their sound was rising and interfering with the token booth clerks' work. Gorvetzian told them to move up to the MUNY spot on the mezzanine. "If you explain to them the reason why," he says, "and maybe offer them an alternate, that's fine. It's communication."

The situation confronting Owens is somewhat different. His wide mezzanine is frequently used by groups that play drums or otherwise perform at high volume levels, attracting large audiences. During our interview I noted that in recent months freelance Andean groups had been playing in that spot every day. I commended Owens for accommodating them at a time when other stations seemed to be restricting freelancers. But his response painted a picture of enforcement practices that differed significantly from the accounts provided by musicians:

> There is one group that spends quite a few hours on the station. It's pretty much like an eight-hour job. And I'm really not accommodating of them. I've tried to have them removed by the police, and it seems these police officers, they are quoting [musicians'] First Amendment rights. And they [the musicians] come back. The idea is to try to make this station hostile to them. . . . I've asked them a couple of times to see their permit, and they've said, "Well, I left it at home." I said, "The next time either you have to have it, or you can't play." The police officer there didn't want to bother them. Since they had amplification, he should at least—the amplification should have been cut off. . . . So now they feel they have a place they can play without being harassed. I like their music. One of the clerks complained that she couldn't hear the customers. The music has a very loud tone to it.

Similar accounts from this and other sources indicate that some officers hesitate to enforce the subway music regulations for fear they might be sued for civil liberties violations. By default, they become allies of the musicians. This tentative truce is actually the result of misinformation. Two groups—officers and musicians—are protecting themselves against ambiguous regulations. Meanwhile the station manager, also misinformed, is left frustrated.

Some officers may be invoking constitutional law because they prefer not to look like the "heavy" or because they enjoy the music. Indeed, Owens describes another situation in which he felt that an audience was clearly causing congestion in his area, yet he found two officers standing by and enjoying the performance. In rare instances Owens has had to ask his supervisor to call the transit police district command, which has ordered the officers to move or eject the musicians regardless of personal feelings.

Although Cherry may make his multicomplex station inhospitable to many musicians, he recognizes the benefits offered by the music. He is pleased when "different musicians come" to his station, where "every color and stripe" passes through. "They are able to touch all cultures," he says. Cherry may be too busy to stop and enjoy the music, but he has noticed its calming effects. "What do they say—music soothes the beast?" He believes it creates a sense of community. "It's bringing people together, and they're communicating. . . . People relate to music. It's a thing of togetherness." Moreover, although he approves of the way in which MUNY controls subway music, he feels less of a need to ask for MUNY members' permits once their faces become familiar to him. Finally, Cherry says that if his boss were to tell him that subway music is to be allowed "all over," he would accommodate it.

Gorvetzian says that subway music can "get you in a good mood." He personally loves the saxophone players in his passageway and the a capella MUNY group called Solo. He volunteers that musicians make the station safer. "The more people are around, the safer it is." In fact, he believes subway music prevents "vicious bodily crimes," and he has never heard of pickpocketing occurring in audience circles. He thinks the music creates a sense of community, defined in terms of focused interaction. "People are interacting. That's the way it's supposed to be, instead of everybody's at each other's throats."

Gorvetzian has positive interactions with musicians, most often with freelancers. He has learned the informal schedule in his passageway and has talked with both the flutist, who plays from ten o'clock until noon, and the saxophone player (Sam Brown) who follows. He has asked, "Why are you over here?" and they have explained that they make "decent money" in that spot. He has also asked the flutist, who plays one song over and over, to "change his tune," although Gorvetzian has found that "working down here, you sort of tune things out after a while." In turn, the flutist has told Gorvetzian that he is "the best station manager I've ever seen!" Gorvetzian reports that he does not feel conflict when his personal insights differ from the regulations. "I can get in trouble for not following what's set down here," he explains. But he adds, "You can bend a little."

Owens remarks that most of the music in his 42nd Street station is very good. He prefers some of the MUNY jazz ensembles because they create an air of "sophistication" and improve public perception of the station. By contrast, he feels that some of the freelancers, such as breakdancers, make the area feel busy and out of control, although he has seen some MUNY groups produce these effects as well. As for his personal tastes, Owens especially likes the Andean musicians even though he knows they are not all part of MUNY. He has dropped dollars in their cases, bought their cassettes, asked them, "Is this just a stepping stone?" and "wished them the best." He understands that this is how they earn their living. Thus he occasionally experiences a conflict. He likes the music but "it gets to the point where they're here quite a few hours. . . . You have to enforce the rules." He feels that the riders who stand around the Andean groups block traffic and inconvenience the majority. Ultimately, he agrees that "a little music is worth the crowd . . . to a point."

TA Employees

They count and dispense tokens eight and a half hours a day. They disinfect stations, clearing out urine, feces, vomit, hypodermic needles, and trash. They announce incoming trains and herd riders into cars. They monitor subway schedules and make sure that conductors report to work. They oversee the hourly employees and fill in for the station managers. And they all answer riders' questions. They are the railroad (token booth) clerks, cleaners, platform conductors (or passenger controllers), train dispatchers, and station supervisors. Their schedules are demanding and their jobs are in some respects tedious, but they are hardly fazed by the unexpected. For instance, one morning I was administering a survey to a platform conductor who was suddenly called away because a rider had fallen down a staircase and was bleeding from his head.

In the winter of 1993 I conducted a survey of thirty TA employees. My sample consisted of thirteen token booth clerks, seven platform conductors, five cleaners, four station supervisors, and one assistant dispatcher. There were approximately twice as many men as women among the respondents, and half identified themselves as African American or black, consistent with Jim Dwyer's report that 42 percent of the city's 51,000 transit workers are African American.[2]

Seventeen respondents reported hearing subway music almost every day. The majority hear it in the afternoons and evenings. When asked what they like about the music, employees responded in much the same way as those who had completed my rider survey. Over one-third (twelve) described the music's positive emotional effects, including its ability to reduce stress, to provide diversion or entertainment, and to improve mood. Seven preferred music that accorded with their personal tastes. Significantly, five approved of the music because they had noticed that it improves riders' experience of the subways. Two expressed neutrality, and one disliked it. Among their responses were the following:

> "Calms the atmosphere down some."
>
> "They're entertaining while waiting for a train. And if it's really good I'll miss a train or two."
>
> "Some sound very nice. The courage to comment and sing is something special."
>
> "I like the sound of music in the subways because it seems to calm the passengers."
>
> "I pay it no mind."

Almost half the respondents (thirteen) indicated that they dislike the music when it is too loud. The next largest cluster, close to one-third of the sample (nine), offered no negative comment. Four asserted that musicians obstruct traffic. Three disapproved of the music because it did not suit their tastes. These were some of the responses:

> "They sometimes play too loud and in combination with other noises can be very annoying."
>
> "Not during rush hours! It's hard to hear!"
>
> "There's enough noise already. It draws crowds—prevents passengers from moving freely and prevents you from hearing announcements."
>
> "Only a few of them are talented. Most of them just annoy the passengers and employees."
>
> "There's nothing not to like! Very fascinating."

Eleven respondents had talked to subway musicians. Over two-thirds of these (eight) had offered positive feedback. The same proportion had asked to see the musicians' MUNY permits or had told them to move. Almost two-thirds of the entire sample (nineteen) reported donating to musicians. Of these, most (thirteen) had based their decision on personal taste, but over one-third (seven) had also donated because "the musicians looked like they needed the money."

Over one-third (eleven) of all my respondents indicated a preference for jazz groups, although, like my sample of subway riders, some enjoyed a combination of styles, such as "rhythm and blues, jazz, rock," or "classical and contemporary," or "jazz, gospel, steel drummers, a capella singers, South Americans, classical, folk-rock." Only ten of these employees said they knew what Music Under New York was, and of that portion half either did not explain what it was or thought it referred to New York subway musicians in general.

Respondents were given a list of statements with which to agree or disagree. Twenty-six out of thirty had heard some very talented musicians in the subways. Twenty-three had seen riders enjoying subway music. The same number had found some music too loud. Nineteen agreed that musicians make the subways more pleasant, and the same number had been exposed to music in the subways which they had not heard previously. Subway music had triggered memories for over half (seventeen) of the respondents. Eleven reported that some subway music had interfered with their job. Almost the same number (ten) agreed that musicians make the subways feel safer. Eight affirmed the right to make music in the subways even if they disliked what was being performed. Five respondents preferred MUNY members to freelancers. Four confirmed that some musicians leave litter behind them. Two felt that only MUNY members should be allowed to play. Some of those who disagreed commented: "Wouldn't be fair" and "Everybody should play." Almost two-thirds of the respondents (nineteen) would like the TA to eliminate homeless people from the subways. Almost one-third (nine) would support the same policy toward itinerant vendors, and a few (three) would also part with subway musicians. These responses actually seemed to reflect a range of political views. For instance, one employee commented: "If you get rid of the homeless, you've got to get rid of all [three groups]. They all have the same rights."

A full three-quarters of this sample (twenty-two) agreed that subway music creates a sense of community. Respondents provided their own qualifications and elaborations. "In a loose sense," one said. Another commented: "People gather around and start talking. They get friendly. It takes a lot of the edge off the hustling and bustling of New York City."

When asked to explain the TA regulations on subway music, one-third of the respondents either had no comment or admitted that they did not know the rules. The same proportion believed that MUNY members alone may legally perform. Six made comments about restrictions on volume, crowding, or soliciting donations. Two asserted that subway music is simply not allowed, and two stated that there essentially are no regulations. These were some of the responses:

> "They are not allowed unless they have a permit."
>
> "Music is not supposed to be played in the subways unless in the designated areas."
>
> "Besides MUNY technically they're not supposed to ask for money."
>
> "No amplifiers. [But] expressing yourself is a basic human right."
>
> "It's not permissible unless the source (personal) is connected to a headphone."
>
> "They change with pressure."
>
> "There are no rules, to my knowledge."

Respondents were asked whether time-place-manner restrictions were necessary and, if so, how they would design them. With respect to time, over half (seventeen) would permit musical performances in the afternoons only or in combination with other times of day. Seven would defer to the TA. Three would leave the decision to the musicians.

Nineteen respondents would allow musicians to play only on mezzanines or in combination with platforms or passageways. One-third would defer to the TA on appropriate spots, although many of these respondents were the ones who also offered their own opinions.

In this survey, "manner" was defined as volume level. Just over one-third of the sample (eleven) preferred to leave the TA in charge of establishing a decibel ceiling, although some of these same respondents said "it depends on the music" or "the way they play now is fine" or the music needed to be "softer" than it is now. One-third responded that appropriate volume depends on musical style. Five said that "now is fine."

One question described the ban on amplified music on the platforms, specifying the initial fine (at least fifty dollars) and the fact that nonamplified musicians are authorized to stay. Two-thirds of the sample (twenty) considered the amp ban unfair or misguided. Under one-quarter (seven) found it acceptable. Their assessments included the following:

> "Good rule! Except when the drummers are playing too loud, but it is still a natural sound."
>
> "On the surface, unfair. But controllable."
>
> "Some drummers and trumpet players are worse than the ones using amplifiers."
>
> "I think everyone needs to be fined. Don't just penalize one without punishing the other."
>
> "Needs to be reviewed."
>
> "Unfair."

Respondents were asked to comment, using their own observations, on transit police officers' treatment of subway musicians. One-third expressed approval. Six stated that officers do not bother musicians but did not indicate whether or not they considered that to be a good enforcement practice. Five were more clearly critical, paralleling station manager Owens's report that officers tend not to enforce the regulations on their own initiative and are reluctant to be seen as the "heavy." These were some of the responses:

> "Friendly."
>
> "If too loud, ask to leave. If not in designated areas, ask to leave the system."
>
> "Some enjoy it, some don't, depending on the music."
>
> "The same way they relate to anything else in the system: if you complain they tell the person you're complaining about that. They don't care, but someone else does."

Fewer respondents had observed any interaction between musicians and station managers. Fifteen reported that it is positive or that managers regulate the music effectively. One remarked that the relationship depends on the managers' musical tastes.

> "Very good relationship."
>
> "They really don't get involved—unless [the music] creates a crowd. . . . They tell the police . . . if it interferes with service."
>
> "Biased in the same way as transit police."

Finally, respondents were asked who, ideally, should formulate the subway music regulations. Eighteen indicated that TA employees should be involved, and an even greater proportion (twenty) believed that subway riders should have a say. Exactly half would include the transit police, and almost half (fourteen) would invite TA officials. Just over one-quarter of this sample thought that MTA executives and musicians should have a voice in the process.

A few employees offered final comments:

> "In the passageway [next to] where I work, sometimes there are four musicians all playing different music at the same time and arguing for spots. Grand Central is another station with plenty of musicians. The larger the station the more noise. If you let musicians play, you must let homeless sleep, etc. You must let vendors do their things and so on and so on."
>
> "Subway musicians can be entertaining after a tough day at work. They can also cause serious traffic problems on the platforms. So I guess they have good points as well as bad."
>
> "Riders are not too adversely affected by the current situation. There are certain types [of music] for certain types [of people]. Some ignore it, and some respond. We can't please everybody because sometimes the music is extremely disruptive. Loud music affects clerks working in the booths and passengers trying to hear messages. You have to draw the line."
>
> "I hope one day they make it, get something out of it. Get discovered. So many different cultures."

Concession Stand Workers

Record Mart, Times Square BMT Mezzanine: Luc

The Record Mart has been a permanent fixture on the Times Square BMT mezzanine, one short staircase below the shuttle area, for the last thirty-five years. Under old yellow signage, a sliver of space features rows of obscure album covers, mainly of Latino artists, whose contents are broadcast seven days a week on the store's stereo. Hidden from view is a much larger storage area, as well as owner Jesse Moskowitz's cramped office, which shakes every time a shuttle train enters or leaves the station. Moskowitz formerly ran a second outlet in a subway station on 14th Street, but when the MTA closed it down for renovation and offered it back at a higher rent, he decided to devote himself to the Times Square store.

Although he hardly appears old enough, Luc has been working with Moskowitz for twenty-three years. He knows a great deal about what goes on in his station, including subway music, which he hears daily. He observes that certain types of music are performed at certain times of day. Andean musicians play in the mornings, and breakdancers, jazz bands, and hip hop bucket drummers perform in the afternoons. He is not sure whether this schedule is the result of an informal agreement among performers, or whether "it just happens." Musicians perform on the mezzanines on his level and across from the shuttle. Spot selection, Luc reports, depends in part on "police action." If officers chase musicians off one mezzanine, they "move up or down." Luc calls this musician-officer interaction "mouse and cat."

Luc personally prefers the Andean groups, whose music he considers "quieter, smoother, nicer." He has noticed that some of them are MUNY members but that most are not. Then, in an about-face, Luc says he prefers the MUNY roster. He finds that they are more aware of "the law." They do not block staircases or play too loud. By contrast, the freelancers seem to him to hold the philosophy that "louder is better," that volume attracts larger audiences. In the end Luc concludes, "Any kind I like. As long as they're not too loud." It would be nice, he says, to hear Haitian music performed in the subways; Haiti is his country of origin.

Although Luc personally does not find subway music annoying, he says that it interferes with the Record Mart's business in two ways. First, when a group performs on the BMT mezzanine, its audience may impede the traffic flow from the BMT platforms. When that happens, Luc says, riders look for a detour and miss the store entirely. Second, loud music drowns out the recordings the Record Mart plays to attract customers. This second conflict is unique to a music concession and explains why Luc feels subway music is good "in stations with no record store." And yet it is not clear whether subway musicians compete with the Record Mart; at times they may actually help business. Luc reports that some Latin American riders have asked him whether he carries recordings of the Andean music played by the subway musicians in his station.

Lately, the Record Mart has been disturbed by loud musicians, bucket drummers in particular. Luc remarks, "After a while it sounds more like banging." Customers ask him, "How do you stand the noise?" The store calls the transit police to regulate the musicians' volume and crowds. But the police, Luc says, "don't worry about it at all. They don't want to come." When they do arrive, they tell him, "There's no problem. It's just people playing music." "What about the noise level," he asks, and the fact that the audience is "blocking passageways?" Ninety percent of the time, he says, the officers decide it is "not a problem." At that point, Luc explains, "we have to go higher." The store calls the district command, which instructs the officers to take action. Luc cannot understand why the officers "do not want to touch" the situation.

Luc has no complaints about the regulations themselves. If officers enforced them, he says, the music would not interfere with the store's business. If the musicians respected the decibel ceiling and the distance requirements, Luc believes, they would be "legal." He is not sure whether musicians are required to have a license. He has asked some of them, and they have answered: "We don't. We just have to watch out for police."

Luc indicates that an official schedule incorporating all musicians would minimize conflicts. Currently some groups compete for the Times Square spots by arguing, fighting, or setting up on the musicians who are already there. In spite of these problems, Luc affirms subway music: "It brings more life to the station."

Newsstand, Grand Central Station: Gayas Rathod

At one end of the "Number 7" platform, a concession stand selling reading material and candy is open daily from six o'clock in the morning until one o'clock the following morning. Gayas Rathod, an immigrant from India, has been the manager for the last seven years. He is a fairly young man with wide green eyes and a quick laugh.

Gayas hears subway music on his platform almost daily, in the afternoons and at night. He is not aware of any informal schedule; different people perform there each day. Gayas hears Spanish (Andean) music, drumming, guitar playing, and violins. Laughing, he reports that a homeless man also sings there. Personally, Gayas likes pop music. Sometimes he enjoys the South American musicians with their drums. "Not understand," he says, "but like it to hear." He says he would also like to hear music performed from his culture.

The only music that bothers him is the bucket drumming. Some customers suggest that he call the transit police to have the drummers removed. "How you standing every day here?" they ask him. He does not complain, partly for fear of retaliation. "I can't tell somebody angry, drug."

But in fact the volume of the music hardly interferes with Gayas's business. "*This* noise," he says, pointing to the train roaring into the station. Instead, he feels the musicians hurt his business at night by drawing riders away from his stand. "Stuck over there," he says, "don't spend money on candy." Gayas recognizes that the musicians make riders feel safer at times when the platform is fairly deserted: he explains that people do not like to stand by themselves. Similarly, he believes that he and his business partner give riders a sense of safety when musicians are not around.

Gayas says that he has "no business" with musicians, but they exchange greetings with him when they buy soda from his stand. In turn, sometimes Gayas walks over and asks them to change dollars for him from their donations.

Gayas does not see how the transit police could further control these musicians since officers spend limited time on the platform. Furthermore, he would not want them to increase their control. "No, no like. No money is why they play. If no job, how I feel? He needs money. Cold outside. Come down here."

Gayas has no personal interest in changing the subway music regulations. He is not easily disturbed by any activity on the platform. "Here same thing day, night, no difference." If he could change anything, he would ask some musicians to play closer to his stand. He thinks they would bring him more business.

George's Florist, Roosevelt Avenue Mezzanine

George has managed his flower stand for the last twenty years, keeping it open from 7:00 A.M. to 7:00 P.M. Monday through Saturday, and later when he has additional customers. Two young Mexican men, Miguel and Juan, assist him. George is a tall, serious man who at unexpected moments reveals his sense of humor. While he works he sometimes listens to Mediterranean music—a sign of his Greek heritage—at low volume on a tape recorder.

George very rarely hears subway music in his station. When he does, it is usually on Fridays after 3:00 P.M. and it is performed directly across from his stand. Much as he loves music, he would rather not have any performances on his mezzanine. The problem is not that the music interferes with his work. Rather, it is "the noise," he says. "It's too much. Try six hours here with no music, no noise, just the noise of the trains, and you'll understand." George concedes that "a half hour, an hour would be okay. Five hours is too much." If musicians played Mediterranean music, he says, "I could probably stand for a lot more." Similarly, Juan says that if the musicians played mariachi, a Mexican musical style, he would understand it and tolerate it better.

George thinks it is good that riders enjoy subway music, but their experience is significantly different from his; they hear it only briefly. He, too, might enjoy it "if I was passing by in another train station. I'd stop ten minutes and listen to it." He thinks the music makes riders feel better about the subways, but not necessarily safer. In his opinion, big crowds draw pickpockets and make the stations less safe, although he admits that he has never seen pickpocketing occur in a subway music audience. As for the effects on his business, George believes they are minimal. The music neither brings him nor disturbs his customers.

Many of George's comments about volume levels relate to a hip hop drummer named Tony Walls, better known as Tony Pots and Pans because he has created an entire drum set out of found metal objects. In 1993 the MUNY program added Tony to its roster, and one of his designated three-hour performance spots is the mezzanine at Roosevelt Avenue. "He's good. He's very good," George says. "But after a half hour, I could choke the guy. I could kill him. If I could have him here a half hour every day, I would. I would bring him here myself." Tony and George say hello to each other, and George has never said: "Hey, you bother me" to Tony. "Everybody's entitled to make a buck whenever he can," George says. "I don't think it's my place to tell him how or how not to play. If it bothers me, it's my problem. It's my choice to be here with the good or the bad, and it's his choice to do what he wants to do."

It is George's impression that all the musicians who play at Roosevelt Avenue have MUNY permits, although he does not know whether permits are required. He sees transit police officers allowing musicians to play and moving them only when they are blocking traffic. He has not seen anything "violent or rude" in musician-officer interactions, and he concludes that the transit police are doing a good job in regulating subway music.

If George could change the rules, he would limit performances to two or three hours. He is not aware that MUNY assigns spots for three-hour intervals; many Andean groups play on his mezzanine for four to seven hours at a time.

George would also limit the volume, although he does not see a way to change the decibel level of pots and pans. He mentions that the official MUNY spot in his station is located not directly across from him but farther down the mezzanine. If the musicians played in that spot, they would not sound as loud to him, and he might not need them to lower their volume. In that case, he says optimistically, he might even be able to listen to the music longer without developing a headache.

Newsstand, Grand Central Shuttle: Mohammed Shapon

In the passageway outside Station Manager Gorvetzian's office where freelance musicians perform, there is also a newsstand. Mohammed Shapon, a soft-spoken young man from Bangladesh, has worked there for twenty months. Prior to that he worked in Grand Central Station's other newsstand, which is owned by the same franchise. Mohammed's stand is open from 6:00 A.M. until midnight, Monday through Saturday. He himself works ten hours a day.

Mohammed hears subway music virtually all the time. He reports that it begins after eight in the morning and continues until six at night. In the passageway he hears flutists, saxophonists, and bucket drummers. Mohammed thinks the music is "terrible." It's "too much shout." He is put off by it, moreover, because he is not familiar with the musicians' repertoires. While working, he often listens to Bangladeshi music on a Walkman, which, he says, he would enjoy hearing performed by a subway musician.

The performers he truly enjoys are the young breakdancers who appear on the nearby mezzanine on Friday and Saturday evenings. Mohammed likes the fact that they are "physically working. Hard labor. Like circus. I like kids." The dancers buy batteries and candy from him. They show him when they make fifteen dollars in fifteen minutes. He says they speak nicely to him. In turn, he sometimes leaves his stand to give them a donation.

The flute and saxophone players bother Mohammed because they play the same pieces repeatedly for five or six hours. His customers offer sympathy: "The same thing every day?" He would be able to tolerate it better if they varied their repertoires: "Different gonna be nice."

Mohammed says that the bucket drummers' volume interferes with his work. He finds it hard to hear what his customers are requesting and he has "to talk with them shoutly." In general he feels that the passageway musicians have a negative effect on his business. He claims that riders run past his store, trying to distance themselves from the loud music. "After finish the work," he explains, "everybody's feeling tired," and additional sound bothers them.

On the other hand, Mohammed believes that musicians increase riders' sense of safety. When "somebody's here," they do not feel alone. The musicians do not make him feel safer, however. Since his stand is located in a wall of the passageway, they cannot see him when he is in trouble. He reports that the riders themselves have passed by without noticing that someone was in the process of stealing his goods.

According to Mohammed, the transit police never regulate subway musicians. "They don't bother them," he says. Once he spoke to two officers about a bucket drummer in the passageway. He complained that he was losing business because he could not hear his customers and asked the officers to move the musician. "I can't do that," they replied. Apparently the volume disturbed Mohammed personally because his solution to the situation was to use earplugs. "What can I do?" he asks. "That is [the musician's] business, this is my business. Never told little softer. Here is totally freedom—whatever they like, they can do. If he didn't think about me, I can't tell him nothing. He not listen to me."

If Mohammed could alter subway music, he would lower the volume, but he would not necessarily change the musicians' hours. His impression is that they schedule themselves well according to an informal agreement. If given the choice, though, he would prefer to have them play farther away from his stand. "Why not?" he smiles.

Flower Stand, Times Square Shuttle Mezzanine: Vula

To the side of the old concession gates, there is a small shed almost completely concealed by buckets of wrapped flowers. Inside, a diminutive Greek woman named Vula sits up against a shelf and arranges bouquets. During the winter Vula wears a bulky sweater and ties a scarf around her face. With her head tucked she looks a bit like a nesting bird. Every day, her son George works with her, and her daughter Angela arrives in the afternoons. A young black man named Elgin also helps her. Relatives and friends from home visit regularly and chat with Vula, although they generally have to shout to make themselves heard above the din of the trains and the volume of the music.

Vula has managed her flower stand for seventeen years. Her late husband began there twenty years ago. Until the mid-1980s, the shuttle mezzanine was busy with concessions, including Nedick's, coffee shops, and newsstands. The MTA shut them down as part of a collaborative effort to redevelop the Times Square area above and below ground. When the city's real estate market foundered, so did the project. To date the concessions remain filthy holes, occasionally revealed, behind blackened gates. When the stores were removed, musicians and breakdancers began to fill the empty mezzanine, and MUNY also designated it as one of the program's spots.

Vula, who works seven days a week, reports that musicians perform in the shuttle spot at all times of day, every day except Sunday. During our interview I asked Vula what she likes about the music. "Me no understand," she said. "Everything the same. No understand the music." She says, though, that she would enjoy a performance of Greek music underground.

The broad shuttle mezzanine is the chosen spot for young bucket drummers such as Larry Wright who come to play on most weekday afternoons. Vula finds the drumming, which she calls "ba ba boom," altogether too loud. Her children report that it interferes with business. They cannot hear their customers. George said that customers ask him: "How do you stand it with this noise?" I asked him what he replies. "Nothing—what can I say?" George mimed holding his ears until the drummers leave.

Angela said that the music occasionally brings them customers. Usually audience members come over only to ask for change, which they then donate to the musicians. Some buy flowers in order to receive change. Some buy flowers for the musicians.

I asked Vula what she thinks of the large audience circles that form around the musicians who perform on her mezzanine. "Nothing to do. Lazy. No work. Maybe like it, no like. Some people steal. Maybe small children, baby okay. Lot of people stand. I dunno."

Approximately eight years ago, when hip hoppers began to perform in the shuttle area, they did not speak to Vula. But within a month, they started to greet her: "Hi, Mama, how're you?" Today virtually all the subway musicians who play in that spot, freelancers and MUNY members, call Vula Mama or Mommy. During our interview, I asked her to explain the history of her name change. As is often their practice, a few bucket drummers were sitting to the side of Vula's shed, waiting for a saxophone player to finish. Vula called one of them over, a young man named JR, and asked him to answer my question. JR tentatively smiled. "We call her Mommy because, she like our mother down here. She tell us when the police come, which police is here, the good police, the bad police. . . . She get a lot of respect."

Once it had been revealed that Vula acts as the drummers' decoy, she proudly offered other examples of her positive interactions with musicians. The drummers introduce their friends to her and tell her about special events in their lives. They often deposit their money with her in the morning and return to collect it in the evening. Olmedini the subway magician arrives in the mornings with a bag, which he places in the refrigerator where Vula stores her flowers, and he picks it up at the end of the day. "Don't ask," Vula says. "No problem. I dunno. Trust."

The network extends even further. Customers call her Mama. Transit police officers call her Mama. "Everybody same, friend: black, white, crazy people. 'Mommy, need fifty cents for a coffee.' 'Okay, take fifty cents.' 'Mommy, need flowers free.' 'Okay, take it.'" Clearly this public trust is motivated to a considerable extent by the need for

Hip hop drummer JR plays plastic construction buckets and the metal gates over the old Times Square shuttle concession stands. Photo by Dennis Connors

self-preservation and as such it has its limitations. For instance, when Vula has a headache she falsely reports to the drummers that a tough officer is on duty. Her relationship with them does not allow her to communicate her needs directly. On the other hand, one could argue that people can only pull such pranks on each other once they have developed a certain degree of closeness.

Years ago, Vula used to approach drummers during their performances and ask them to move farther away or to draw their audience members in because they were brushing against and breaking her flowers. Some audience members made harsh remarks, calling her a racist for attempting to contain African American expression. But ironically, Angela says, the drummers heeded Vula's advice and found that they earned more money when riders stood closer to them. Since that period of negotiation, Vula has not been personally troubled by crowding.

Vula and her children have mixed feelings about the transit police's enforcement practices. Angela observed that some officers are "very strict" and eject musicians who have no MUNY permit. When these officers appear, the bucket drummers automatically stop playing. Other officers are "very soft" and let the musicians continue. Angela has decided that some officers are intimidated by the large audiences that "boo" them when they try to stop performances. George said that officers generally report to the musicians and the audience which concession worker has complained, as if to clear themselves of responsibility. George does not appreciate this practice; he calls it "unprofessional." It hurts business, and apparently it is one of the reasons that Vula no longer seeks police assistance in negotiating with musicians.

Angela and George believe that MUNY members are musicians who play at a moderate volume level. Yet, they expressed approval of the saxophone player who performed during our interview, not realizing that he was a freelancer. Moreover, they cannot understand how MUNY could have accepted Tony Walls when, in their judgment, he is much louder than Larry Wright, who freelances.

Angela has many ideas about how to improve the subway music scene at Times Square. She thinks the transit police should not rotate their officers every six months because it is familiarity with the area that enables them to regulate the space. She also thinks that "the people who run the music program" should develop a survey in order to collect station managers' and concession stand workers' opinions and recommendations.

In the early 1990s the TA Station Design Department developed an interim plan for renovating the Times Square station. Escalators and ramps are to be installed in compliance with the Americans with Disabilities Act, and lighting and communications systems will be upgraded. Meanwhile, according to a TA source, the MTA Real Estate Department will "relocate" Vula's stand as well as the Record Mart. The reason? Public safety. Both obstruct traffic, and worse, both are "visual impediments," interfering with transit police surveillance of deserted areas. Neither the TA nor the MTA plans to conduct a survey like the one Angela suggested or to otherwise look into what Vula and her stand mean to people who frequent the Times Square station. They will uproot Mama, never learning that she helps to regulate subway music or that her flower stand is one of the few familiar, safe places in the subways that people virtually call home.

9

Prospects for Change

When I ask New York subway musicians if they have ever considered organizing politically to improve the conditions under which they perform, I receive a number of different responses. Some laugh and advise me that art transcends politics. A few have no desire to put energy into helping their colleagues advance their careers. Others explain, almost tragically, that they have to devote their time to staying one step ahead of the police. Some freelancers say they come underground to escape the demands of organizations; in their opinion, subway music should remain ad hoc and independent.

I find it especially tough to challenge this last view. On the other hand, when musicians lament that they are not in MUNY and look astonished when I inform them of the rights they already have as freelancers, I worry about the status quo. At such moments I am reminded of the distinction Paul Chevigny makes between litigation and politics. "An action by a court is effective," he says, "only when the parties accept the action and change their behavior in response to it."[1] In the 1980s musicians proved that, in crisis situations, they were capable of banding together to change their legal status underground, but they did not sustain an organization to inform all musicians of their rights and responsibilities. Periodically, however, individual performers appear on the scene who successfully organize their colleagues. In this chapter I describe the Street Artists' Guild in Boston and Cambridge, Massachusetts, which has operated for almost a quarter century, and the United Street Artists, which has recently called particular attention to the interests of hip hoppers in New York. Next I recommend how, with relatively little effort, New York subway musicians could collectively transform the politics of subway space. I conclude by reflecting on the ways in which, as individual artists, they transform it already.

The survival of the Street Artists' Guild is largely due to the commitment of its founder, Stephen Baird, often called the "dean" of street performing. Baird has been organizing his colleagues for over two decades, and he spends his winters researching the history of his calling. In 1972, motivated by his experiences in the antiwar movement, he dropped out of chemical engineering school at Northeastern University and took up singing in the streets of Boston. When police officers ticketed him and threatened him with arrest, Baird tracked down his city's street music ordinance and discovered it had not been revised since the 1870s. It contained antiquated restrictions, requiring women who performed, for instance, to be accompanied by men. With the help of a public attorney and the American Civil Liberties Union, Baird pressured the city of Boston to legalize street music and to implement a nonselective permit system.[2]

Together with the handful of performers working on Boston streets at the time, Baird formed the Street Artists' Cooperative, which later became the Street Artists' Guild. The guild publishes a newsletter, which informs street performers across the nation about recent court decisions that might affect them and about street festivals around the world. Locally, the guild is a self-help organization whose members convene meetings when government threatens to restrict or eliminate their performance spaces. A crisis of this sort led to the formation of a subgroup called the Subway Artists' Guild.

In 1986 the Massachusetts Bay Transportation Authority discontinued the Music Under Boston program, which had scheduled selected musicians, including those who used amplifiers, to play in designated spots on subway platforms.[3] According to Stephen Baird, musicians continued to freelance in various stations with no regulation and no problems until subway police began to eject them on the basis of a catch-22. Officers claimed that a permit was needed when in fact no permit system existed. Police harassment was at times quite severe; some officers demanded payoffs from musicians in exchange for the opportunity to perform.

The Subway Artists' Guild wanted to work out an agreement with the MBTA to allow musicians to perform, subject only to time-place-manner restrictions, but officials canceled many appointments. Finally, the guild enlisted the support of a state senator and a civil liberties attorney. Threatened with litigation, the MBTA agreed to meet.

At the meeting, the musicians presented a document outlining how they would perform underground. They would use amplification devices and keep their volume at an unspecified, reasonable level. They would sell recordings of their own music. They would apply for performance licenses from the MBTA. (Some musicians disapproved of this level of bureaucracy, but Baird believed it would train officers not to harass musicians.) Above all, musicians would abide by a self-imposed scheduling system. While planning for this meeting, the musicians had realized that, in Baird's words, "there's different needs for different artists." They had decided to allocate time slots in the most popular stations by holding daily coin tosses; to post sign-up sheets at a second cluster of stations; and to regulate a third cluster through an informal "first-come, first-serve" policy. The MBTA accepted the document (although the guild is still waiting for an official signature), and the musicians have generally abided by its terms.

Like their counterparts in other cities, guild members tend to be reluctant to put time into organizing. Baird encourages them to become "political animals" so that "the political power is there when you need it." For instance, in the winter of 1986 the MBTA unexpectedly began broadcasting Christmas carols on subway platforms. The musicians contacted a state senator whose reelection campaign they had worked on, and he pressured transit officials to turn off the music. Subsequently Baird received a letter from then-governor Michael Dukakis apologizing for any inconvenience the recorded music might have caused the guild's members at a time of year that was financially critical to them. Another crisis began in 1992 when the MBTA unveiled its plan to install 145 television monitors with audio components on station platforms. These "T-TVs," as they were dubbed, threatened to drown out subway music.[4] The guild moved into action. Members made their position known to the MBTA, arranged strategy meetings, spoke to the news media, and asked their audiences to sign petitions opposing the plan. Since then the MBTA has assured them that the monitors will remain silent (although Baird still regrets that the corporate-sponsored visual images will monopolize a public forum). Political organizing involves considerable work, but for the guild's street performers and subway musicians it has proven effective.

The Street Artists' Guild defines its politics not only in terms of its confrontations with government agencies but also in terms of its relationships with audience members and local establishments. Thus, some of its actions actually restrict performances. In 1987, for instance, while demanding their rights in the subways, guild members were also holding meetings to address problems with the street performing scene in Harvard Square.[5] Some musicians were using large amplifiers powered by car batteries, which greatly increased their volume and drowned out other performers. In response to neighborhood complaints, local police were cracking down on all performers, amplified and acoustic. The guild approached a Cambridge council member, Baird says, who helped pass ordinances authorizing the use of amplification and also establishing a decibel ceiling for the square. The guild resolved to censure uncooperative musicians by distributing protest cards among their audiences. And it reasserted its expectation that local police would support street performers' efforts to regulate themselves.

The guild establishes links within various social and cultural networks. Members perform at local benefits and organize street festivals with social service agencies. Representing the guild and his other organization, the Folk Arts Network, Baird helps to open coffeehouses and applies for grants to support interns at a local college radio station. He explains that these sorts of interactions benefit guild members, winning them allies in crisis situations and providing them with access to other venues. (Coffeehouse managers love them because they bring their street and subway audiences with them.) In turn, networking radicalizes Boston's established arts community by putting it in contact with the street.

There is, nevertheless, a difference of opinion on whether street and subway performers should organize politically. Sally Harrison-Pepper contends that Boston's street performers have lost their spontaneity because they enjoy local government sanction. "Without licenses," she says, "the courage to perform must be recreated daily,"[6] and she prefers that test of commitment. But the atmosphere of a street or subway performing scene is also shaped by the character of a city and its performance spaces. Boston and Cambridge, for instance, are well known for their folk music scenes and college campuses. Thus, over the years, Stephen Baird has been able to distribute instruments and puppets among students in Harvard Yard and present an elaborate show. Indeed, a licensing system may not be the organizational mechanism of choice in every city. But surely even the veteran New York subway musician who missed the days when subway music was banned entirely and he did not have to compete with inconsiderate colleagues for performance spots would agree: there is nothing romantic about police harassment.

Police harassment is one of the main reasons that Robert Turley founded the United Street Artists, also known by its patriotic acronym, USA. Before arriving in New York in 1988, Turley had lived in Detroit and Las Vegas, where he had played funk music on electric bass in nightclubs and casinos. In 1990 he launched his musical career in New York by performing in the streets. On his first day out, he met hip hop drummers and breakdance troupes. Turley, who is white, was familiar with hip hop from the predominantly African American neighborhood in Detroit where he was raised. He began to share spots with these performers and later formed a duo with a drummer named Tyrone Hamlette, better known as Lock. They call themselves "RobOnBass" and "LockOnDrums."

In time, Turley learned that a number of hip hop street performers were abandoning their calling and turning to drug dealing. Money, they explained, was not the only incentive; they also found that police harassed them less as drug dealers than as street performers. Turley tried to persuade one of these friends, who went by the name of Professor Pop, to return to performing, but in late 1992 Pop was killed in a drug-related incident. Determined not to allow Pop's death to pass without notice, Turley contacted Lou Young of *NBC News*, who then produced a local segment on street performers and police harassment. Producers of the *Phil Donahue Show* saw Turley on the segment and invited him to appear on their December 30th program devoted to street performing. Some of Turley's colleagues met in his home to watch the program, and that night the USA was founded. In 1993 the USA held bimonthly meetings in a West Side church to discuss problems, goals, and organizing strategies.

From the outset, the USA articulated issues of race and class relevant to street and subway performance in New York. One of its primary goals is to encourage young people from disadvantaged neighborhoods to consider street performing both as a social outlet and as an economic opportunity at a time when few other real jobs are available to them.

The USA's second main objective is to fight the police harassment that affects all street and subway performers. Yet, in an informal inter-

Robert Turley, founder of the United Street Artists ("USA"), plays TrebleBass accompanied by his partner, Lock, at the Times Square shuttle spot. Photo by Dennis Connors

view Turely described incidents that suggest government and private interests are cracking down with particular force on hip hoppers. In the winter of 1993, for example, a breakdance troupe set up outside of Bergdorf Goodman, an elegant clothing store in Manhattan's "gilt-edged" commercial district, in the same spot where Christmas carolers had been welcomed. Police told the dancers that the store's management "doesn't want you here." Street robot dancer Mega Flash Martinez was also arrested for performing on Fifth Avenue. According to Martinez's report, police officers threw him against a store window with such force that the glass shattered, then they detained him in jail for two days. They charged him with kicking the window himself, but an eye witness corroborates Martinez's account.

Hip hoppers are also constrained in the subways. Plastic bucket drummers and breakdancers are issued summonses for "obstructing traffic" and "disorderly conduct" in situations where the validity of the charges is debatable. One bucket drummer reports that a police officer ordered him to stop because he was not playing an instrument. Clearly the officer was not aware that other instruments have similar origins. Steel pans, for instance, were created in the Caribbean out of oil drums imported from the United States.

Turley reports that the MUNY program did not accept him because his music was not "suitable for the subways" and that MUNY administrators told Ayan Williams's Float Committee street dance troupe not to bother auditioning. According to the USA's accounts, private directives and public policy in New York have encoded particularly negative social attitudes toward street and subway performers who represent the cultural expressions associated with the black underclass.

As early as 1990 Turley became politically active, looking for channels through which to change street performing regulations in New York. He wrote letters to then-mayor David Dinkins proposing a nonselective permit system. Together with Art Eisenberg, legal director of the New York Civil Liberties Union, he met with attorneys at the Department of Parks and Recreation and proposed revisions to its permitting requirements. He spoke with the Consumer Affairs Committee of the city council and was invited to draft a new street performing ordinance. He never did, and judging from the council's handling of the cabaret laws, a single street performer might wait years before action was taken on such a proposal. Finally in 1993, with the help of his counsel, Robert T. Perry, Turley filed a lawsuit in federal district court challenging the constitutionality of the street performing policies and enforcement practices of the police and parks departments (see Appendix 2). He is suing for one million dollars in actual and punitive damages.

Turley believes that the USA represents the interests of all New York City street and subway performers. Yet at the meetings I attended, the participants were mainly young African American and Latino men who had joined together to defend their rights. Another indication that the USA represents particular interests is that some of the street performers and subway musicians interviewed for this book were skeptical of the USA's motives.

Like the musicians in Harvard Square, Turley and other USA members use amplifiers and speakers powered by car batteries, which are much larger than the Maxi Mouse amps that most street and subway musicians use. Turley explains that the Mouse distorts the low frequencies of the unusual instrument he now plays, called a TrebleBass, and that his speaker produces a better-quality sound. It is the "creative choice" argument from the *Carew-Reid* case with a new twist. Some of my sources report, however, that Turley and other colleagues use their large speakers quite simply to increase their volume and drown out the "competition." Turley, a very articulate person, says he is willing to work out conflicts with fellow performers. My other sources say that they have tried and have been met with aggression. For these reasons some street performers and subway musicians wonder whether the USA is not simply attempting to expand its members' freedoms at the expense of others'.

Robert Turley may very well remove these doubts. The presiding judge in his case assigned him the task of providing the court with model street performing regulations. Thus Turley can begin the process of combining litigation on constitutional rights with a discussion of collective responsibilities in public space.

Allies can also help improve the politics of street and subway performance. In 1992 Steve Zeitlin, executive director of City Lore: The Center for Urban Folk Culture, and I began the Street Performers' Advocacy Project. Together with Robert T. Perry; urban sociologist Kim Edel; Naomi Schrag, a student at New York University School of Law; and subway musicians Steve Witt, Ricardo Silva, Bruce Edwards, Marcial Olascuaga, and Jorge Cabrera, we decided that our long-term goal would be to draft a booklet, "Know Your Rights," clarifying the regulations in New York for performers, police, and hearing officers alike. The booklet may also list legal and social services available to performers, review options for conflict resolution, and survey performers about the kinds of change they might like to see in public policy. Although I was concerned that a project initiated by audience members might not be accepted, a number of subway musicians have responded enthusiastically, and Gene Russianoff of the New York Public Interest Research Group has expressed interest in collaborating with us. Ultimately, the project aims to inform and to foster dialogue among all those involved in the city's street and subway performing scenes.

Subway musicians in New York have yet to form a broad-based self-help organization, but the USA, the Street Performers' Advocacy Project, and even MUNY demonstrate that, individualism notwithstanding, many are willing to join a group, or even more than one group, to improve their working conditions. If they did decide to organize and change the subways' performance frames, they could assemble a formidable list of potential allies. For instance, in addition to riders, NYPIRG, and the local news media, they could contact Kurt Masur, conductor of the New York Philharmonic, who organized street musicians in the former East Germany.[7] Meanwhile, to promote a greater sense of community among themselves, they could look inward and work on developing a collective memory. Unfortunately the activists of the 1990s have run the risk of reinventing the wheel, for few had ever heard of the *Manning* case, Lloyd Carew-Reid, or Subway Troubadours Against Repression.

In the four years that I studied the New York City subway music scene, I observed, and learned to accept, the inevitable turnover among musicians. Jorge and Patricio Aguirre of Los Andinos returned to Cuenca, Ecuador, and decided to remain there. Marcial Olascuaga and César Dueñas of Anthology began studying English in order to combine performing with steady, nonmusical jobs. Francisco Rodríguez of Antara del Barrio decided to focus on his visual art and his poetry, which he presents, along with his music, in more established cultural venues. At least one of the young musicians who contributed to this study tragically died of AIDS. Michael Christopher and Steven Blue disappeared as mysteriously as they came, perhaps to perform on the streets of other cities or to answer other callings. Meanwhile, new musicians such as Jessel Harris and Asheba arrived, and happily, veterans such as Jim Graseck and Sam Brown never left.

Guitarist Peter Barkman once told me that the subway music scene has an ebb and a flow, and I think the metaphor is very fitting. Musicians come and go, and the transit police have their periods of attack and retreat. But in the late 1980s, police cracked down on musicians more or less predictably for using amplifiers on platforms, for disregarding orders to lower their volume, or for engaging in some form of "disorderly conduct." The 1990s have seen a more disturbing trend. Many officers advise musicians that unless they have a MUNY permit, they have no right to perform. Indeed, the error itself is not difficult to understand. Officers need uniform rules; they cannot understand how musicians can be legitimate both with and without permits. But there are MTA executives and TA officials who know about the error and they are not putting an immediate stop to it. Until the authorities openly condemn such rule inventions, MUNY will serve what apparently was its original purpose, namely, to displace and censor freelance musicians, including MUNY members who "double" as freelancers.

MUNY includes many exceptional performers, but a number of them would be freelancing in the subways anyway. And while MUNY assumes the right to determine what legitimate culture is underground, its administrators have difficulty determining how to present some of that culture. For instance, until 1993 there were no hip hoppers on the MUNY roster. Then, perhaps to avoid charges of bias, the program accepted Tony "Pots and Pans" Walls and scheduled him at spots for three hours at a time, to the utter dismay of some concession stand workers and some TA employees. If MUNY is truly committed to promoting musical performance as a public art tradition, it should "open up" more of the city's 469 stations, feature music from underrepresented cultures, address real needs in struggling musicians' lives, and help musicians negotiate difference with others in the subways' informal social network.

Like MUNY, the TA regulations reflect the authorities' continued ambivalence toward subway music. The rules adopted in 1989 authorize the music as a form of expressive activity but arbitrarily ban amplifiers on platforms. It seems clear that the amp ban is not a reasonable time-place-manner restriction. The volume studies used to justify it are methodologically invalid and the safety studies are, from all indications, nonexistent.[8] MTA and TA arguments essentially hold musicians responsible for the unintelligible public address system, antiquated police radio equipment, crowds waiting for delayed trains, and urban noise resulting from decades of poor planning decisions (which the city council claims to have addressed in 1993 by revising its "unnecessary noise" ordinance to prohibit "unreasonable noise").[9]

As defendants in the *Carew-Reid* case, the authorities contended that the amp ban would help to ensure public safety and convenience. But it has proven to be little more than an administrative convenience, avoiding the noise problem it purported to address. It is also divisive, promising to protect riders from performers, and pitting amplified against acoustic musicians (if not also white against black musicians). Thus it undermines the musicians' ability to act like a community and to function as allies of the transit police. If some subway music is performed at an unacceptable volume, and indeed it seems that not all loud music is a "creative choice," the TA can establish a reasonable and culturally sensitive decibel ceiling and equip transit police officers with meters to enforce it. Compliance would surely be increased by enfranchising all musicians, including hip hoppers, through a single scheduling system (where necessary) that they would administer themselves with the help of the transit police.

MTA and TA corporate management strategies further obscure subway music's positive effects. The station manager program may improve customer service underground, but it also turns stations into fiefdoms, controlled environments in which spontaneous activity is limited. Between the MUNY program, the amp ban, the rule inventions of the transit police, and the discretionary decisions of station managers, subway musicians are being discouraged to an extent that even the TA proposed rules did not suggest. Judging from the frequency with which musicians are forced to scuttle from spot to spot or out of the system entirely, official performance frames and erroneous enforcement are reducing the amount and variety of music underground.

It seems the authorities control the music in these ways because they are not entirely willing to acknowledge that the subways have become a socially accepted performance space for vernacular music as well as a broad-based meeting place. The MTA sponsors MUNY because the program has promotional value for the transit system, and the TA authorizes freelancers because the courts have given it no other choice. Nevertheless, reluctance is not an adequate explanation. Why do they acquiesce when the transit police use safety and sanitation arguments to clear the stations of musicians?

Paul Chevigny provides an answer when he explains why it took so long to eliminate the cabaret laws. Quite simply, local government did not consider small jazz clubs important. Similarly, the MTA and TA may recognize that riders enjoy the entertainment, and individual transit executives such as Robert Kiley may applaud it as part of the culture of New York, but at base they do not view subway music, or the lives and interests of subway musicians, as terribly important. Thus the TA shifts perspectives easily and degrades musicians along with other "disorderly" people in the stations. The authorities' "quality of life" program is billed as a way to increase public safety, but it is merely the latest effort to produce a controlled community underground by labeling entire categories of people as "others" and removing them so as not to offend the sensibilities of affluent middle-class commuters. The Port Authority and Penn Station have adopted similar strategies. Ironically, all these agencies celebrate the public space roles of musicians and vendors by appropriating them; by piping in Muzak or establishing selective permitting systems, they keep out the very individuals who invented the roles in the first place in an effort to survive.

I have no doubt that some riders approve of such policies. But I believe this book has shown that subway music is important to many people. Moreover, judging from what goes on in the audience circles, riders feel secure when they can interact in ways that reduce alienation. The MTA and TA should be collaborating with the subways' informal social network on nurturing urban diversity underground. They should also be actively reminding elected officials of the systemic disorder that is the real source of New Yorkers' mounting insecurity.[10]

In the spirit of the remarkably populist public hearings in 1989, the TA should create channels of communication through which the subways' many populations might address any problems they encounter with subway music scenes. They could discuss whether people on platforms are captive audiences, whether performances are ever feasible in train cars, what kinds of consideration concession stand workers may expect, and which forms of self-regulation the police ought to encourage. The TA should also enlist musicians' help in conducting the station-by-station survey suggested at the 1989 hearings. All this information could be used to narrowly tailor the rules and make them reflect the subways' architectural and cultural realities more accurately. Indeed, the survey results and interviews I have presented demonstrate that people are already communicating informally; the TA simply needs to develop reliable methods of listening to what is being expressed through words and other exchanges.

The current trend in public space policy, however, is just the reverse. In January 1994 Rudolph Giuliani was elected mayor of New York on the promise that he would "restore order." To lead the city into battle,

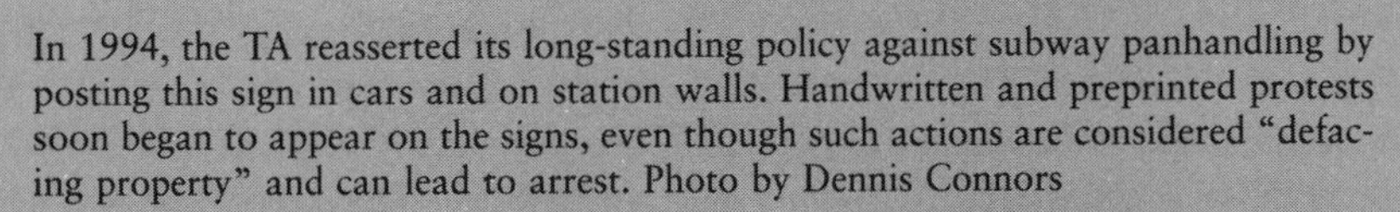

In 1994, the TA reasserted its long-standing policy against subway panhandling by posting this sign in cars and on station walls. Handwritten and preprinted protests soon began to appear on the signs, even though such actions are considered "defacing property" and can lead to arrest. Photo by Dennis Connors

Giuliani appointed William Bratton commissioner of the New York City Police Department—the only municipal agency spared severe budget cuts.[11] Bratton, formerly chief of the transit police, has pledged to implement George Kelling's broken windows theory citywide. In a 42-page document titled *Reclaiming the Public Spaces of New York*, Bratton and Giuliani enumerate the targets of their "quality of life" crusade. Topping the list of "others" are "squeegee men" (young underclass New Yorkers, primarily black men, who stand at major traffic intersections and clean car windshields in return for donations), and "aggressive" panhandlers.[12] Many more are also being criminalized in the name of civility. Notably, the document does not mention street performers, but a few musicians report that the number of hospitable spots above ground has diminished.

Some subway musicians have expressed concern that the Giuliani administration may crack down on their calling. Although the subways do not fall directly under the city's jurisdiction, the political climate above ground can change official attitudes underground. Shortly after Giuliani entered office and the MTA and TA introduced their antipanhandling campaign (see Appendix 1), some musicians reported that they too were experiencing increased police harassment. But government would have a difficult time imposing additional legal restrictions on subway music. Activist musicians have ensured that the constitutionality of their performances is beyond dispute, and ultimately it is impossible to stop people from expressing themselves, especially in one of the few spaces where a truly shared public culture exists.

Musicians have positively transformed the subways of New York since 1904 when the first IRT line opened, and even earlier than that. Almost a century later, in spite of restrictions, the city's subway music scene is more vibrant and culturally diverse than its counterpart in Massachusetts and, according to some of my sources, in major transit systems the world over. Much as they may differ in terms of personality, cultural origins, class background, age, aspirations, and talent, the musicians all help to sustain a viable independent forum. They also humanize what in spite of welcome renovations remains a harsh, if not hostile, environment.

The musicians initiate a peculiarly urban form of interaction in which a most heterogeneous population converges to affirm and explore identity. Across the "stage," these partners create scenes with unusual limits and possibilities. Though they may not make the musical discoveries of aficionados in self-selected venues, riders and subway workers transcend everyday struggles and tensions by participating in moments of social and cultural transformation. Some musical traditions reinforce the identities of specific individuals, but the music is also a vehicle of communication that accommodates and articulates the complex identities of many audience members. This process defies standard assumptions about how New Yorkers, perhaps how urban people in general, understand themselves and each other. Some riders do leave these scenes with more knowledge than they brought with them. In April 1994 in a Times Square station passageway, I noticed that a young African American man walking next to me was whistling the melody being played by an Andean group in a nearby spot. "You know it," I commented to him. "Yeah," he smiled. "I hear them every day. I like their music." Some of us are exposed to particular musical styles in the subways for the first time, and as they transform our personal cultural repertoires, they enrich our lives.

Subway space facilitates highly textured instances of focused interaction. For instance, on Thursday, March 10, 1994, at nine o'clock at night, Motown guitarist Roger Ridley was singing in his booming, gritty voice on the Times Square IRT platform. Four teenagers waiting for the train gathered at Ridley's side and harmonized and improvised with him. An audience circle quickly fell into place. Riders beamed, and the applause after each song was tremendous. (It was the first time that a subway music scene made me cry.) The teenagers brought to mind images of doo-woppers on Brooklyn street corners in the 1950s. This crew, however, was Latin American, African American, and Asian American. They symbolized the multicultural future of this city and rendered it optimistic. Ironically, Ridley was using a Mouse amp that night, and he could have been stopped or ticketed by a transit police officer. That government would weaken this informal social control or block cross-cultural flow in a city plagued by violence and racial conflict is unconscionable.

When there is widespread economic and political disorder, street and subway life proliferates. The most effective way to eliminate it is to make private spaces available in which people may thrive. Yet, even if a multitude of local affordable cultural venues suddenly opened in New York, there would still be a need for subway music's "transitory community." Its significance can only have increased since the 1980s, for in the same decade that the music was deemed constitutionally protected expression, the courts allowed channels of communication

Roger Ridley, Motown r&b guitarist, on the Times Square BMT platform. One subway fan, who owns a recording company, featured Ridley in a video and distributed it in Europe. As a result, Ridley was invited to perform overseas. Photo by Dennis Connors

to pass into private hands and government leased or sold public assembly spaces to the most affluent members of society. When people walk over to subway music circles, they signal that they need more than packaged, mediated, and controlled cultural experiences in their lives. There is something mysterious, exciting, and meaningful to them about being directly involved in spontaneous, open, messy, unique urban cultural moments.

At base, this book has been about changing perceptions. Let me provide one final example. On a recent sunny day, I bumped into Sam Brown shining shoes alongside the New York Public Library. He pointed to a folding chair.

"Have a seat and watch the parade."

"What parade?" I asked unimaginatively.

"Why, the people passing by."

Over the course of a day, New Yorkers have the choice of seeing the diverse population that constitutes this city either as an annoyance or as a source of learning and a cause for celebration. Subway music gives public encounters form and focus. It enables vastly different lives to intersect. If repeated often enough in the same stations, it renders many people—musicians, panhandlers, junkies, parents with children, working-class and white-collar commuters—real and familiar to one another. As a result strangers begin to appear nonthreatening and actually safe. This contact becomes a valued part of New Yorkers' vast repertoire of relationships.

Through the vehicle of music, time is suspended and heightened in the circle. In the moment between gathering and dispersing, people have a chance to develop a feel for the city and, at least temporarily, to feel that the city is okay. Many of these issues merit further consideration, but the responses I have collected during this study strongly suggest that subway music promotes the kind of public trust that is so desperately needed in contemporary urban society.

It is always striking when a subway musician sets up in front of a huge commercial billboard, one of the myriad images that insist on telling us what we should own and who we should be. The musician starts to play, a circle forms, and within the cacophony of subway space we listen to the harmonies and enjoy who we already are.

APPENDIX 1

Subway Homelessness

The term "homeless" is to a great extent a misnomer. Some of the individuals in the subways who are folded into this category may have access to private spaces in which to sleep or keep their belongings. They may, however, suffer from addictions, mental disabilities, or extreme poverty. Not all of them panhandle. Some have jobs, and some receive government support. The subway system provides them with shelter or with social and financial contacts. For clarity's sake, I continue to use the term "homeless" in its undifferentiated sense.

Subway homelessness has a history. Destitute New Yorkers have slept underground at least since the Great Depression.[1] During the 1980s their numbers increased dramatically because of major disorder, produced in part by the Reagan administration's attempts to dismantle the social welfare system created during the Great Depression; the failure of New York governors Carey and Cuomo to provide adequate community-based services to deinstitutionalized mentally challenged New Yorkers; the city council's resistance to passing legislation banning both the warehousing of apartments and the demolition of single-room occupancy units; and the Koch administration's reluctance to find alternatives to the warehousing of people in dangerous, costly public shelters.

Faced with this growing crisis, Mayor Ed Koch revived LaGuardia's campaign to restore order by eliminating itinerant activity in general and homeless people in particular, only without demonstrating LaGuardia's concern for the poor. Koch in effect drew up the blueprints for what has come to be known in New York as the "quality of life" campaign. In February 1985 he advised Robert Kiley, then chair of the MTA, to conduct nighttime "sweeps" and eject homeless people sleeping in the waiting area of Grand Central Terminal.[2]

Four years later, in April 1989, the MTA held its public hearings on the proposed rules for "non-transit use of transit facilities," which reasserted the long-standing TA ban on panhandling in the subways. In the same month, the city council reviewed a "street sweep" bill which proposed to authorize a city agency to remove homeless people from the streets and take them to shelters.[3] Also in the same month, the New York City Department of Parks and Recreation held hearings on its revised rules authorizing the park police to eject homeless people who had brought their belongings onto park grounds. After receiving testimony from homeless people and their advocates, the department removed the language that criminalized homelessness.[4] In short, the government agencies in charge of the city's three major public spaces attempted to solve the "homeless problem" by shuttling homeless people from one public space to another.

In September 1989 the MTA resolved to handle the situation with compassion through its Homeless Outreach Program. Robert Kiley contracted with the Human Resources Administration, the Division of Substance Abuse Services, ADAPT, and the Bowery Residents Committee to match clients with social services. Although the MTA reported success, the Coalition for the Homeless stated that the program's visibility primarily helped politicians and relegated other homeless people to lower positions on waiting lists for the same services.[5]

The following month, the TA assumed an aggressive stance when it introduced Operation Enforcement, the promotional name given to the newly adopted rules. Operation Enforcement prohibited panhandling, sleeping, washing, and lying down in the subways. It called for the removal of benches from station platforms, and of lockers from Grand Central Terminal as well as seats from phone booths there. In a letter to the MTA and TA, Gene Russianoff and Joseph Rappaport of NYPIRG objected to these measures. "Riders want to be part of the answer," they reported, "not . . . an excuse for such acts of official vandalism."[6] Indeed, the contradictions in the MTA and TA approaches reflected the agencies' divergent priorities but also riders' conflicting desires to support compassionate, long-term solutions and to be immediately shielded from people with their hands outstretched.[7]

In response to Operation Enforcement, two homeless men filed a class action against the MTA, the TA, Metro-North Commuter Railroad, the Port Authority of New York and New Jersey (which had imposed a similar ban on panhandling in its bus terminal), and state attorney general Robert Abrams (because the case challenged a statute under the New York State Constitution). With George Sommers as their counsel, the plaintiffs in *Young v. New York City Transit Authority* charged that the ban on panhandling violated the constitutional right of homeless people to express themselves in public space. They observed, furthermore, that the MTA and TA had authorized charities to solicit and musicians to collect donations in the subways; the Fourteenth Amendment, they contended, guaranteed panhandlers equal protection under the law.[8]

Judge Leonard B. Sand of the federal district court granted the plaintiffs a preliminary injunction, affirming the right to panhandle in the subways. Agreeing with Sommers that a ban on panhandling alone amounted to content-based discrimination, Judge Sand recognized the class issue involved. He concluded his decision: "A true test of one's commitment to constitutional principles is the extent to which recognition is given to the rights of those in our midst who are the least affluent, least powerful and least welcome."[9]

The MTA and TA appealed the *Young* and *Carew-Reid* decisions at the same time. Just as the Court of Appeals for the Second Circuit reversed the injunction on the amplification ban, it upheld the authorities' right to reimpose the panhandling ban throughout the subway system. Judge Frank X. Altimari, writing the majority opinion for *Young*, focused on *conduct* rather than on First Amendment rights. He held that riders experienced panhandling as a form of "assault," and he chastised the lower court for having overlooked the "common good." Judge Altimari did not simply ignore the case's larger context: he rejected the notion that panhandlers' speech has significant political and social content.[10]

The plaintiffs in *Young* tried to appeal the court of appeals decision, but the Supreme Court declined to hear the case,[11] whereupon Sommers turned his attention to the streets. As counsel to the plaintiffs in *Loper v. New York City Police Department*, he challenged the constitutionality of the panhandling ban above ground.[12] Like Judge Sand, Judge Robert W. Sweet of the federal district court accepted the argument that the ban was a form of content-based discrimination. In an eloquent decision, Judge Sweet wrote:

> As civilization has moved forward, people have learned time and again that suppressing speech and conduct deemed contrary to society's sense of order merely masks the underlying disorder. . . . Walking through New York's Times Square, one is bombarded with messages. . . . Giant billboards and flashing neon lights dazzle; peddlers hawk; preachers beseech; the news warily wraps around the old Times building; the Salvation Army band plays on. One generally encounters a beggar, too. Of all these solicitors, though, the only one subject to a blanket restriction is the beggar.[13]

On appeal, the police department lost the *Loper* case. This was a major victory for panhandlers; it affirmed that they may exercise their First Amendment rights in the streets. In an informal interview, Sommers explained the difference in the outcomes of *Young* and *Loper*. In *Loper* there was no denying that the streets are a traditional public forum in which speech is constitutionally protected. Sommers speculates that the police department never appealed the decision farther because the Supreme Court would have upheld the ruling, setting a "bad precedent" for other law enforcement agencies intent on removing panhandlers. By contrast, in recent years courts have been inclined to uphold government assertions that transportation terminals are nonpublic forums, which do not have to accommodate panhandling or other kinds of solicitation. One of the most significant precedents is *International Society for Krishna Consciousness v. Walter Lee*, in which the Supreme Court affirmed the Port Authority's right to ban solicitation from its terminals even if First Amendment activity is involved.[14] Close to twenty-five years after *Wolin* and *St. Clair*, cases that, according to some civil liberties attorneys, deemed transportation terminals to be traditional public forums, the majority opinion in *ISKCON v. Walter Lee* held that they are nonpublic forums. Sommers has not reopened *Young* out of concern that the subways might also be deemed a nonpublic forum, perhaps setting a "bad precedent" for free expression underground. But, he observes, the panel of judges that heard *ISKCON* was almost evenly divided in its opinion, indicating that the Court's position on the forum issue is far from resolved. At least, Sommers reasons, the constitutionality of panhandling is now beyond dispute and homeless people may legally ask for donations above ground.

Meanwhile, enforcement of the subway panhandling ban has been inconsistent. Already in January 1991 transit police officers were abandoning Operation Enforcement, frustrated by the policy's ineffectiveness and reluctant to sweep homeless people into the streets during the winter. Determined to continue the campaign against "rule violators," Chief William Bratton convened a task force that developed more compassionate strategies for removing homeless people from the subways.[15] But, relying on their own discretion, many officers preferred to ignore homeless people's presence and activities. Conversely, one of the officers I interviewed confessed that he occasionally slips some of these individuals a dollar to persuade them to leave the subways for the day.

In December 1993 Mayor-elect Giuliani announced his decision to appoint William Bratton commissioner of the New York City Police Department. During initial interviews Bratton stated his intention to apply the broken windows theory underlying Operation Enforcement to police work citywide. At the top of his list of targeted offenders were "squeegee" windshield cleaners and "aggressive" panhandlers.[16] By focusing on conduct, Bratton, like other law enforcement officials, sidestepped the constitutional, class, and racial issues involved.

Giuliani and Bratton have proposed to merge the city, transit, and housing police departments (a plan that Bratton strongly opposed as chief of the transit police), but meanwhile the subways do not fall directly under the jurisdiction of the NYPD. It seems more than coincidental, however, that in January 1994 the MTA, TA, and transit police launched their own "quality of life program." This time, they targeted riders, who were advised to give to charities, not to panhandlers. Black-and-white antipanhandling posters, totaling forty thousand dollars, appeared in subway cars and stations. The posters depicted a cartoon bubble supposedly containing the thoughts and fears of a rider confronted by a panhandler; the internal monologue ended: "Sorry. No money from me." Station managers' customer service stands were stocked with flyers explaining why riders should not assist panhandlers. "Don't give to lawbreakers on the subway," public address systems warned people. And the transit police undercover "quality of life task force" stepped up the department's patrol strategy by arresting panhandlers found to be "repeat offenders."

The MTA Homeless Outreach Program introduced by Robert Kiley has been replaced by MTA/Connections, administered by the authority and operated by a private organization contracted through the municipal Gouvernor's Hospital, to "assist homeless people out of the transit system and into permanent housing." MTA/Connections reports that in an eighteen-month period, with an annual budget of one million dollars paid by the TA, Long Island Rail Road, and Metro-North Commuter Railroad, it has placed 195 clients in treatment or residential facilities.[17]

Through press releases and the news media the authorities have defended their decision to implement compassionate and aggressive strategies simultaneously, explaining that both approaches are responses to customer fears about personal safety. The authorities have not, however, reported the results of a recent customer survey, which revealed that between 1988 and 1992 (overlapping with Operation Enforcement) there was an increase in the number of riders who felt that transit police officers treat homeless people and panhandlers too harshly, and a *decrease* in the number of riders who feel intimidated into giving money on subway trains. In its analysis of these findings, the MTA acknowledges that "external factors" are responsible for many subway space problems, but it decides to continue chasing after the victims of the real disorder.[18]

The histories of homeless people and musicians underground are more intertwined than some in either group might care to admit. In the early part of this century, politicians and some members of the public considered both to be beggars and undesirables. Until 1985 a single regulation prohibited both from expressing themselves in the subways. A few of my sources believe that the TA decided to restrict freelance music along with panhandling to shift attention away from its plan to rout homeless people.

Of course, musicians are compared to panhandlers because both depend on donations from the public. This similarity helps to explain why some officers close musicians' instrument cases and warn them not to "solicit." But the TA regulations authorize musicians to accept donations; they do not explicitly allow "passing the hat," which very few musicians do (except in subway cars), perhaps because they want to avoid the comparison with panhandling or the charge of "disorderly conduct." Some musicians do walk around the audience circle with cassettes and CDs, but they are cautious, since unlicensed commercial activity is prohibited underground and the TA has not made commercial licenses available for selling original recordings.

Both musicians and panhandlers failed to change the rules through litigation, but the musicians have been able to continue performing for donations (without amplifiers on platforms) because the rules explicitly authorize subway music. Some homeless people who followed the *Carew-Reid* and *Young* cases resent musicians for their relative legitimacy. Some have decided to sing or play music themselves, in the words of a homeless man named Robert, "to avoid starvation." In turn, some musicians resent being compared to panhandlers; the link seems to reinforce their already marginal status in the established arts world. On the other hand, Lloyd Carew-Reid would have liked to file a joint suit with the plaintiffs in the *Young* case, to fight for the legal protection of all free expression in the subways. The authorities, meanwhile, continue to link musicians and panhandlers politically. Musicians report that when the latest antipanhandling campaign began, the transit police stepped up the crackdowns on them as well.

Legal and public policy frames, however, do not by themselves determine actual relationships. Informal contact between musicians and homeless people is striking on social, cultural, and political levels. They find ways to negotiate and even share space and attention. Musicians greatly appreciate the donations that homeless people make (which are often more generous than those made by affluent riders). Subway music scenes are in fact some of the only spaces in the city where homeless people can enjoy equal social and political status with others. There is at least the potential for all participants to be rendered less frightening and more real to one another. More than once during my research I observed relatively affluent commuters and homeless people standing in front of musicians, engaged in conversation.

APPENDIX 2

New York Street Music

Whereas subway music occurs in an interconnected space traveled by an exceptionally heterogeneous population, the street music scene in New York consists of public space environments that attract more particular audiences.[1] During their lunch hour, young professionals gather around Andean and jazz bands in Liberty Plaza in the Wall Street area. On weekends, young people looking for entertainment with an "edge" congregate in Washington Square Park. Theater- and moviegoers cheer breakdancers and stand-up comics while waiting on line along Broadway in Times Square.

In 1970 Mayor John Lindsay signed a bill abolishing licensing requirements for street musicians, and since then New York has regained its reputation as one of the most hospitable American cities for street entertainment.[2] Some musicians, however, would disagree. In informal interviews some of my sources reported that officers with the New York City Police Department had moved them, ejected them, fined them, confiscated their instruments, and arrested them. Indeed, such actions may be within the bounds of police authority under the ambiguous noise, safety, and conduct codes of the city. In some instances police claim to be responding to complaints made by those merchants who consider street musicians to be negative competition.[3] In other situations officers' discretionary decisions may actually be based on personal taste or mood, which is why Harrison-Pepper calls them "the ultimate theater critics."[4]

Although the city no longer has a uniform licensing system above ground, it has a sound amplification permit requirement. Robert Turley, founder of the United Street Artists, investigated and discovered that the daily charge for a sound amplification permit, twenty-nine dollars, exceeds the *annual* fee for permits in Boston and Atlantic City. According to Turley, the police precincts, which issue the permit, often refuse to grant it to him, arguing that he will obstruct traffic—before inspecting the spots he has requested. In addition, the city noise code does not specify a decibel ceiling for street music, and the precincts impose arbitrarily low limits on Turley's volume.

In December 1993, with Robert T. Perry as his counsel, Turley filed a lawsuit in federal district court challenging the constitutionality of the sound amplification permit requirement. The case also challenges the double standard applied by the police in granting permits to government- and corporate-sponsored musicians while withholding them from freelance street musicians; major performances funded by private interests are held in the same spots that are denied to Turley. And whereas MUNY members receive free permits to perform in the Duffy Square traffic triangle, Turley must pay for the same opportunity. In *Turley v. New York City Police Department and New York City Department of Parks and Recreation*, Turley invokes the Fourteenth Amendment, demanding equal protection under the law.

The court case also challenges the constitutionality of the more elaborate catch-22 embedded in the rules and regulations of the Department of Parks and Recreation. In 1990 Betsy Gotbaum was appointed parks commissioner and during her tenure street musicians who wanted to use amplifiers when performing in city parks were required to apply for the twenty-nine-dollar permit from the police as well as a twenty-five-dollar "Special Events" permit from her department. Yet when Turley and other musicians approached the parks, they were told that the special events permit was no longer being issued. Parks rules specify, moreover, that special events permits must be requested twenty-one days in advance. If these regulations were uniformly enforced, they would effectively censor spontaneous street music in city parks.[5]

In the fall of 1992 the park police began to crack down on the use of amplifiers by musicians who performed on weekends along the popular 72nd Street transverse in Central Park. Apparently, one reason for the increased enforcement was that some musicians were using large amplifiers powered by car batteries, which produce considerably more volume than Mouse amps. Yet the department did not publicly articulate this concern, and the park police made erratic discretionary decisions. For instance, they confiscated the Mouse amp of a jazz ensemble that had been performing peacefully along the transverse for ten years (and whose leader had accompanied some of the jazz "greats" in previous decades). It took four months for the ensemble to retrieve its Mouse. One of the members reported to me that the loss of that small increase in volume had meanwhile translated into a loss of income.

The parks department regulations and uneven enforcement practices have produced various contradictions. One example is the Mayor's Council on the Environment Green Market at Union Square, a colorful, fragrant space in lower Manhattan where regional farmers sell their produce directly to New Yorkers. The market managers and security guard, who either circulate or sit at a center table, have developed an elaborate public trust. Customers ask them questions and engage them in long conversations. Homeless people leave money and belongings with them for safekeeping. In the words of security guard Islam Muhammad, "We deal with the whole spectrum of humanity here. . . . This is *our* community; we're not gonna let anyone fluff [the disadvantaged members] off!"

In 1990 the park police entered the market and fined a guitarist who played there regularly for using a Mouse amp. The managers' initial reaction was outrage: they began collecting customers' signatures on a protest petition. Since, however, the market is located on parks property—on a lot adjacent to Union Square Park—it must abide by department rules. It was then, manager Joel Patraker said, that he instituted "Joel's Law." He negotiated with the park police to allow acoustic musicians to perform without having to apply for special events permits.

In time, the managers decided that acoustic music was "more in harmony" with the market's atmosphere. During informal interviews they told me that their farmers and customers preferred acoustic music, although no formal surveys had been conducted. They also reported that, partly in deference to area residents, they did not allow the use of drums in the market (which could provoke charges of content-based discrimination).

Ironically, although street musicians in the market may not use Mouse amps, the parks department issues permits to musical groups to play in the Union Square Park bandshell. Among these groups are highly amplified rock banks that aggravate the market's customers.

The department does not consult the market staff on these permitting decisions; instead, the managers report customer complaints and farmers' reduced sales retroactively. Most ironic of all, amplified street music is welcomed in other green markets across the city which are not located on park property.

A clear example of the parks department's double standard with regard to government-sponsored entertainers and street musicians is the SummerStage concert series. Every summer Central Park presents free concerts on its stage at 72nd Street. Featured guests, some of whom are world renowned, represent a wide range of cultures and musical styles. In 1991 I surveyed 108 people in Central Park, and the vast majority of my respondents approved of SummerStage. They made such comments as, "It's a good way to get more people in and using the park. It's also the least they can do for all the taxes I pay!"

But SummerStage also reflects a shift in public policy toward corporate management of the city's park system; it is another effort to privatize and control musical performances. The concert series is underwritten by corporate sponsors, and at each event, inflated plastic beer cans and rice boxes swing in the air. Clearly, the parks department, whose budget is meager, and its private partner, the Central Park Conservancy, have decided to seek additional revenue from private sources. But in fact, large concerts require a considerable amount of work and are not all that lucrative for the parks to present.[6]

Over time, the SummerStage lineup has become exclusive. According to one of my sources, the series began informally in the early 1980s and was held in the Naumberg bandshell (the site disputed in the *Rock against Racism* case). Local arts organizations and community groups were invited and paid to arrange performances, but in a matter of years those same groups were charged a fee to participate. In 1990 SummerStage moved to a newly constructed stage, just to the east of the bandshell, which is generally unavailable for independent public concerts. While street musicians are prevented from using Mouse amps, the new SummerStage uses a sound system so powerful that, it is rumored, the police stationed around the concert area are furnished with earplugs. So many East Side residents complained about the noise that the parks department spent over ten thousand dollars on sound consultants and in 1992 SummerStage's volume level was reduced from 115 to 102 decibels.[7]

Indeed, just as the subways have, albeit unofficially, had multiple functions for years, so have city parks.[8] Some people use them for recreation and free expression; others rely on them as refuges from the chaotic city and as places of quiet contemplation. Thus in my 1991 survey, respondents suggested a variety of reasonable time-place-manner restrictions for street music in Central Park. Some said that any conflict involving musicians could be resolved through self-regulation. In the words of one respondent: "Central Park is certainly large enough for one to either listen or escape from music."

In 1994 the newly elected mayor, Rudolph Giuliani, appointed Henry Stern as parks commissioner, the same post he had held in the Koch administration of the 1980s. Some of my sources recall that Stern was more hospitable than Gotbaum toward street musicians in Central Park. Indeed, once advised of Robert Turley's lawsuit, the department under Stern began issuing special events permits to them. But, just months after resuming his position, Stern resolved to restrict other types of musical performance. In May, a confrontation between audience members and police officers at a punk rock concert in Tompkins Square Park led Stern to announce that the department would become more selective in granting permits for independent public events. Norman Siegel, executive director of the New York Civil Liberties Union, responded that his organization was prepared to represent rejected permit seekers in court and to challenge the constitutionality of regulations that amounted to content-based discrimination.[9]

Decades after Lindsay abolished street music licenses, city agencies and private sponsors are attempting to contain unsponsored musicians by regulating them, managing them, and replacing them with official events. The parks department, for example, seems to have waged war against public bandshells. Commissioner Gotbaum's administration fought and lost a lengthy court battle to tear down the Naumberg bandshell in Central Park and replace it with a tourist center. Meanwhile in Tompkins Square Park, which developed a reputation in recent years as the site of clashes between homeless squatters and police, the bandshell has been officially demolished; one of my sources says it was built in the 1960s to promote cross-cultural exchange among the ethnically diverse residents of the neighborhood. Subway musician and Lower East Side activist Roger Manning reports that the parks department has also begun to crack down on bongo players in Tompkins Square to appease area residents who have complained about the volume. Ironically, says Manning, the drummers used to play inside the bandshell, which kept their sound within the park's borders.

Another battle has been waged on the streets. New York City zoning laws have allowed many developers to build additional stories on their buildings in exchange for such public amenities as outdoor plazas. Yet when street musicians set up in those plazas, private security guards often chase them away. Business Improvement Districts have had similar effects on performances. Although intended to improve neighborhoods by uniting merchants and residents and providing additional sanitation and security, the BIDS essentially privatize many commercial strips in New York.[10]

Street festivals have become a familiar sight in New York during the spring and summer months, and street musicians often perform between vendors' international stands. A handful of companies produce these festivals, however, standardizing and controlling them and, in some cases, charging musicians for spots. And since 1993, Manhattan's Financial District has been the site of an annual week-long Buskers Fare, showcasing a wide variety of entertainment in downtown public spaces; yet less than a handful of New York City street performers are invited to participate.[11] The officials and "professionals" who manage and control street musicians believe that they are accommodating public space activity while ensuring public convenience. But their approach imposes restrictions on free expression that are of questionable constitutional validity, and it imposes structure on experiences valued for their spontaneity.

Thus, the actual status of New York City street music remains complicated and tenuous. Nevertheless, the existing performance frames allow for a degree of flexibility. For instance, local park officials may use their discretion in enforcing the street music regulations. Until 1994, Arne Abramowitz served as administrator of Flushing Meadows Corona Park in Queens. He welcomed the Andean musicians who occasionally performed in his public space. In his view, street music "is like fresh air."

Notes

Preface

1. Edward T. Hall, *The Hidden Dimension* (New York: Doubleday, 1966), p. 52.

Introduction—Venturing Down

1. Deborah Sontag, "Unlicensed Peddlers, Unfettered Dreams," *New York Times*, June 14, 1993, A1.
2. The names given to these stations indicate major commercial institutions or districts in their vicinity. In reality, only Grand Central and Times Square are so designated by the Transit Authority. The Port Authority station is adjacent to the bus terminal known by this name but is operated by the TA, not by the Port Authority of New York and New Jersey.
3. Patricia J. Campbell, *Passing the Hat: Street Performers in America* (New York: Delacorte Press, 1981), p. 101.
4. For the term "circle," see Sally Harrison-Pepper, *Drawing a Circle in the Square: Street Performing in New York's Washington Square Park* (Jackson: University Press of Mississippi, 1990). I use it broadly to describe various audience configurations.
5. Lawrence W. Levine, *Highbrow Lowbrow: The Emergence of Cultural Hierarchy in America* (Cambridge: Harvard University Press, 1988), p. 9.
6. I use the term "authorities" to refer to the quasi-governmental MTA and TA, not to law enforcement agents, as is often the practice. Jim Dwyer, in *Subway Lives: 24 Hours in the Life of the New York City Subway* (New York: Crown, 1991), pp. 221–22, maintains that the MTA is "a symbol of independent authorities that are beyond the control of elected officials." Nevertheless, he adds, the chief executives of authorities are aware that one of their primary responsibilities is to shield the elected officials who appointed them from public criticism.

1 Setting Up

1. Harrison-Pepper, *Drawing a Circle*, p. xiv.
2. Simon Frith, *Sound Effects: Youth, Leisure, and the Politics of Rock 'n' Roll* (New York: Pantheon, 1981), p. 29.

3. Campbell, *Passing the Hat*, p. 12.

4. Herbert I. Schiller, *Culture, Inc.: The Corporate Takeover of Public Expression* (New York: Oxford University Press, 1989), p. 101.

5. Paul Chevigny, *Gigs: Jazz and the Cabaret Laws in New York City* (New York: Routledge, Chapman, and Hall, 1991), p. 168.

6. Ibid., p. 77.

7. The Federal Immigration Act was revised in 1965. Since then, according to Sheldon S. Wolin, "the images of homogeneity have been strained further by the global dislocation occasioned in part by American political and economic policies. These have caused thousands of human beings, many of them Asians and Hispanics, to flee their homelands for the United States, thereby helping to produce new differences and to accentuate existing ones." See "Collective Identity and Constitutional Power," in *The Constitution and the Regulation of Society*, ed. Gary C. Bryner and Dennis L. Thompson (Provo, Utah: Brigham Young University, 1988), p. 101.

8. David Toop, *The Rap Attack: African Jive to New York Hip Hop* (Boston: South End Press, 1984), p. 14.

9. Ibid., pp. 8, 14–15.

10. Ibid., pp. 15–16, 100, 12.

11. William H. Whyte, *City: Rediscovering the Center* (New York: Doubleday, 1988), p. 39, quoting Judge Marven E. Aspen's ruling in *Friedrich v. Chicago*: "If the City chooses to renew the ordinance [banning street performing] next year, it would be well advised to consider the passing of the breakdancing phenomenon in its evaluation."

12. Clifton Hood, *722 Miles: The Building of the Subways and How They Transformed New York* (New York: Simon and Schuster, 1993), pp. 11–12. Other sources estimate ridership at 3.5 million.

13. Harrison-Pepper, *Drawing a Circle*, p. xv: "Unlike much conventional theater, the street performer works in a 'found' environment and must inscribe his meaning upon it."

14. Whyte, *City*, p. 35.

15. Harrison-Pepper, *Drawing a Circle*, p. 39.

16. Ibid., p. 22.

17. Toop, *Rap Attack*, p. 22. He does not feel, however, that this film does justice to hip hop or to black street culture. He calls its street performing scene a "revisitation of Bill 'Bojangles' Robinson teaching Shirley Temple how to tap."

18. A *New York Times* critic asserted: "Abolish the diabolical street pianos and hand organs which disseminate these vile tunes in all directions and which reduce the musical taste of the children in the residence streets to the level of that of the Australian bushman, who thinks noise and rhythm are music." Levine, *Highbrow Lowbrow*, pp. 216–17. These issues will be examined in greater detail in Chapter 4.

19. Harrison-Pepper, *Drawing a Circle*, pp. xv, xvi.

20. Ibid., p. 26.

21. Brian J. Cudahy, *Under the Sidewalks of New York* (Lexington, Mass.: Stephen Greene Press, 1988), p. xiii.

22. Hood, *722 Miles*, p. 215.

23. Jim Dwyer, *Subway Lives*, p. 4.

24. Ibid., pp. 119–21, 202–4.

25. Harrison-Pepper, *Drawing a Circle*, p. 43.

26. The term comes from Sally Harrison, "Drawing a Circle in Washington Square Park," *Studies in Visual Communication* 10 (Spring 1984): 68–83.

27. Ruth H. Finnegan, *The Hidden Musicians: Local Music in a Small English Town* (Cambridge: Cambridge University Press, 1989), pp. 6–12.

28. Ibid., p. 338.

29. This is not to deny that positive social interaction often spontaneously occurs between individual riders, especially when a child is involved, but it is rare for such good will to develop into a collective experience other than in the context of subway music scenes. Perhaps a similar effect is now triggered by Asian vendors who walk through the train cars displaying shopping bags full of toys, eliciting laughter and eye contact. Some of them have developed routines, making them the subways' latest entertainers.

30. Chevigny, *Gigs*, pp. 54–56, 4.

31. *Carew-Reid v. Metropolitan Transportation Authority*, docket no. 90-7143, *Brief of Defendants-Appellants*, February 1990, p. 7; Metropolitan Transportation Authority, Marketing Research Division, Memorandum from Peter Harris to Andrew Hyde, "Citywide Survey Results," May 9, 1988, p. 8.

2 *The Beat Goes On: History*

1. Hood, *722 Miles*, pp. 42–48.

2. Dwyer, *Subway Lives*, p. 147.

3. *New York World*, February 27, 1870, quoted in Beach Pneumatic Transit Company, *Illustrated Description of the Broadway Pneumatic Underground Railway with a Full Description of the Atmospheric Machinery and the Great Tunneling Machine* (New York: S. W. Green, 1870), pp. 16–17, in New-York Historical Society.

4. "Rapid Transit Tunnel Begun," *New York Times*, March 25, 1900, 2.

5. The term "patrician" comes from Hood, *722 Miles*, chap. 5.

6. Individual subway lines were constructed with municipal funds and were initially operated by private companies. Transit officials and riders used the companies' acronyms to identify trains. The acronyms have since been replaced by a color-coded number and letter system, but many New Yorkers still use them, to the possible bewilderment of newcomers.

7. "Our Subway Open, 150,000 Try It," *New York Times*, October 28, 1904, 1.

8. "Subway Open," *Evening Post*, October 27, 1904, 1–2.

9. Ibid.

10. "Our Subway Open."

11. Hood, *722 Miles*, pp. 95–96.

12. "Bay Ridge Celebrates the Beginning of Work on Fourth Avenue Subway Extension," *New York Times*, October 27, 1912, sec. 3, p. 6.

13. Schiller, *Culture, Inc.*, pp. 103–4.

14. "Celebrate Opening of Subway Link," *New York Times*, July 1, 1924, 23.

15. "Business Men Fete Opening of Subway," *New York Times*, September 10, 1932, 6.

16. "Fifth Avenue Station of Subway Opened," *New York Times*, March 23, 1926, 29.

17. Hood, *722 Miles*, p. 212.

18. "New Subway Line on 6th Ave. Opens at Midnight Fete," *New York Times*, December 15, 1940, 1.

19. Hood, *722 Miles*, pp. 227, 259.

20. New York State, *Public Authorities Law*, bk. 42, sec. 1201 (McKinney's Consolidated Laws of New York Annotated, 1982). The Metropolitan Transportation Authority was created in the late 1960s to coordinate the region's subway, bus, and commuter railroad systems.

21. "Carolers Take Yuletide Spirit Down to the Subway," *New York Times*, December 13, 1956, 44.

22. Ibid.

23. Miss E. Laurel, letter to Joseph E. O'Grady, chairman, New York City Transit Authority, December 7, 1964, TA Archives, file "Noise—Rapid Transit—1964—0-250—Complaints."

24. Paul J. Keleti, acting secretary, New York City Transit Authority, letter to Raymond Hagan, Esq., December 23, 1964, ibid.

25. Steve Witt, "Piped-in Subway Music? What about the Subway Musicians?" in "The Street Singer's Beat," *Downtown* (clipping, n.d., n.p., furnished by Steve Witt).

26. Campbell, *Passing the Hat*, pp. 8–9.

27. Ibid., p. 9, citing Wickham Boyle, *On the Streets: A Guide to New York City's Buskers* (New York: Department of Cultural Affairs, 1978).

28. Ibid., p. 10.

29. Robert Briffault, *The Troubadours* (Bloomington: Indiana University Press, 1965), pp. 17–23. Translated from the original, *Les Troubadours et le sentiment romanesque* (Paris, 1948).

30. George Robinson, "The Klezmatics: Making a Difference with Music That's Different," *Jewish Sentinel*, October 20, 1993, A4.

31. Toop, *Rap Attack*, p. 32.

32. Amy Tan, *The Kitchen God's Wife* (New York: G. P. Putnam's Sons, 1991), p. 121.

33. Vincent Thomas, arranger, *Cryes of Olde London* (London: London, Goodwin, and Tabb, 1925), Introductory Note.

34. Thomas Turino, *Moving Away from Silence: Music of the Peruvian Altiplano and the Experience of Urban Migration* (Chicago: University of Chicago Press, 1993), pp. 1, 46–47, 64.

35. Ibid., pp. 3–4, 140.

36. Ibid., p. 146.

37. Ibid., pp. 184, 3.

38. See Turino's bibliography for articles on indigenous cultures in Andean countries other than Peru.

39. Silva recalls that the controversial political party Sendero Luminoso (Shining Path) recruited young members at the Sunday afternoon performances, but he believes that the majority of the people attended to hear the music and to experience a feeling of "connection" with their original culture.

40. To varying degrees Andean musicians in New York see themselves as expressing resistance to cultural imperialism by embedding their traditions in musical innovation; a few, though, are notorious among their colleagues for exploiting the popularity of the resistance message for their own financial gain.

41. Roi Ottley and William J. Weatherby, eds., *The Negro in New York: An Informal Social History, 1626–1940* (New York: Praeger, 1967), pp. 25–26, originally prepared by the Federal Writers Project.

42. Ibid., p. 26: "Not a part of the main stream of the town's social life, Negroes found needed fellowship in these gatherings."

43. Frith, *Sound Effects*, p. 16.

44. James Lincoln Collier, *Louis Armstrong: An American Genius* (New York: Oxford University Press, 1983), p. 28; Richard Meryman, *Louis Armstrong: A Self-Portrait* (New York: Eakins Press, 1971), pp. 10–14.

45. Hettie Jones, *Big Star Fallin' Mama: Five Women in Black Music* (New York: Dell, 1974), pp. 40–42. Success, however, had its price. Steve Chapple and Reebee Garofalo state that in the early twentieth century, black women in the music business were stereotyped to a far greater extent than their white counterparts as "readily available sex objects." Steve Chapple and Reebee Garofalo, *Rock 'n' Roll Is Here to Pay: The History and Politics of the Music Industry* (Chicago: Nelson-Hall, 1977), p. 274.

46. Laurence Bergreen, *As Thousands Cheer: The Life of Irving Berlin* (New York: Viking Press, 1990), p. 12.

47. Campbell, *Passing the Hat*, p. 11.

48. *Code of Ordinances of the City of New York, Adopted March 30, 1915*, comp. Arthur F. Cosby (New York: Banks Law, 1915), pp. 250–51. Brooklyn already had such an ordinance in 1897. See *Ordinances of the City of Brooklyn*, as found in *General Ordinances of the City of New York under the Greater New York Charter*, comp. George Whitfield Brown Jr. (New York: Banks Law, 1901), pp. 203–4, in Municipal Reference and Research Center, New York City Department of Records and Information Services.

49. Stephen Baird, quoted in Campbell, *Passing the Hat*, p. 11.

50. Interborough Rapid Transit Company, Subway Division, *Rules and Regulations for the Government of the Operating Officers and Employés of the Interborough Rapid Transit Company, Subway Division, to Take Effect October 1, 1904* (1904), pp. 76, 80, in New-York Historical Society.

51. Manhattan Railway Company, *Rules and Regulations for the Government of the Operating Officers and Employés of the Manhattan Railway Company* (1890), rule 285, p. 57, in New-York Historical Society.

52. Levine, *Highbrow Lowbrow*, pp. 36–37.

53. *Rules of the Suburban Rapid Transit Company* (1886), in New-York Historical Society, rule 85, p. 18: "News agents will not be allowed to cry their papers on the Company's property. No pedlers [*sic*] or beggars will be allowed on or around the stations."

54. Joseph Cunningham and Leonard O. DeHart, *A History of the New York City Subway System* (microform; New York: The authors, 1976), pt. 1: *The Manhattan Els and the I.R.T.*, p. 65.

55. Federal Writers' Project, *The WPA Guide to New York City* (1939; New York: Random House, 1982), p. 406.

56. "Hurdy-Gurdy Fees Abolished by Mayor," *New York Times*, March 8, 1935, 23.

57. New York City, Municipal Archives, Department of Records and Information Services, Fiorello H. LaGuardia files, Department of Licenses, microfilm roll 13, frame 000828, roll 18, frame 000986.

58. Quoted in "Mr. LaGuardia Warned," *New York Times*, April 21, 1935, sec. IV, p. 8.

59. "A Few Relics Wanted," *New York Times*, April 16, 1935, 20. LaGuardia outlines his arguments in a letter to Mrs. F. S. Stebbins, May 14, 1935, in Municipal Reference and Research Center, New York City Department of Records and Information Services.

60. "The Hurdy-Gurdy," *New York Times*, April 20, 1935, 12; "A Plea for the Organ Grinder," *New York Times*, January 24, 1936, 18.

61. "German Band Is Banned," *New York Times*, January 3, 1936, 21; "Organ Grinders Will Go on Radio to Fight Ban," *New York Times*, January 11, 1936, 17; "Mary Lewis Joins Hurdy-Gurdy Plea," *New York Times*, January 23, 1936, 25; "Organ Grinders to Go," *New York Times*, January 17, 1936, 21; New York City, Board of Transportation, *Rules and Regulations Governing Employees Engaged in Operation: Independent City-Owned Rapid Transit Railroad* (1938), chap. 1, pt. I, rule 25.

62. Thomas Kessner, *Fiorello H. LaGuardia and the Making of Modern New York* (New York: Penguin, 1989), p. 12.

63. Frith, *Sound Effects*, pp. 27–30.

64. Harrison-Pepper, *Drawing a Circle*, pp. 24–26. It is also worth noting, as Stephen Baird does, that Vietnam veterans sing on the streets of Boston and other major American cities.

65. Joe Klein, *Woody Guthrie: A Life* (New York: Alfred A. Knopf, 1980), p. 214.

66. Chapple and Garofalo, *Rock 'n' Roll*, pp. 235–42.
67. Ibid., pp. 49–52.
68. Toop, *Rap Attack*, p. 84.
69. Ibid., p. 32. The white teenagers who sang doo-wop on the street corners at that time were predominantly Italian American. Like their African American counterparts, their performances contained echoes, however unconscious, of their community's particular cultural traditions. For a detailed analysis, see Anthony J. Gribin and Matthew M. Schiff, *Doo-Wop: The Forgotten Third of Rock 'n' Roll* (Iola, Wis.: Krause, 1992).
70. Ibid., p. 86. Robinson notes that rap emerges from harsher conditions than doo-wop and therefore often sounds more "aggressive and volatile."
71. Campbell, *Passing the Hat*, p. 68.
72. Chevigny, *Gigs*, pp. 94–95; "Lead-Paint Bill Signed by Mayor," *New York Times*, June 12, 1970, 20.
73. "39 'Don'ts' Listed in Subways' Code," *New York Times*, February 17, 1967, 39.

3 The Partners: Subway Musicians and Their Audiences

1. Campbell, *Passing the Hat*, pp. 12–13.
2. Frith, *Sound Effects*, p. 86.
3. Chapple and Garofalo, *Rock 'n' Roll*, pp. 270, 293–96.
4. Douglas Martin, "Rush-Hour Recitals for a Chinese Violinist," *New York Times*, July 24, 1994, sec. I, p. 1.
5. Robert Cantwell, *Bluegrass Breakdown: The Making of the Old Southern Sound* (Urbana: University of Illinois Press, 1984), p. 273. Cantwell says, moreover, that musical crossover occurred during encounters between black slaves and Irish immigrants (also discriminated against in that period).
6. Chapple and Garofalo, *Rock 'n' Roll*, pp. 245–46.
7. My use of the term "fusion" is to be distinguished from fusion jazz, a style made popular in the 1980s.
8. Chevigny, *Gigs*, p. 44.
9. Steve Witt, "Ogarro Interviewed," in "The Street Singer's Beat," *Downtown*, March 13, 1991, clipping, n.p., furnished by Steve Witt.
10. New York State, *Official Compilation Codes, Rules, and Regulations of the State of New York*, title 21, chap. XXI, Metropolitan Transportation Authority, subchap. F, New York City Transit Authority.
11. Michael Lydon discussed these three motivations in "New York City Subway Orpheus," *Atlantic Monthly* (June 1990): 24–28.
12. See *Goldstein v. Town of Nantucket*, 477 F.Supp. 606 (1979); *Davenport v. City of Alexandria, Va.*, 710 F.2d 148 (1983).
13. Cantwell, *Bluegrass Breakdown*, pp. 150–55.
14. Meetings between Peruvian and Ecuadorian musicians may be even more significant if, as one tells me, political tensions between their countries make such cultural encounters unlikely back home.
15. Cantwell, *Bluegrass Breakdown*, pp. 28, 214.
16. Ibid., p. 182.
17. Ibid., p. 151.
18. Turino, *Moving Away from Silence*, p. 235.
19. Cantwell, *Bluegrass Breakdown*, pp. 152–53.
20. Jane Jacobs, *The Death and Life of Great American Cities* (New York: Random House, 1961), p. 69.

4 Boundaries and Bridges: Relationships in Public Space

1. See, for example, Edward T. Hall, *The Hidden Dimension*; William H. Whyte, *City*; Tony Hiss, *The Experience of Place* (New York: Knopf, 1990); and Amanda Dargan and Steven Zeitlin, *City Play* (New Brunswick, N.J.: Rutgers University Press, 1990).
2. Levine, *Highbrow Lowbrow*, p. 56.
3. Dargan and Zeitlin, *City Play*, p. 29.
4. Campbell, *Passing the Hat*, p. 160.
5. Turino, *Moving Away from Silence*, p. 114.
6. Whyte, *City*, p. 67.
7. Jacobs, *Death and Life of Cities*, p. 50.
8. Whyte, *City*, p. 91.
9. Dargan and Zeitlin, *City Play*, p. 106.
10. Harrison-Pepper, *Drawing a Circle*, p. 126.
11. Whyte, *City*, p. 175.
12. Erving Goffman, *Behavior in Public Places: Notes on the Social Organization of Gatherings* (New York: Free Press of Glencoe, 1963), pp. 244–48.
13. Ibid., pp. 246–47.
14. Finnegan, *Hidden Musicians*, p. 306.
15. Ibid, p. 322.
16. See Richard Sennett, ed., *Classic Essays on the Culture of Cities* (Englewood Cliffs, N.J.: Prentice-Hall, 1969).
17. Edward B. Fiske, "Now, Whites Are Minority in New York," *New York Times*, March 22, 1991, B1–2.
18. Turino, *Moving Away from Silence*, p. 99.
19. Turino observes that "cross-cultural" studies have tended to presume cultural homogeneity within communities. Instead, he analyzes "similarities and differences between groups of people, as well as between individuals who typically would be thought of as belonging to the same 'culture,' the same ethnic group, or at least the same society." Ibid., p. 8.
20. James C. McKinley, Jr., "Dinkins, in TV Speech, Defends Handling of Crown Heights Tension," *New York Times*, November 26, 1992, 1. The mayor did propose measures involving meaningful interaction, such as "classroom lessons to stop bigotry and a program to promote cultural exchanges between black and Jewish groups."
21. Metropolitan Transportation Authority, Arts for Transit Office, promotional brochure (1990), p. 11. Furnished by the Arts for Transit Office.
22. Klein, *Woody Guthrie*, pp. 431–33.
23. Andrew Ross, *No Respect: Intellectuals and Popular Culture* (New York: Routledge, Chapman, and Hall, 1989), p. 41.
24. Frith, *Sound Effects*, pp. 28, 30.
25. Frith, *Sound Effects*, p. 101.
26. Ross, *No Respect*, p. 70.
27. In *Culture, Inc.*, Herbert Schiller notes that "a prediction made in the mid-1980s that by 1995 almost 90 percent of all communication facilities (including newspapers, broadcast outlets, cable systems, telephone lines, relays, and satellites) would be in the hands of fifteen companies is close to realization well before that date" (p. 35). Schiller's work was released years after Frith's *Sound Effects*, but the trends were already well under way.
28. Dargan and Zeitlin, *City Play*, p. 170.
29. Turino, *Moving Away from Silence*, pp. 13, 114.
30. Frith, *Sound Effects*, pp. 158–60.

31. Simon Frith and Howard Horne, *Art into Pop* (London: Methuen, 1987), pp. 176–77.

32. Chevigny, *Gigs*, p. 94.

33. George L. Kelling, "The Contagion of Public Disorder," *City Journal* (Spring 1991): 58, 60–61.

34. See also Marshall Berman, "Take It to the Streets: Conflict and Community in Public Space," *Dissent* 33 (Fall 1986): 476–85.

35. Jacobs, *Death and Life of Cities*, p. 32.

36. Deirdre Carmody, "Transit Goals Being Met, Gunn Says," *New York Times*, September 19, 1985, sec. II, p. 6.

37. Dwyer, *Subway Lives*, p. 36: "In 1983, the year before David Gunn arrived, there were 172 newsstands in subway stations. Today, 52 remain."

38. Ibid.

39. Gene Russianoff, staff attorney, and Joseph G. Rappaport, Straphangers' Campaign coordinator, New York Public Interest Research Group, letter to then newly appointed TA president Alan F. Kiepper, February 5, 1990. Furnished by NYPIRG.

40. Jacobs, *Death and Life of Cities*, p. 56.

41. Ulf Hannerz, *Exploring the City: Inquires toward an Urban Anthropology* (New York: Columbia University Press, 1980), p. 110.

42. New York Public Library, "Rules and Regulations Governing Public Behavior in the Library," Rule 4: "Users of the library are expected to maintain an acceptable standard of personal hygiene. Unpleasant body odor which may offend other patrons of the library is unacceptable. Shirts and shoes must be worn; bare feet are not permitted."

43. Hiss, *Experience of Place*, p. 90.

44. Michael Walzer, "Pleasures and Costs of Urbanity," *Dissent* 33 (Fall 1986): 473.

5 Music Under New York: Official Sponsorship

1. Turino, *Moving Away from Silence*, pp. 219, 231.

2. The first contemporary effort was actually the TA's installation of sepia murals in the 42nd Street (Bryant Park) IND-IRT passageway in 1971, but there appears to be no direct connection between that project and more recent MTA programming. Helen A. Harrison, "Subway Art and the Public Use of Arts Committee," *Archives of American Art Journal* 21.2 (1981): 9–10.

3. Ibid., p. 11.

4. Ellis Henican, "Kiley Bolts for Door, Joins the Out Crowd," *New York Newsday*, November 27, 1990, 3.

5. Arts for Transit Office, promotional brochure, p. 1.

6. Cudahy, *Under the Sidewalks*, p. 7.

7. Harrison, "Subway Art," p. 10.

8. Ibid., pp. 3–9. Conservative papers had opposed the project from the start, charging that the left-wing PUAC was engaged in "un-American" activity. Harrison, however, does not attribute the project's demise to this reaction.

9. Ibid., p. 12; U.S. Department of Transportation, Urban Mass Transportation Administration, "Design and Art in Public Transportation Projects," Circular UMTA C 9400.1, January 19, 1981, in State Transportation Library, Boston, Mass.

10. Arts for Transit Office, promotional brochure, p. 1.

11. MTA, "Citywide Survey Results," p. 6.

12. Pamela Allara, "The Arts Fall in Line: The Station Modernization Program at the MBTA." Introduction to promotional brochure, in State Transportation Library, Boston, Mass.

13. Massachusetts Bay Transportation Authority, "Subways Are for Music in Boston," press release no. 77-7-150, July 1, 1977, in State Transportation Library, Boston, Mass.

14. Robin Toner, "The M.T.A. Presents: Music to Soothe the Subway Rider," *New York Times*, September 13, 1985, sec. I, p. 1.

15. James Brooke, "Subway Musician Challenges the Law," *New York Times*, July 13, 1986, sec. I, p. 27.

16. Steve Witt, "Another Extraordinary Talent Doing His Thing in the Subway," in "The Street Singer's Beat," *Downtown*, December 19, 1990, clipping, n.p., furnished by Steve Witt.

17. MPL Productions, "Judge for Yourself," promotional flyer for fourth annual MUNY audition, 1989.

18. Schiller, *Culture, Inc.*, p. 98.

19. "Plaintiffs' Complaint Dated November 20, 1989," *Carew-Reid v. MTA*, docket no. 90-7143, *Joint Appendix*, p. 45.

20. MTA, "Citywide Survey Results," p. 9.

6 Sounds and Silence: Regulating Subway Music

1. New York State, *Official Compilation Codes, Rules, and Regulations of the State of New York*, title 21, chap. XXI, Metropolitan Transportation Authority, subchap. F, New York City Transit Authority, 1050.6(c).

2. James Howard, subway musician, testifying at MTA Public Hearing on Proposed Rules for Non-Transit Use of Transit Facilities, MTA boardroom, April 13, 1989.

3. Laurence H. Tribe, *Constitutional Choices* (Cambridge: Harvard University Press, 1985), p. 188.

4. Ibid., p. 190.

5. Laurence H. Tribe, *American Constitutional Law* (Mineola, N.Y.: Foundation Press, 1988), p. 986 n.2.

6. Chevigny, *Gigs*, p. 66–67, 94–95, 106.

7. *Wolin v. Port of New York Authority*, 392 F.2d 83 (1968).

8. *People v. St. Clair*, 288 N.Y.S. 2d 388 (Criminal Court of New York County, 1968) at 391, quoted from "Testimony of Arthur Eisenberg before the New York Transit Authority in Response to Proposed Rules for Non-Transit Use of Transit Facilities, April 14, 1989," p. 2, furnished by the MTA freedom of information officer.

9. See, for example, *Winters v. New York*, 333 U.S. 507 (1948) at 510, as cited in "Testimony of Arthur Eisenberg," p. 4.

10. New York Civil Liberties Union, "The Rights of Subway Musicians: Round Two," *N.Y. Civil Liberties* 35 (March 1987): 3.

11. *People v. Roger Manning*, Criminal Court of the City of New York, docket no. 5NO38025V, 1985.

12. *Carew-Reid v. Metropolitan Transportation Authority*, docket no. 90-7143, *Joint Appendix*, pp. 34–35. See also Brooke, "Subway Musician Challenges the Law."

13. New York City Transit Authority, *Proposed Rules for Non-Transit Use of Transit Facilities*, January 20, 1989, pp. A-1, A-2. See Appendix 1 for a brief discussion on soliciting donations and "passing the hat" in the subways.

14. Lydon, "New York Subway Orpheus," p. 25.

15. MTA, "Citywide Survey Results," p. 8.

16. *Proposed Rules*, pp. A-4, A-7, A-8, and A-9.

17. David E. Pitt, "MTA Turns Down Volume on Subway Platform Music," *New York Times*, August 26, 1989, sec. I, p. 27.

18. Testimony of Christina North at the Manhattan public hearing, p. 49. Transcripts of testimony were furnished by the MTA freedom of information officer.

There is a difference of opinion on whether the views expressed at the hearings were representative. In 1994 a TA source told me that rider mail received at the time was "overwhelmingly in favor of the proposed rules" and even supportive of a complete ban on subway music. Under the Freedom of Information Act, I requested copies of all the letters on this topic compiled in 1989. I received a total of eleven letters written by riders. Four supported the proposed rules. Seven opposed them and praised the musicians.

19. Steve Witt, "A Party for the Bureaucrats," in "The Street Singer's Beat," *Downtown*, April 26–May 3, 1989, clipping, n.p., furnished by Steve Witt.

20. *Proposed Rules*, p. A-5.

21. *Proposed Rules*, pp. A-4 and A-5.

22. Notice how many of the musicians pictured in this book position themselves in the center of the platforms, against the trash cans, to stay out of the traffic flow.

23. *Proposed Rules*, pp. A-5 and A-9.

24. *Proposed Rules*, p. A-4.

25. *Lehman v. Shaker Heights*, 418 U.S. 298 (1974) at 304; and see Tribe, *American Constitutional Law*, pp. 910 n. 43, 941 n. 84.

26. "Plaintiffs' Complaint Dated November 20, 1989," *Carew-Reid v. MTA, Joint Appendix*, pp. 26–27.

27. "Affidavit of Michael Lydon in Support of Plaintiffs' Motion for Preliminary Injunction Dated December 4, 1989," ibid., pp. 90–96.

28. "Affidavit of Peter Barkman in Support of Order to Show Cause Dated November 20, 1989," ibid., pp. 84–86.

29. *Carew-Reid v. MTA*, 903 F.2d 914, 1990 U.S. APP. (2nd cir. NY 1990) at 917.

30. "Affidavit of Carol E. Meltzer in Opposition to Plaintiffs' Motion for Preliminary Injunction Dated December 4, 1989," in *Carew-Reid v. MTA, Joint Appendix*, pp. 103–5.

31. "Affidavit of Lloyd Carew-Reid In Support of Order to Show Cause Dated November 20, 1989," and "Opinion and Order of the District Court Dated January 5, 1990," ibid., pp. 82, 20–21.

32. *Carew-Reid v. MTA*, 903 F.2d 914 at 917, 918.

33. Ibid. at 919.

34. Ibid. at 916.

35. *Carew-Reid v. MTA*, docket no. 90-7143, *Brief of Defendants-Appellants*, February 1990, p. 7.

36. *Ward v. Rock against Racism*, 109 S.Ct. 2746 (1989).

37. *Carew-Reid v. MTA*, docket no. 90-7143, *Brief of Plaintiffs-Appellees*, February 1990, p. 22. Citations are from *Perry Education Association v. Perry Local Educators' Association*, 460 U.S. 37 (1983) at 45, 46.

38. New York State, *Public Authorities Law*, bk. 42, secs. 1260–79b.

39. *Carew-Reid v. MTA, Brief of Defendants-Appellants*, pp. 22–23. Citation is from *Perry*, 460 U.S., quoting *United States Postal Service v. Council of Greenburgh Civic Associations*, 453 U.S. 114 (1981) at 129–30 and *Greer v. Spock*, 424 U.S. 828 (1976) at 836.

40. Tribe, *American Constitutional Law*, pp. 996–97. Similarly, the court of appeals decided in *International Society for Krishna Consciousness v. Walter Lee*, 113 S.Ct. 37 (1992) that the Port Authority Bus Terminal is a nonpublic forum.

41. Tribe, *Constitutional Choices*, p. 198.

42. Manhattan hearing, p. 174; Brooklyn hearing, p. 62.

7 Walking the Beat: Transit Police

1. New York City Transit Authority, *The New York City Transit Police: Vision for the 1990s* (1991), p. 25.
2. New York City Transit Authority, *The New York City Transit Police Department: History and Organization* (December 1990), "Historical Highlights," p. 2.
3. TA, *Vision for the 1990s*, pp. 2–3, 19.
4. Ibid., pp. 3, 13, 28–32.
5. Ibid., pp. 7, 9, 16.
6. Ibid., p. 17.
7. Michael K. Brown, *Working the Street: Police Discretion and the Dilemmas of Reform* (New York: Russell Sage Foundation, 1988), pp. 37–44.
8. TA, *Vision for the 1990s*, p. 21.
9. Brown, *Working the Street*, p. 129.
10. New York City Transit Police, Civilian Complaint Unit, letter to Susie Tanenbaum, May 14, 1991.
11. Brown, *Working the Street*, p. 196.
12. Ibid., pp. 194–95.
13. TA, *Vision for the 1990s*, p. 7.
14. Brooklyn public hearing transcript, p. 87.
15. TA, *Vision for the 1990s*, p. 7.
16. Ibid., p. 10.
17. Brown, *Working the Street*, p. 37.
18. TA, *Vision for the 1990s*, pp. 7, 13.

8 Music on the Job: Subway Workers

1. For additional perspectives on this cat-and-mouse game, see Craig Castleman, *Getting Up: Subway Graffiti in New York* (Cambridge: MIT Press, 1982); and Alan Riding, "Parisians on Graffiti: Vandalism or Art?" *New York Times*, February 6, 1992, C15.
2. Dwyer, *Subway Lives*, p. 280.

9 Prospects for Change

1. Chevigny, *Gigs*, p. 132.
2. Nick Tate, "Stephen Baird: Streetsinging as Mission," *Cambridge Chronicle*, June 23, 1983, 1.
3. Compare this to the New York City Transit Authority's decision to ban amplified music from the platforms.
4. Marjorie Howard, "Don't Give Us Your T-TV," *Boston Sunday Herald*, January 3, 1993, 11.
5. Dennis Gaffney, "Suitable Entertainment: Street Performers Set Deadline for MBTA Action on Permits," *The Tab*, May 5, 1987, 14.
6. Harrison-Pepper, *Drawing a Circle*, p. 37.
7. Henry Kamm, "The Political Downbeat of Kurt Masur," *International Herald Tribune*, April 24, 1990, 20. It is occasionally suggested that street and subway musicians join Local 802, the musicians' union, but a few who already pay dues feel that the local caters to its most famous clients.
8. Evidently the videotape of the 1989 public hearing, which I watched in the MTA

library four years ago, no longer exists either; to save storage space, the MTA destroys video footage of agency meetings within a matter of months. (Indeed, as indicated in Chapter 6, the written transcript remains.) It was probably the most astounding social history record I have ever seen.

9. Clifford J. Levy, "Transit Plan: To De-Garble Speakers in Stations," *New York Times*, September 13, 1992, 49; TA, *Vision for the 1990s*, p. 2: "The Transit Police radio system, in reality a train dispatch system that had been adapted for police use, fell far below the FCC and National Institute of Justice standards for police or public safety radio"; Larry Sutton, "Solution to a Noisy Problem Takes Council Lots of Time," *Daily News*, January 28, 1993, 6.

10. A similar recommendation was made by New York Civil Liberties Union executive director Norman Siegel at the MTA public hearing on Metro-North and Long Island Rail Road's *Proposed Rules and Regulations concerning Conduct of Customers and Employees*, held in the MTA boardroom, November 14, 1989, transcript, p. 50. Document furnished by the MTA freedom of information officer.

11. Michael Powell, "Sacred Cops," *New York Newsday*, April 4, 1994, A3. Compare this to Fiorello LaGuardia (to whom Mayor-elect Giuliani frequently alluded) who suppressed itinerant activity in the name of modernization but helped lay the foundation of a social welfare system locally and nationally.

12. For more information on the Giuliani administration's attitude toward public space use, see the following *New York Times* articles: Alison Mitchell, "Mayor-Elect's Man," December 3, 1993, A1; Steven Lee Myers, "'Squeegees' Rank High on Next Police Commissioner's Priority List," December 4, 1993, 1; Rick Bragg, "Homeless Seeing Less Apathy, More Anger," February 25, 1994, A1; "Some Free Speech on Mayor's Words," March 17, 1994, B3. Also Michael Powell, "Shelter Squad," *New York Newsday*, August 17, 1994, A3. For evidence that the news media are helping to hasten the demise of Giuliani's campaign by exposing its costliness and absurdity, see these *New York Times* articles: Jonathan P. Hicks, "New York City Exceeds Limit on Overtime," August 9, 1994, B1; and John Kifner, "On Ridding the Jungle of Its Louts," July 20, 1994, B3.

Appendix 1

1. Federal Writers' Project, *WPA Guide to New York City*, p. 402.

2. *Safety Network* (March 1985), New York City Coalition for the Homeless newsletter.

3. Ibid. (April 1989).

4. Ibid. (July 1989).

5. Ibid. (September 1989).

6. Gene Russianoff, staff attorney, and Joseph Rappaport, Straphangers' Campaign coordinator, NYPIRG, letter to Robert Kiley, chair, MTA, and Alan F. Kiepper, president, TA, March 2, 1990. Furnished by NYPIRG.

7. By 1988 the MTA knew from its customer survey that riders wanted real political solutions to subway homelessness: 51 percent of the respondents said that local officials should do something, 16 percent said the state should take responsibility, and 21 percent "look to Federal government for a solution." MTA, "Citywide Survey Results," p. 9.

8. *Young v. New York City Transit Authority*, 729 F.Supp. 341 (SDNY 1990) rev'd. 903 F.2d 146 (2d cir.) cert. denied 111 S.Ct. 516 (1990).

9. Ibid., at 360.

10. Craig Wolff, "U.S. Appeals Court Upholds Ban on Begging in New York Subways," *New York Times*, May 11, 1990, A1. Also Schiller, *Culture, Inc.*, p. 52.

11. Ethan Bronner, "Justices Won't Review NY Subway Begging Ban," *Boston Globe*, November 27, 1990, 3.

12. *Loper v. New York City Police Department*, 99 F.2d 699 2d cir. (1993).

13. Dennis Hevesi, "Judge Upsets Law Banning Street Begging," *New York Times*, October 2, 1992, B1.

14. *International Society for Krishna Consciousness v. Walter Lee*, 113 S.Ct. 37 (1992).

15. "Subway Plan on Homeless is Abandoned," *New York Times*, January 21, 1991, B1.

16. Mitchell, "Mayor-Elect's Man."

17. Metropolitan Transportation Authority, Press Office, "New Program Aimed at Improving Subway Quality-of-Life," press release by John Cunningham, press secretary, and Tito Davila, deputy press secretary, January 10, 1994, pp. 14–15.

18. Ibid., pp. 8, 12–13.

Appendix 2

1. Campbell, *Passing the Hat*, p. 24; Harrison-Pepper, *Drawing a Circle*, p. 39.

2. "Lead-Paint Bill Signed by Mayor"; Chevigny, *Gigs*, p. 95.

3. Harrison-Pepper, *Drawing a Circle*, p. xiv.

4. Ibid., p. 44.

5. *Robert Turley v. New York City Police Department and New York City Department of Parks and Recreation*, Complaint 93 Civ. 8748, December 1993.

6. The department, for instance, received $400,000 from Time Warner Cable for the 1991 Paul Simon concert held on the Great Lawn. "After the City has paid all the overtime for cops and parks workers and so forth, [Gotbaum] might have something like $100,000 left—which she admits is 'not huge,'" reported Dennis Duggan, in "Park Your Concert Right Here," *New York Newsday*, September 1, 1991, 43.

7. "Discord Over SummerStage," *New York Times*, September 13, 1993, sec. 13, p. 8.

8. For an extensive analysis of the negotiations that have shaped Central Park, see Roy Rosenzweig and Elizabeth Blackmar, *The Park and the People: A History of Central Park* (Ithaca: Cornell University Press, 1992).

9. Norimitsu Onishi, "Following Melee, Parks Department Alters Policy on Concert Permits," *New York Times*, June 1, 1994, B3.

10. New York City, Department of Business Services, *Establishing and Operating a Business Improvement District: A Step-by-Step Guide*, 1994.

11. "Official Program: Buskers Fare '94," *Downtown Express*, June 14–27, 1994, 13–16.

Bibliography

BOOKS AND ESSAYS

Bergreen, Laurence. *As Thousands Cheer: The Life of Irving Berlin.* New York: Viking Press, 1990.

Berman, Marshall. "Take It to the Streets: Conflict and Community in Public Space." *Dissent 33* (Fall 1986): 476–85.

Boyle, Wickham. *On the Streets: A Guide to New York City's Buskers.* New York: Department of Cultural Affairs, 1978.

Briffault, Robert. *The Troubadours.* Bloomington: Indiana University Press, 1965. Translated from the original, *Les troubadours et le sentiment romanesque.* Paris: Les Editeurs du Chêne, 1948.

Brown, Michael K. *Working the Street: Police Discretion and the Dilemmas of Reform.* New York: Russell Sage Foundation, 1988.

Bryner, Gary C., and Dennis L. Thompson, eds. *The Constitution and the Regulation of Society.* Provo, Utah: Brigham Young University, 1988.

Campbell, Patricia J. *Passing the Hat: Street Performers in America.* New York: Delacorte Press, 1981.

Cantwell, Robert. *Bluegrass Breakdown: The Making of the Old Southern Sound.* Urbana: University of Illinois Press, 1984.

Castleman, Craig. *Getting Up: Subway Graffiti in New York.* Cambridge: MIT Press, 1982.

Chapple, Steve, and Reebee Garofalo. *Rock 'n' Roll Is Here to Pay: The History and Politics of the Music Industry.* Chicago: Nelson-Hall, 1977.

Chevigny, Paul. *Gigs: Jazz and the Cabaret Laws in New York City.* New York: Routledge, Chapman, and Hall, 1991.

City Lore. *I've Been Working on the Subway: The Folklore and Oral History of Transit.* New York City Transit Museum, 1989.

Collier, James Lincoln. *Louis Armstrong: An American Genius.* New York: Oxford University Press, 1983.

Cudahy, Brian J. *Under the Sidewalks of New York.* Lexington, Mass.: Stephen Greene Press, 1988.

Cunningham, Joseph, and Leonard O. DeHart. *A History of the New York City Subway System* [microform]. New York: The authors, 1976.

Dargan, Amanda, and Steven Zeitlin. *City Play*. New Brunswick, N.J.: Rutgers University Press, 1990.

Dwyer, Jim. *Subway Lives: 24 Hours in the Life of the New York City Subway*. New York: Crown, 1991.

Federal Writers' Project. *The WPA Guide to New York City*. New York: Random House, 1939; rpt. 1982.

Finnegan, Ruth H. *The Hidden Musicians: Local Music in a Small English Town*. Cambridge: Cambridge University Press, 1989.

Fischler, Stan. *Uptown, Downtown: A Trip through Time on New York's Subways*. New York: Hawthorn, 1976.

Frith, Simon. *Sound Effects: Youth, Leisure, and the Politics of Rock 'n' Roll*. New York: Pantheon, 1981.

Frith, Simon, and Howard Horne. *Art into Pop*. London: Methuen, 1987.

Goffman, Erving. *Behavior in Public Places: Notes on the Social Organization of Gatherings*. New York: Free Press of Glencoe, 1963.

Gribin, Anthony J., and Matthew M. Schiff. *Doo-Wop: The Forgotten Third of Rock 'n' Roll*. Iola, Wis.: Krause, 1992.

Hall, Edward T. *The Hidden Dimension*. New York: Doubleday, 1966.

Hannerz, Ulf. *Exploring the City: Inquiries toward an Urban Anthropology*. New York: Columbia University Press, 1980.

Harrison, Helen A. "Subway Art and the Public Use of Arts Committee." *Archives of American Art Journal* 21.2(1981): 3–12.

Harrison, Sally. "Drawing a Circle in Washington Square Park." *Studies in Visual Communication* 10 (Spring 1984): 68–83.

Harrison-Pepper, Sally. *Drawing a Circle in the Square: Street Performing in New York's Washington Square Park*. Jackson: University Press of Mississippi, 1990.

Hiss, Tony. *The Experience of Place*. New York: Alfred A. Knopf, 1990.

Hood, Clifton. *722 Miles: The Building of the Subways and How They Transformed New York*. New York: Simon and Schuster, 1993.

Jacobs, Jane. *The Death and Life of Great American Cities*. New York: Random House, 1961.

Jones, Hettie. *Big Star Fallin' Mama: Five Women in Black Music*. New York: Dell, 1974.

Kelling, George L. "The Contagion of Public Disorder." *City Journal* (Spring 1991): 57–64.

Kessner, Thomas. *Fiorello H. LaGuardia and the Making of Modern New York*. New York: Penguin, 1989.

Klein, Joe. *Woody Guthrie: A Life*. New York: Alfred A. Knopf, 1980.

Levine, Lawrence W. *Highbrow Lowbrow: The Emergence of Cultural Hierarchy in America*. Cambridge: Harvard University Press, 1988.

Love, Edmund G. *Subways Are for Sleeping*. New York: Harcourt Brace, 1957.

Meryman, Richard. *Louis Armstrong: A Self-Portrait*. New York: Eakins Press, 1971.

Ottley, Roi, and William J. Weatherby, eds. *The Negro in New York: An Informal Social History, 1626–1940*. New York: Praeger, 1967. Originally prepared by the Federal Writers Project.

Rosenzweig, Roy, and Elizabeth Blackmar. *The Park and the People: A History of Central Park*. Ithaca: Cornell University Press, 1992.

Ross, Andrew. *No Respect: Intellectuals and Popular Culture*. New York: Routledge, Chapman, and Hall, 1989.

Schiller, Herbert I. *Culture, Inc.: The Corporate Takeover of Public Expression*. New York: Oxford University Press, 1989.

Sennett, Richard, ed. *Classic Essays on the Culture of Cities*. Englewood Cliffs, N.J.: Prentice-Hall, 1969.

Tan, Amy. *The Kitchen God's Wife*. New York: G. P. Putnam's Sons, 1991.
Thomas, Vincent, arranger. *Cryes of Olde London*. London: London, Goodwin, and Tabb, 1925.
Toop, David. *The Rap Attack: African Jive to New York Hip Hop*. Boston: South End Press, 1984.
Tribe, Laurence H. *American Constitutional Law*. Mineola, N.Y.: Foundation Press, 1988.
——. *Constitutional Choices*. Cambridge: Harvard University Press, 1985.
Turino, Thomas. *Moving Away from Silence: Music of the Peruvian Altiplano and the Experience of Urban Migration*. Chicago: University of Chicago Press, 1993.
Walzer, Michael. "Pleasures and Costs of Urbanity." *Dissent* 33 (Fall 1986): 470–75.
Whyte, William H. *City: Rediscovering the Center*. New York: Doubleday, 1988.

LEGAL AND GOVERNMENT DOCUMENTS

Allara, Pamela. "The Arts Fall in Line: The Station Modernization Program at the MBTA." Introduction to promotional brochure, n.d., State Transportation Library, Boston, Massachusetts.
Carew-Reid v. Metropolitan Transportation Authority 903 F.2d 914, 1990 U.S. APP. (2nd cir. NY 1990); docket no. 90-7143, *Brief of Defendants-Appellants*, February 1990; *Brief of Plaintiffs-Appellees*, February 1990; *Joint Appendix*, December 1989.
Davenport v. City of Alexandria, Va. 710 F.2d 148 (1983).
Eisenberg, Arthur. Testimony before the New York Transit Authority in Response to Proposed Rules for Non-Transit Use of Transit Facilities, April 14, 1989. Furnished by the MTA freedom of information officer.
Goldstein v. Town of Nantucket 477 F.Supp. 606 (1979).
Interborough Rapid Transit Company. Subway Division. *Rules and Regulations for the Government of the Operating Officers and Employés of the Interborough Rapid Transit Company, Subway Division, to Take Effect October 1, 1904*. 1904. New-York Historical Society.
International Society for Krishna Consciousness v. Walter Lee 113 S.Ct. 37 (1992).
Keleti, Paul J., acting secretary, New York City Transit Authority, letter to Raymond Hagan, Esq., December 23, 1964. TA Archives, file "Noise—Rapid Transit—1964—0-250—Complaints."
Laurel, Miss E., letter to Joseph E. O'Grady, chairman, New York City Transit Authority, December 7, 1964. TA Archives, file "Noise—Rapid Transit—1964—0-250—Complaints."
Lehman v. Shaker Heights 418 U.S. 298 (1974).
Loper v. New York City Police Department 99 F.2d 699 2d cir. (1993).
Manhattan Railway Company. *Rules and Regulations for the Government of the Operating Officers and Employés of the Manhattan Railway Company*. 1890. New-York Historical Society.
Massachusetts Bay Transportation Authority. "Subways Are for Music in Boston." Press release no. 77-7-150, July 1, 1977. State Transportation Library, Boston, Massachusetts.
Metropolitan Transportation Authority. Arts for Transit Office. Promotional brochure, 1990. Furnished by Arts for Transit Office.
——. Marketing Research Division. Memorandum from Peter Harris to Andrew Hyde. "Citywide Survey Results." Prepared by director Peter Harris, May 9, 1988.
——. Policy and Planning Department. Arts for Transit Division. *1994 Budget: Explanation of Professional Services Expenses* and *Explanation of Variances in Other-than-*

Employee-Compensation Costs. Furnished by the MTA freedom of information officer.
——. Press Office. "New Program Aimed at Improving Subway Quality-of-Life." Press release by John Cunningham, press secretary, and Tito Davila, deputy press secretary, January 10, 1994.
——. Testimony at MTA Public Hearing on Metro-North and Long Island Rail Road's *Proposed Rules and Regulations concerning Conduct of Customers and Employees*, November 14, 1989. Transcripts furnished by the MTA freedom of information officer.
——. Testimony at MTA Public Hearings on *Proposed Rules for Non-Transit Use of Transit Facilities*, April 13, 27, May 4, 11, 1989. Transcripts furnished by the MTA freedom of information officer.
New York City. *Code of Ordinances of the City of New York, Adopted March 30, 1915*. Compiler and annotator Arthur F. Cosby. New York: Banks Law, 1915.
——. *General Ordinances of the City of New York under the Greater New York Charter*. Compiler and annotator George Whitfield Brown Jr. New York: Banks Law, 1901.
——. Board of Transportation of the City of New York. *Rules and Regulations Governing Employees Engaged in Operation: Independent City-Owned Rapid Transit Railroad*. 1938.
——. Department of Business Services. *Establishing and Operating a Business Improvement District: A Step-by-Step Guide*. 1994.
——. Municipal Archives. Department of Records and Information Services. Fiorello H. LaGuardia files. Department of Licenses. Microfilm roll 13, frame 000828; roll 18, frame 000986.
——. New York Public Library. "Rules and Regulations Governing Public Behavior in the Library." As posted in the Mid-Manhattan branch library at 40th Street and Fifth Avenue in Manhattan.
——. Office of the Mayor. Fiorello H. LaGuardia, letter to Mrs. F. S. Stebbins, May 14, 1935. Municipal Reference and Research Center, New York City Department of Records and Information Services.
——. Office of the Mayor and New York City Police Department. *Police Strategy No. 5: Reclaiming the Public Spaces of New York*. 1994.
New York City Transit Authority. *Proposed Rules for Non-Transit Use of Transit Facilities*. January 20, 1989.
——. Transit Police. Civilian Complaint Unit. Letter to Susie Tanenbaum, May 14, 1991.
——. *The New York City Transit Police Department: History and Organization*. December 1990.
——. *The New York City Transit Police: Vision for the 1990s*. 1991.
New York State. *Official Compilation Codes, Rules, and Regulations of the State of New York*. Title 21. Chapter XXI. Metropolitan Transportation Authority. Subchapter F. New York City Transit Authority.
——. *Public Authorities Law*. Book 42, sections 1201, 1260–79b. McKinney's Consolidated Laws of New York Annotated, 1982.
People v. Roger Manning. Criminal Court of the City of New York, docket no. 5NO38025V, 1985.
People v. St. Clair 288 N.Y.S. 2d 388. Criminal Court of New York County, 1968.
Port Authority of New York and New Jersey. Rules and Regulations. As posted in the bus terminal on 42nd Street and Eighth Avenue in Manhattan.
Robert Turley v. New York City Police Department and New York City Department of Parks and Recreation. Complaint 93 Civ. 8748, December 1993.
Rules of the Suburban Rapid Transit Company. 1886. New-York Historical Society.

Russianoff, Gene, staff attorney, and Joseph G. Rappaport, Straphangers' Campaign coordinator, New York Public Interest Research Group, letter to TA president Alan F. Kiepper, February 5, 1990; letter to MTA chair Robert Kiley and TA president Alan F. Kiepper, March 2, 1990. Furnished by NYPIRG.

U.S. Department of Transportation. Urban Mass Transportation Administration. "Design and Art in Public Transportation Projects." Circular UMTA C 9400.1, January 19, 1981. State Transportation Library, Boston, Massachusetts.

Ward v. Rock against Racism 109 S.Ct. 2746 (1989).

Winters v. New York 333 U.S. 507 (1948).

Wolin v. Port of New York Authority 392 F.2d 83 (1968).

Young v. New York City Transit Authority 729 F.Supp 341 (SDNY 1990) rev'd 903 F.2d 146 (2d cir.) cert. denied 111 S.Ct. 516 (1990).

NEWSPAPER AND MAGAZINE ARTICLES, NONGOVERNMENTAL PROMOTIONS

"Bay Ridge Celebrates the Beginning of Work on Fourth Avenue Subway Extension." *New York Times*, October 27, 1912, sec. 3, p. 6.

Beach Pneumatic Transit Company. *Illustrated Description of the Broadway Pneumatic Underground Railway with a Full Description of the Atmospheric Machinery and the Great Tunneling Machine*. New York: S. W. Green, 1870.

Bragg, Rick. "Homeless Seeing Less Apathy, More Anger." *New York Times*, February 25, 1994, A1.

Bronner, Ethan. "Justices Won't Review NY Subway Begging Ban." *Boston Globe*, November 27, 1990, 3.

Brooke, James. "Subway Musician Challenges the Law." *New York Times*, July 13, 1986, sec. I, p. 27.

"Business Men Fete Opening of Subway." *New York Times*, September 10, 1932, 6.

Carmody, Deirdre. "Transit Goals Being Met, Gunn Says." *New York Times*, September 19, 1985, sec. II, p. 6.

"Carolers Take Yuletide Spirit Down to the Subway." *New York Times*, December 13, 1956, 44.

"Celebrate Opening of Subway Link." *New York Times*, July 1, 1924, 23.

Coalition for the Homeless. *Safety Network*, March 1985–January 1990. New York City Coalition for the Homeless newsletters.

"Discord over SummerStage." *New York Times*, September 19, 1993, sec. 13, p. 8.

Duggan, Dennis. "Park Your Concert Right Here." *New York Newsday*, September 1, 1991, 43.

"A Few Relics Wanted." *New York Times*, April 16, 1935, 20.

"Fifth Avenue Station of Subway Opened." *New York Times*, March 23, 1926, 29.

Fiske, Edward B. "Now, Whites Are Minority in New York." *New York Times*, March 22, 1991, B1–2.

Gaffney, Dennis. "Suitable Entertainment: Street Performers Set Deadline for MBTA Action on Permits." *The Tab*, May 5, 1987, 14.

"German Band Is Banned." *New York Times*, January 3, 1936, 21.

Henican, Ellis. "Kiley Bolts for Door, Joins the Out Crowd," *New York Newsday*, November 27, 1990, 3.

Hevesi, Dennis. "Judge Upsets Law Banning Street Begging." *New York Times*, October 2, 1992, B1.

Hicks, Jonathan P. "New York City Exceeds Limit on Overtime." *New York Times*, August 9, 1994, B1.

Howard, Marjorie. "Don't Give Us Your T-TV." *Boston Sunday Herald*, January 3, 1993, 11.
"The Hurdy-Gurdy." *New York Times*, April 20, 1935, 12.
"Hurdy-Gurdy Fees Abolished by Mayor." *New York Times*, March 8, 1935, 23.
Kamm, Henry. "The Political Downbeat of Kurt Masur." *International Herald Tribune*, April 24, 1990, 20.
Kifner, John. "On Ridding the Jungle of Its Louts," *New York Times*, July 20, 1994, B3.
"Lead-Paint Bill Signed by Mayor." *New York Times*, June 12, 1970, 20.
Levy, Clifford J. "Transit Plan: To De-Garble Speakers in Stations." *New York Times*, September 13, 1992, 49.
Lydon, Michael. "New York City Subway Orpheus." *Atlantic Monthly* (June 1990): 24–28.
McKinley, James C., Jr. "Dinkins, in TV Speech, Defends Handling of Crown Heights Tension." *New York Times*, November 26, 1992, 1.
Martin, Douglas. "Rush-Hour Recitals for a Chinese Violinist." *New York Times*, July 24, 1994, sec. I, p. 1.
"Mary Lewis Joins Hurdy-Gurdy Plea." *New York Times*, January 23, 1936, 25.
"Mr. LaGuardia Warned." *New York Times*, April 21, 1935, sec. IV, p. 8.
Mitchell, Alison. "Mayor-Elect's Man." *New York Times*, December 3, 1993, A1.
MPL Productions. "Judge for Yourself." Promotional flyer for fourth annual MUNY audition. 1989.
Myers, Steven Lee. "'Squeegees' Rank High on Next Police Commissioner's Priority List." *New York Times*, December 4, 1993, 1.
"New Subway Line on 6th Ave. Opens at Midnight Fete." *New York Times*, December 15, 1940, 1.
New York Civil Liberties Union. "The Rights of Subway Musicians: Round Two." *N.Y. Civil Liberties* 35 (March 1987): 3.
"Official Program: Buskers Fare '94," *Downtown Express*, June 14–27, 1994, 13–16.
Onishi, Norimitsu. "Following Melee, Parks Department Alters Policy on Concert Permits." *New York Times*, June 1, 1994, B3.
"Organ Grinders to Go." *New York Times*, January 17, 1936, 21.
"Organ Grinders Will Go on Radio to Fight Ban." *New York Times*, January 11, 1936, 17.
"Our Subway Open, 150,000 Try It." *New York Times*, October 28, 1904, 1.
Pitt, David E. "MTA Turns Down Volume on Subway Platform Music." *New York Times*, August 26, 1989, sec. I, p. 27.
"A Plea for the Organ Grinder." *New York Times*, January 24, 1936, 18.
Powell, Michael. "Sacred Cops." *New York Newsday*, April 4, 1994, A3.
——. "Shelter Squad." *New York Newsday*, August 17, 1994, A3.
"Rapid Transit Tunnel Begun." *New York Times*, March 25, 1900, 2.
Riding, Alan. "Parisians on Graffiti: Vandalism or Art?" *New York Times*, February 6, 1992, C15.
Robinson, George. "The Klezmatics: Making a Difference with Music That's Different." *Jewish Sentinel*, October 20, 1993, A4.
"Some Free Speech on Mayor's Words." *New York Times*, March 17, 1994, B3.
Sontag, Deborah. "Unlicensed Peddlers, Unfettered Dreams." *New York Times*, June 14, 1993, A1.
"Subway Open." *Evening Post*, October 27, 1904, 1–2.
"Subway Plan on Homeless Is Abandoned." *New York Times*, January 21, 1991, B1.
Sutton, Larry. "Solution to a Noisy Problem Takes Council Lots of Time." *Daily News*, January 28, 1993, 6.

Tate, Nick. "Stephen Baird: Streetsinging as Mission." *Cambridge Chronicle*, June 23, 1983, 1.

"39 'Don'ts' Listed in Subways' Code." *New York Times*, February 17, 1967, 39.

Toner, Robin. "The M.T.A. Presents: Music to Soothe the Subway Rider." *New York Times*, September 13, 1985, sec. I, p. 1.

Witt, Steve. "A Party for the Bureaucrats." In "The Street Singer's Beat," *Downtown*, April 26–May 3, 1989. Clipping, n.p., furnished by Steve Witt.

——. "Another Extraordinary Talent Doing His Thing in the Subway." In "The Street Singer's Beat," *Downtown*, December 19, 1990. Clipping, n.p., furnished by Steve Witt.

——. "Ogarro Interviewed." In "The Street Singer's Beat," *Downtown*, March 13, 1993. Clipping, n.p., furnished by Steve Witt.

——. "Piped-in Subway Music? What about the Subway Musicians?" In "The Street Singer's Beat," *Downtown*. Clipping, n.d., n.p., furnished by Steve Witt.

Wolff, Craig. "U.S. Appeals Court Upholds Ban on Begging in New York Subways." *New York Times*, May 11, 1990, A1.

Index

Page references to illustrations are in italics.